DISCOVERING SCIENCE

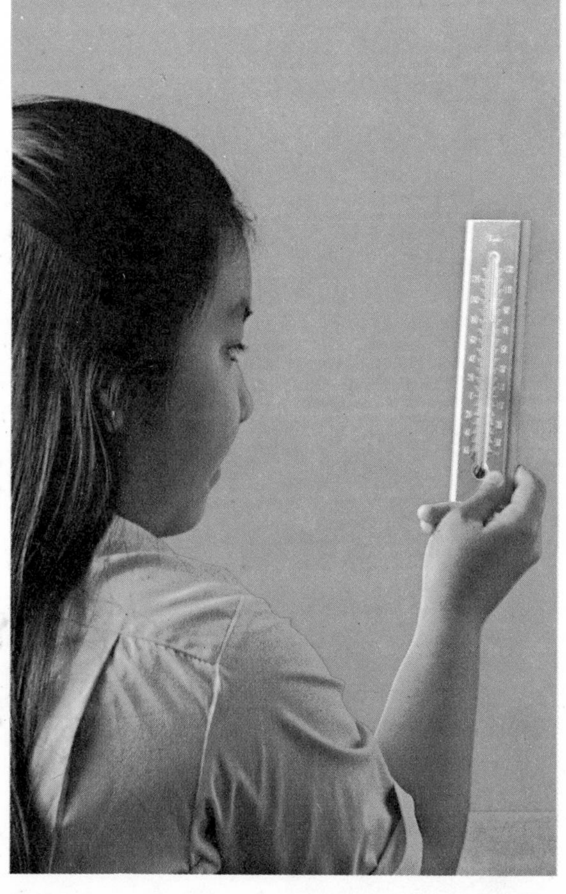

Albert Piltz

U.S. Office of Education
San Francisco, California

Roger A. Van Bever

Detroit Public Schools
Detroit, Michigan

Dr. Piltz is a professional employee in the U.S. Office of Education. No official support or endorsement by the Office of Education is intended or should be inferred.

1975 Printing

CHARLES E. MERRILL PUBLISHING CO.

A Bell & Howell Company
Columbus, Ohio

A Merrill Science Text

Consultant Science Teaching Specialist
Ben B. Strasser

Illustrations by:

L. F. Cary • J. D. Firestone Associates
William M. Hutchinson • Pat and Paul Karch
Miss Irma Wilde

A MERRILL SCIENCE TEXT

THE DISCOVERING SCIENCE PROGRAM

DISCOVERING SCIENCE Series K-6
by Piltz, Blough, Costa, Roche, and Van Bever

DISCOVERING SCIENCE Equipment Kits 1-6

DISCOVERING SCIENCE Evaluation Program 3-6

DISCOVERING SCIENCE Skillcards Intermediate Levels

ISBN 0-675-02454-4

Published by
CHARLES E. MERRILL PUBLISHING CO.
A Bell & Howell Company
Columbus, Ohio 43216

Printed in the United States of America

CONTENTS

Photograph Credits

Cover photograph by Paul W. Nesbit. Other photographs: American Airlines, p. 215, p. 326 top; Courtesy of the American Museum of Natural History, p. 306-307, p. 332; Armco Steel Corporation, p. 64; AVCO Systems Division, p. 250-251; Baron-Blakeslee, Inc., p. 51; Bell Telephone, p. 209 bottom right, p. 271 right; Lester V. Bergman and Assoc. Inc., p. 22; The Boeing Company, p. 272 left; Bunker Hill Company, p. 32; Bureau of Reclamation, p. 211 bottom center; Bureau of Sport Fisheries and Wildlife, p. 329 bottom; Celestron Pacific, p. 222; Bruce Charlton, p. 3, p. 4, p. 7, p. 8, p. 9, p. 14 right, p. 16, p. 17, p. 18, p. 20 bottom, p. 21, p. 23, p. 25, p. 26, p. 27, p. 28, p. 30, p. 48, p. 53, p. 56, p. 79, p. 81, p. 87, p. 91, p. 102, p. 103, p. 104, p. 105, p. 106, p. 110 top-bottom left, p. 111 top, p. 114, p. 115, p. 119, p. 123 right, p. 126, p. 129, p. 130, p. 132, p. 135, p. 143, p. 146, p. 147, p. 158, p. 162 bottom, p. 164, p. 195, p. 197 center-bottom, p. 201, p. 207, p. 209 top, p. 213, p. 241, p. 265, p. 276-277, p. 279 top, p. 285, p. 286 top, p. 288, p. 293 left, p. 294, p. 295, p. 296, p. 297 left, p. 298 top right-bottom p. 299 top, p. 301, p. 302; Columbia Broadcasting System, p. 49; Columbus Dispatch Magazine, p. 291; Courtesy Carolina Biological Supply Company, p. 297 right; Courtesy CCM; General Biological Inc., Chicago, p. 300; Walt Craig, p. 150-151, p. 168 right; Denver Museum of Natural History, p. 327 top; Dept. of Photography, Ohio State University, p. 268 top; Dow Chemical Co., p. 214 right; ESSA photo, p. 161, p. 175 bottom, p. 187; Field Museum of Natural History, p. 317 top center, p. 318, p. 321; Photo by GAF Corporation, U.S.A., p. 204 bottom right, p. 205 center, p. 211 bottom left; Ewing Galloway, NY., p. 226; Philip Gendreau, NY., p. 212 right; General Dynamics Electric Boat Co., p. 110 bottom right; Geophysical Instrument and Supply Co., p. 185; Photo, Malcolm S. Hayden, p. 204 top left; Lil Junas, p. 211; Kenn Knowlton, p. 155 left; Harold M. Lambert Studios, p. 46, p. 112-113; Phyllis S. Lewis, p. 159 top right; Lick Observatory Photograph, p. 229; Marathon Oil Company, p. 111 bottom; Massie-Missouri Resources Div., p. 303 left; Meston's Travels, p. 34-35, Photographs from the Mount Wilson and Palomar Observatories, p. 224, p. 225, p. 248, p. 268 bottom; Ed Nano, p. i, p. 76, p. 96, NASA p. 108, p. 175 top, p. 188, p. 220-221, p. 227, p. 228, p. 232, p. 262 bottom, p. 269, p. 270, p. 271 left, p. 272 center right, p. 273; National Center for Air Pollution Control, p. 191 top right; National Coal Association, p. 10; National Education Association Publishing: Di Dio, p. 2; Paul W. Nesbit, p. 155 right, p. 156, p. 159 center right, p. 163 center, p. 166 top left, bottom left-right, p. 178, p. 191 bottom, p. 194 left, p. 196 bottom, p. 204 bottom left, p. 206 top, p. 214 left, p. 331; Ohio Department of Natural Resources Photo, p. 212; Rex Chainbelt Inc., Pacific Flush Tank Div., p. 217; Pan American Airways, p. 39; Geo. W. Park Seed Co., p. 179; Ria C. Parody, p. 31; Photo Courtesy Chas. Pfizer and Co., Inc., p. 298 top left; Portland Cement Association, p. 123 left; Allan Roberts, p. 199, p. 310 left, p. 312, p. 328 left, p. 329 top, p. 330 bottom; H. Armstrong Roberts, p. 205 bottom, p. 209 bottom left; Rust-Oleum Corporation, Evanston, Illinois, p. 20 top left; Science Service, p. 163 top; Will Sheppard, p. 266; Alvin E. Staffan, p. 162 top, p. 279 bottom, p. 310 right, p. 319 bottom, p. 321, p. 330 top; State of Colorado, O. Roach, Photographer, p. 192; TWA Ambassador, p. 84-85; J. W. Thompson, p. 299 bottom; Union Pacific Railroad, p. 14 left, p. 197 top; University of Houston, p. 10; Official U.S. Air Force Photo, p. 223; USDA Photo, p. vi-l, p. 169, p. 191 top left, p. 196 top left, p. 212 left, p. 278, p. 286 bottom, p. 293 right, p. 303 right, p. 323, p. 326 bottom, p. 328 right; W. F. Lee U.S. Geological Survey, p. 196 top right, p. 216; United States Lines Co., p. 100; Official U.S. Navy Photos, p. 92, p. 176, p. 218, p. 262 top; U.S. Soil Conservation Service, p. 24, p. 165, p. 180-181, p. 194 right, p. 198; U.S. Steel Corporation, p. 54-55; Roger A. Van Bever, p. 317 bottom; Edward J. Webster, p. 19; Western Union, p. 66, p. 71; Wide World Photos, p. 206 bottom, p. 319 top; W.W. Williams Co., p. 327 bottom; Woods Hole Oceanographic Institution, p. 207, p. 209 right column center, p. 210; Jerome Wyckoff, p. 166 top right; Yerkes Observatory Photograph, p. 231.

1

Working With Chemicals

Look at the burning wood. Is the wood changing? What do you think will be left when the fire goes out?

Name some other changes. In some changes, it is easy to get the original matter back again. Water can be changed to ice and then changed easily back to water. But could the ashes of wood be changed easily back to wood again?

There are many, many kinds of materials and many, many kinds of changes that materials undergo. How many things have you seen change? Discovering what chemicals are and what happens to them can help you to understand changes that take place.

Molecules and Atoms

All matter is made of tiny bits of material called **molecules** (mol′ ə kūlz). The largest molecules are so small that a million of them could fit along a line only one inch long!

There are as many kinds of molecules as there are different kinds of materials. Look around your classroom. Are some things in your classroom made of wood and some of metal? Can you find other kinds of materials? How many kinds of materials can you see? Make a list. Compare it with lists that others have made.

What are some of the ways that materials differ from one another? In what ways can you observe materials to discover these differences?

Materials
Wood
Metal
Leather
Glass
Cloth

Each material is different from others because it is made of different kinds of molecules. Wood molecules are different from metal molecules. Have you ever used sugar in place of salt, or salt in place of sugar? How are these materials alike? How can you tell them apart? Differences in materials depend upon the kinds of molecules of which the materials are made. Their molecules are different in size and shape. But there is a more important difference.

Molecules are made up of even smaller parts called **atoms** (at′ əmz). Materials are different if their molecules are made of different kinds and numbers of atoms.

Elements and Compounds

Some materials have only one kind of atom. These materials are called **elements** (el′ ə mənts). Oxygen, carbon, gold, and copper are examples of elements.

How many of the names of elements on this list do you recognize?

Some Common Elements	
oxygen	hydrogen
sulfur	fluorine
iron	gold
nitrogen	carbon
calcium	phosphorus

Each atom of an element is like all other atoms of that same element. Two atoms of the same element may combine to form a molecule of that element.

Get twelve crayons. Make sure you have six colors and two crayons of each color. Imagine that each crayon represents an atom. How *many* atoms do you have? How many different *kinds* of atoms do you have?

What is a compound?

Can you arrange the crayons so that they represent molecules of elements? Using all twelve crayons, how many "molecules" of elements can you make?

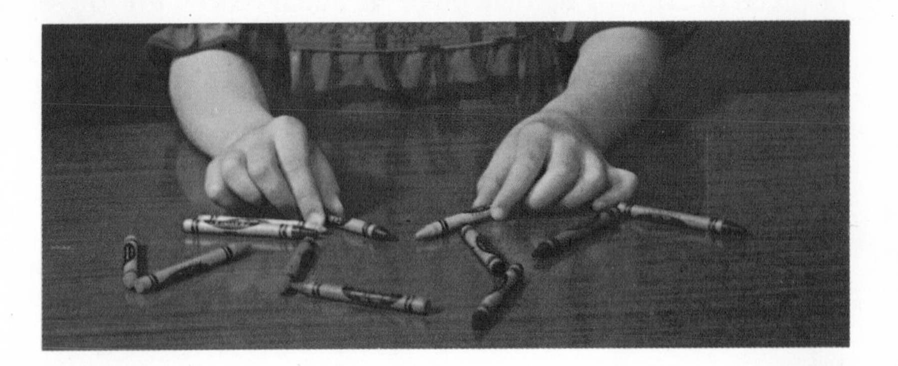

Most molecules are made of more than one kind of atom. These molecules are called **compounds** (kom′ pounds). A compound always has more than one element.

Use six crayons of six different colors. Group them to represent molecules of compounds. How many "molecules" of compounds can you make?

Matter and Change

What do atoms, molecules, elements, and compounds have to do with changes in matter?

Look at the picture of a glass. It is made of molecules of glass. Suppose the glass is broken. Do you think the broken pieces of glass are still made of molecules of glass? Why do you think so or why not?

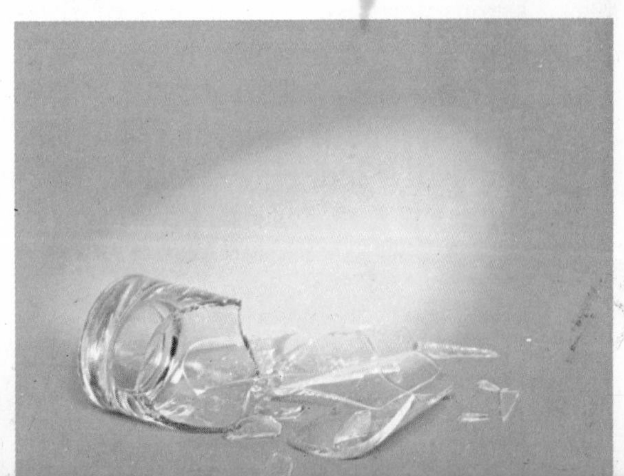

Now look at the picture of a piece of burning paper. When the paper has burned, will the material still be paper? Why do you think so or why not? What is the difference between the way in which the glass was changed and the way in which the paper was changed? Tell about some changes that are similar to the breaking of glass. Name some changes that are similar to the burning of paper.

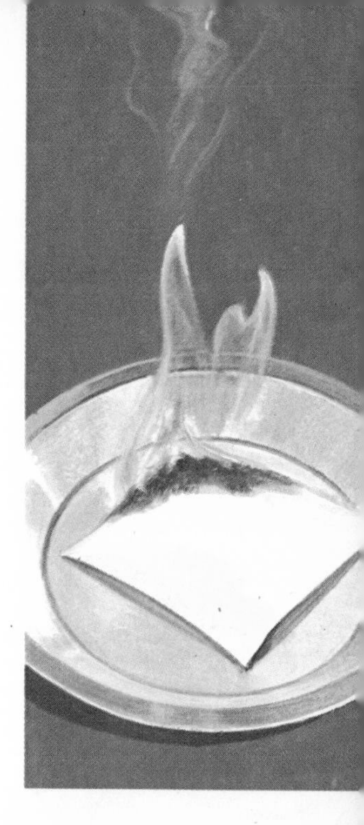

Look at these two lists of changes. Describe what happens in each change. How are all the changes in List A different from all the changes in List B?

List A	List B
1. freezing of water	1. burning of candle
2. cutting of wood	2. burning of paper
3. cutting of paper	3. rusting of hinge
4. crushing of box	4. souring of milk

What is changed when wood is cut? What is changed when a candle burns? What is changed when paper is burned? What is changed when an iron hinge is left in moist air?

Do molecules change in a physical change?

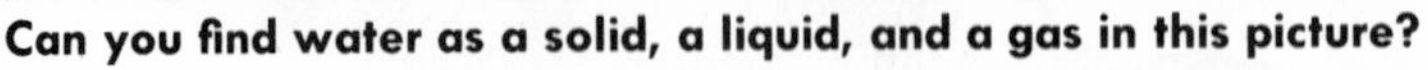

Can you find water as a solid, a liquid, and a gas in this picture?

When a material changes, but it still has the same kind of molecules, the change is called a **physical** (fiz′ ə kl) **change.** A physical change is a change in the size, shape, or condition of an object. Water can be a liquid, a solid, or a gas. What can be done to change liquid water into a solid? What is the solid called? What can be done to change liquid water into a gas? What is the gas called? Each of these changes is a physical change. Can you explain why?

In physical changes, the molecules do not change. The molecules in ice are the same kind of molecules that form water and water vapor. But the molecules in ice are spaced differently from the molecules in water and water vapor. In which form of water are its molecules closest together? In which form are the molecules farthest apart?

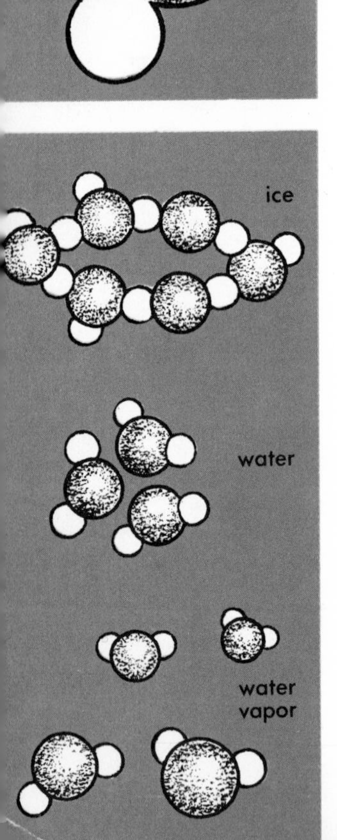

When a material changes and it no longer has the same kind of molecules, the change is called a **chemical** (kem′ ə kl) **change.** A chemical change is a change in the kind of molecules. When a candle burns, new materials are formed. Some of the atoms which are present in the molecules of wax join with atoms of oxygen in the air and form different materials. None of these new materials is like wax because other kinds of molecules are formed. A chemical change forms a different material. This new material has molecules with different kinds and different amounts of atoms from the original material.

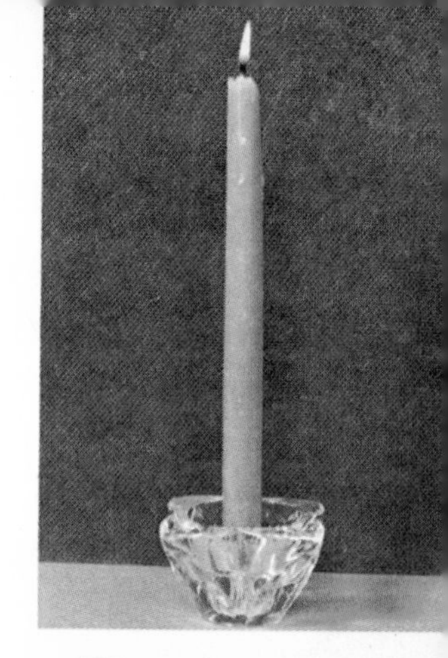

Now can you decide whether the changes in List A are chemical or physical changes? Are the changes in List B chemical or physical changes? (See page 5.)

There are more than one hundred different kinds of elements! In chemical changes, atoms of elements can join in different ways to form millions of different kinds of molecules. Each day, scientists find ways to rearrange atoms and groups of atoms to form new molecules.

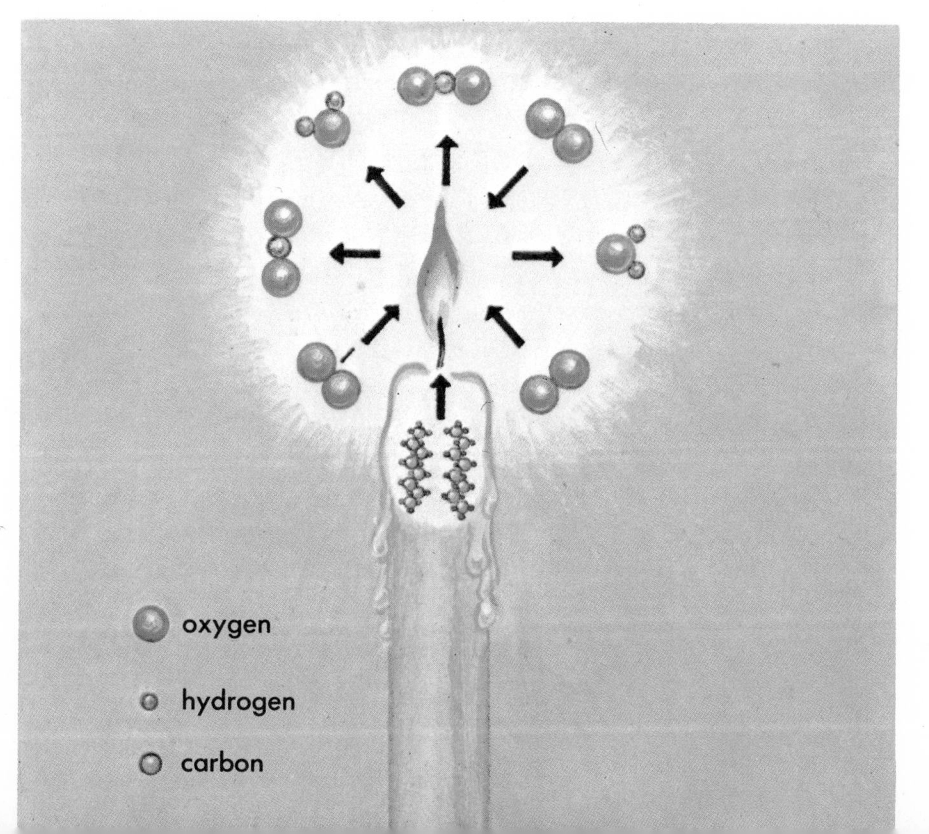

Do some compounds have more than two kinds of elements?

Again use crayons to help you understand how atoms combine and make different molecules. With a red crayon, color a small square on a piece of white paper. Cover the red square with blue crayon. Is the color of the square red? Is it blue? What has happened?

Has a different color formed? Is it like either of the colors you started with? In a chemical change, when atoms join to form a molecule, the molecule is different from any of the single atoms in the molecule.

Can you join red with any of the other colors to get a different color? In the same way, a single element can join with many other kinds of elements to form many different compounds.

To get a different color, you joined the colors of only two crayons. Many kinds of compounds have more than two kinds of elements. Sometimes, many atoms of the same element are part of a single molecule of a compound. Suppose you could join the colors of your crayons in any way you wanted. By using only six colors, you could make hundreds of different colors. Can you understand why there are so many kinds of molecules?

Balls of clay or painted styrofoam balls and some toothpicks may help you to understand more about atoms and molecules. Use different colors to represent different kinds of atoms. Gather twelve beads or balls: three red, three blue, three yellow, and three green. Fasten all the red "atoms" together. This can represent one kind of molecule, a molecule of an element. Why? Fasten two red "atoms" and a yellow "atom" together. This can represent another kind of molecule, a molecule of a compound. Why?

Molecules are many shapes and sizes. Choose any five "atoms" and fasten them with some wire. Try twisting one "molecule" into different shapes. Can a larger or smaller molecule be twisted into more shapes? Use eight or ten "atoms" in a large "molecule" to find out. Which molecules you made represent elements? Why? Which molecules represent compounds? Why?

Can the same atoms be made into different molecules if the atoms are put together differently? On a wire, string five "atoms" together in this order: one blue, three red, and one green. Remember what this "molecule" looks like. Now, take the same "atoms," but string them in a different order: one red, one blue, one red, one green, and one red. Does this "molecule" look different? Replace one of the atoms with a yellow atom. Do you have another kind of molecule?

Scientists have a special kind of "language" to describe what happens when molecules are changed. See if you can understand their language.

What is a chemical symbol?

Coal is one form of carbon.

Describing Chemical Changes

Drawings of molecules and atoms do not look like real molecules and atoms. However, drawings may help you to understand how atoms join in a chemical change to form molecules.

Carbon (kär′ bən) is an element which makes up the black solid called coal. An atom of carbon can be drawn like this:

Oxygen (ok′ sə jən) is an element which is a gas in the air. You must breathe oxygen to stay alive. An oxygen atom can be drawn like this:

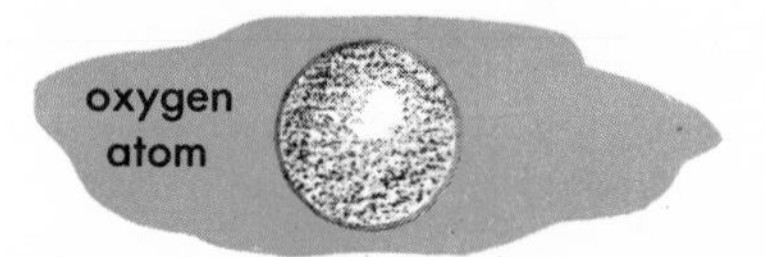

The atoms in a material can join with other kinds of atoms. If carbon and oxygen atoms join, do they form a compound?

How many kinds of atoms does the new molecule have? It is a compound called **carbon dioxide** (kär′ bən dī ok′ sīd). Carbon dioxide is not like either of the elements of which it is made.

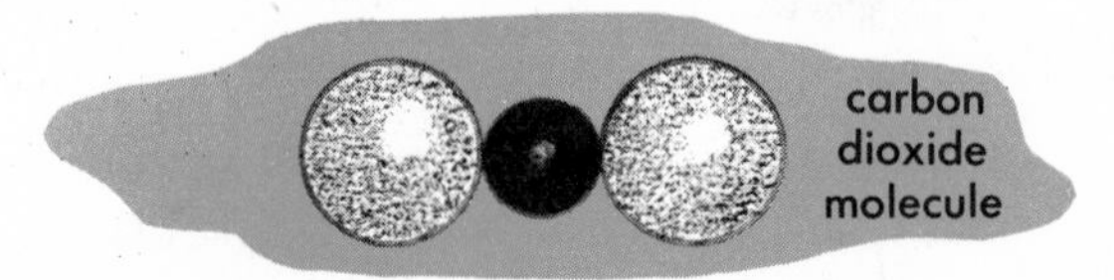

The name of each kind of atom, or element, is often written with only one or two letters. These letters are called **chemical symbols** (sim′ blz). Each element has its own symbol. Look at the names and symbols of some of the chemical elements.

ELEMENTS AND THEIR SYMBOLS

Element	Chemical Symbol	How Used
Silver	Ag	coins
Aluminum	Al	cooking pans
Gold	Au	jewelry
Carbon	C	pencil lead
Calcium	Ca	cement
Chlorine	Cl	swimming pools
Chromium	Cr	auto bumpers
Copper	Cu	electrical wiring
Fluorine	F	plastics
Iron	Fe	nails
Hydrogen	H	fuel
Helium	He	balloons
Mercury	Hg	thermometers
Iodine	I	antiseptics
Potassium	K	fertilizers
Magnesium	Mg	flares
Nitrogen	N	explosives
Sodium	Na	table salt
Neon	Ne	electric signs
Nickel	Ni	coins
Oxygen	O	fuel
Phosphorus	P	matches
Lead	Pb	fishing sinkers
Platinum	Pt	jewelry
Sulfur	S	gunpowder
Silicon	Si	sand
Tin	Sn	steel can coating
Uranium	U	nuclear energy
Zinc	Zn	electric cells

These same symbols are used all over the world, no matter what language is spoken. Why do you think this is important?

Can you use symbols to show how atoms join in a chemical change to form compounds? Instead of drawing a picture of a carbon atom, you can write the symbol "C" to represent a carbon atom.

If you want to show that there is only one atom of a certain kind, you write only the symbol. If you wish to show more than one atom of the same kind, you write a small number beside the symbol for the atom. The symbol for a molecule of oxygen which contains two atoms of oxygen is O_2.

What would you write to show a molecule of carbon dioxide? You can put the symbols for the atoms of carbon and oxygen together, CO_2.

Does carbon dioxide have more than one kind of atom joined together? Is carbon dioxide a compound? When the symbols for its atoms are written together (CO_2), they are called a **chemical formula** (fôr′ myə lə). A formula shows what atoms are in a molecule of a compound and how many atoms of each kind the molecule has. How many atoms of carbon does a carbon dioxide molecule have? How many atoms of oxygen does it have?

Look at the formulas for the compounds shown in this chart.

Name of Compound	Chemical Formula
water	H_2O
salt	NaCl
hydrogen peroxide	H_2O_2
sugar	$C_{12}H_{22}O_{11}$
sand	SiO_2

Name the elements in each compound. (Use the list on page 11.) How many of each kind of atom are in each kind of molecule? What is the total number of atoms in each molecule?

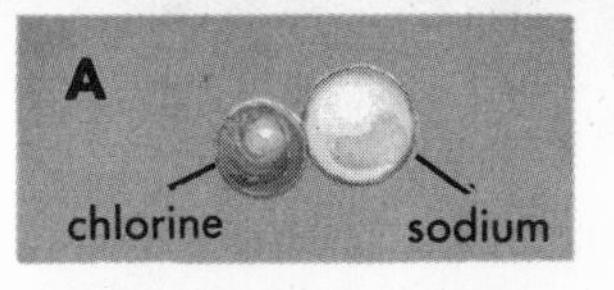

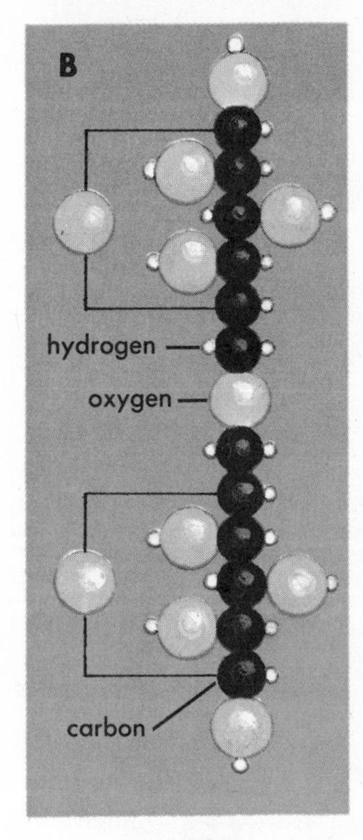

A. Salt molecule
B. Sugar molecule

Chemical Sentences

If you wanted to tell how atoms join to form carbon dioxide, you might say or write it in words like this:

One atom of carbon joins with two atoms of oxygen to form one molecule of carbon dioxide.

Or, you might draw something like this:

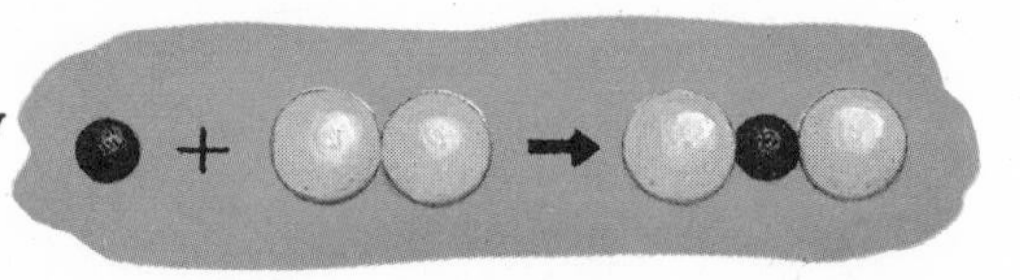

Or, you might use chemical symbols and formulas:

$$C + O_2 \rightarrow CO_2$$

If you use chemical symbols and formulas, you use a **chemical equation** (i kwā′ zhən). Do all three ways tell the same thing? Which way do you think is the fastest and simplest?

What is a water molecule made of?

Water is a compound made up of the elements hydrogen and oxygen. Both elements are part of the air you breathe. Each is a gas. Yet, when atoms of these elements join, they form a liquid that you can drink. When atoms of these elements join, two molecules (four atoms) of hydrogen join with one molecule (two atoms) of oxygen to form two molecules of water. This is how the change could be shown by drawing atoms.

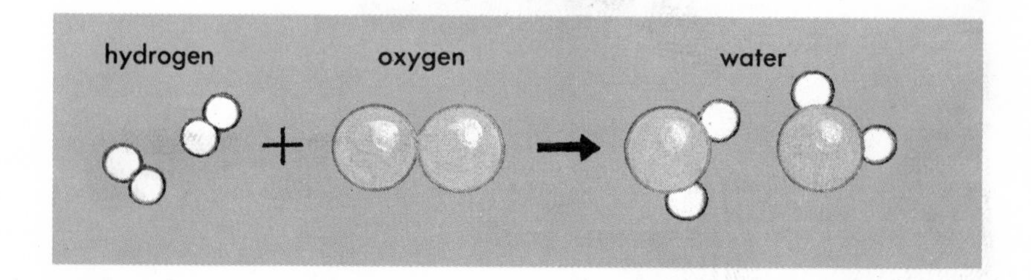

This equation tells the same thing:

$$2\,H_2 + O_2 \rightarrow 2\,H_2O$$

What does a number in front of a symbol tell you?

Understanding that water molecules are made of atoms can help you better understand the difference between a physical change and a chemical change.

"Breaking" a Compound

Can the compound water be a solid, a liquid, or a gas? When a cube of ice melts, its molecules move more rapidly. When water evaporates, its molecules move still faster. Usually, the faster the molecules move, the farther apart they are. No matter what the distance between the molecules, each molecule still has two atoms of hydrogen and one atom of oxygen. Are the molecules still molecules of water? Are melting and evaporation physical or chemical changes? If the molecules are changed, a new material will be formed. If the atoms of hydrogen and oxygen are separated, will they still form water? Is the change a chemical change?

How are molecules of ice, water, and water vapor different? How are the molecules alike?

DISCOVER

How can you separate water into hydrogen and oxygen molecules?

What You Need

carbon rods from 2 flashlight cells
2 pieces of insulated wire, each 1 foot long
quart jar
teaspoon
washing soda (sal soda)
water
small widemouthed jar
2 test tubes
electric cell
magnifying glass

1. Remove one inch of the covering from each end of the wires. Loop one end of one of the wires around a carbon rod and fasten it tightly by twisting. Do the same with the other wire and the other carbon rod.
2. Fill a quart jar with water. Add four teaspoonfuls of washing soda and stir until all of it has dissolved.

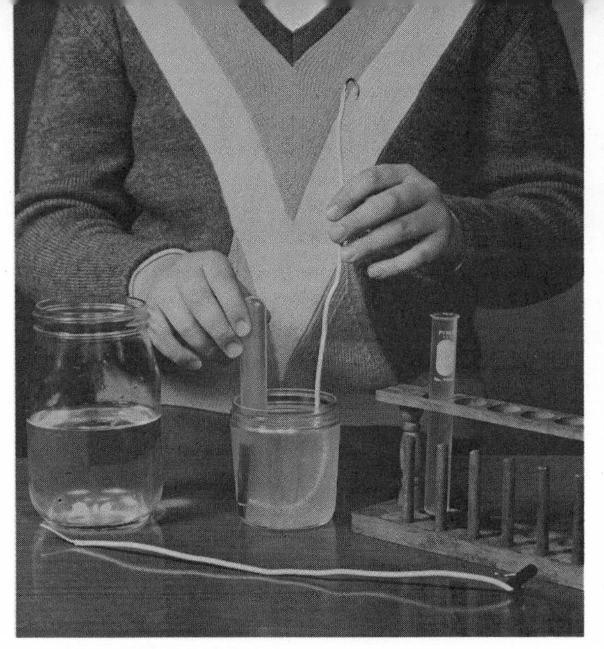

3. Pour half the liquid from the quart jar into a small widemouthed jar. Use some of the remaining liquid to fill the two test tubes completely. While holding a thumb over the opening of one test tube, turn the test tube upside down and place its opening below the top of the liquid in the small jar. The liquid will remain in the test tube.
4. Now put one carbon rod into the opening of this test tube. Make sure the bare wire attached to the carbon rod is also in the test tube. Do this carefully, so that the tube remains filled with liquid. Do the same with the other test tube and carbon rod.
5. Connect the wires to the terminals of an electric cell. Watch the carbon rods carefully with a magnifying glass. What collects on the rods? Allow the action to continue for at least an hour.

Is there less liquid in each test tube? What is pushing the liquid out? What elements are collecting in the test tubes?

What may be used to separate water into hydrogen and oxygen molecules?

Electricity can separate the two kinds of atoms in water molecules. The washing soda helps to start the separation. In one test tube, bubbles of oxygen gas collect. In the other test tube, bubbles of hydrogen gas collect. As the gases fill the test tubes, what happens to the water? More gas should collect in one test tube than in the other. Do you think that the test tube with more gas contains hydrogen gas or does it contain oxygen gas? Give a reason for your answer.

Making a Compound

What gas is formed when oxygen atoms join with carbon atoms? What liquid is formed when oxygen atoms join with hydrogen atoms? Can you use oxygen atoms to form a solid compound?

DISCOVER

How can you form a solid compound with the element oxygen, which is a gas?

What You Need

steel wool	water
glass	paper towels

1. Roll some steel wool into a ball and put it into a glass. Add enough water to cover the steel wool.

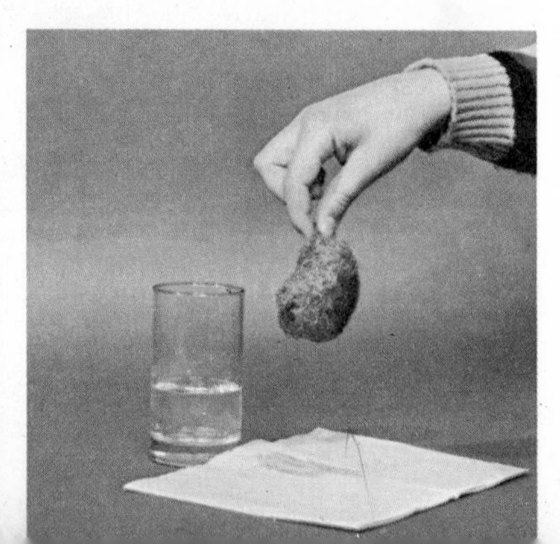

2. Take the steel wool out of the glass. Put the wet steel wool on a piece of paper towel. Let it stand overnight.

Observe the steel wool carefully the second day. What change do you notice? What would you call the new solid that has formed?

The steel wool is made mostly of the element iron (Fe). Air supplied the element oxygen (O). The two elements, oxygen and iron, joined to form a new material. The new material is a solid called "rust." Rust is mostly the compound iron oxide (Fe_2O_3). How many atoms of iron are in one molecule of iron oxide? How many atoms of oxygen are in one molecule of iron oxide?

What effect does moisture have on rusting?

Why do you think this side of a ship has rusted?

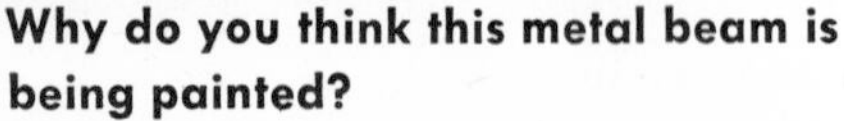

Why do you think this metal beam is being painted?

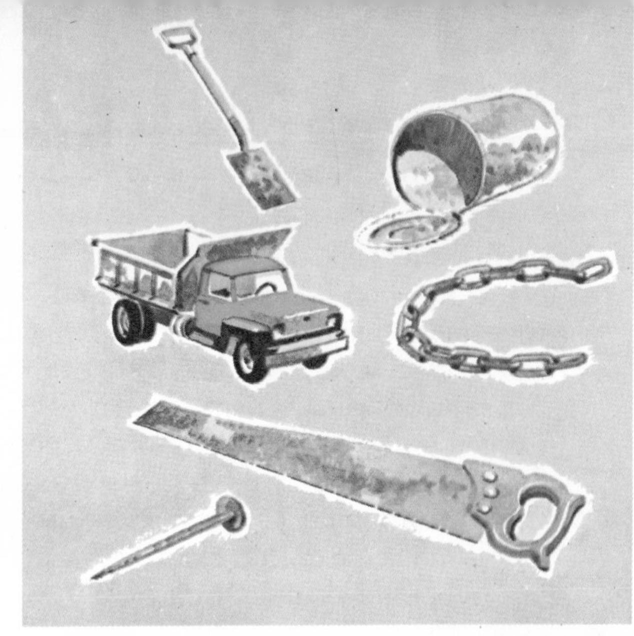

Why do you think these things have rusted?

Usually, rust forms more slowly than it did in your experiment. Oxygen in the air joins with atoms of iron most easily when the air is moist. Is rusting a chemical change? Each year, millions of dollars are spent to replace iron and steel objects which have been damaged by rust. Can you find some materials around your home or school on which rust is forming? What is usually done to keep oxygen in the air away from iron and steel?

In what ways might you find out what this material is?

Testing for Elements and Compounds

Suppose you want to find out what elements are in a compound. You can work with clues, much like a detective. Find out all you can about the material, such as its color, odor, weight, and the way it changes either physically or chemically when mixed with known materials.

When certain elements are heated in a flame, the flame is a particular color. Scientists sometimes identify elements in this way. This is called a **flame test.**

FIND OUT

How can you use a flame test to identify certain elements?

EXPERIMENT

What You Need

alcohol burner
3 spoons
salt ($NaCl$)
boric acid (H_3BO_3)
cream of tartar ($KHC_4H_4O_6$)

1. Have your teacher light the alcohol burner. Darken the room. The alcohol should burn with a pale blue flame.
2. Now, sprinkle salt into the flame. What color is the flame?
3. Repeat the test by sprinkling boric acid into the flame. What color is the flame?
4. Now test some cream of tartar. What color is the flame this time?

Can a flame test be used with all elements?

Flame test for sodium

Flame test for potassium

Flame test for boron

Can you think of another way to make the flame test without sprinkling the test material into the flame?

Sodium (Na) atoms make a flame yellow. When a compound containing sodium is heated, the flame becomes yellow. A yellow flame shows that the compound being tested contains what element? Do you think salt contains sodium? Many other compounds contain sodium. To discover which sodium compound you are investigating, you must make other tests.

A violet flame shows that cream of tartar is a compound containing the element potassium (K). A green flame shows that boron (B) is one of the elements in boric acid. Not all elements burn with a flame that has a characteristic color. Other tests also must be used.

Here is a list of other elements and the color of flame they produce. Ask your teacher for some chemicals which can be safely tested with a flame test.

FLAME TESTS OF SOME ELEMENTS

Element	Flame Color
barium	light green
boron	yellow-green
calcium	red-orange
copper	bright green
lead	light blue
potassium	light violet
sodium	bright yellow
zinc	white-green

Many different kinds of tests may be used to recognize compounds. Sometimes you can recognize a compound by a change in its color when another chemical is added to it.

Try a simple test to see if a material contains the compound called starch.

FIND OUT

How can you test to see if a material contains the compound starch?

EXPERIMENT

What You Need

drinking glass
water
medicine dropper
tincture of iodine
cornstarch
tablespoon

1. Mix a tablespoon of cornstarch in a glass that contains very warm water.
2. Use a medicine dropper to add the iodine, a few drops at a time, to the glass of cornstarch. Stir the cornstarch solution with a spoon each time you add several drops of iodine. Do this until you notice a change in color. What is the color change?

How can you discover if a food contains starch?

What color could be seen when the iodine was added to a material which contained starch? Many of the foods you eat contain starch. Try to find out which foods on this list have the compound starch in them. With dried seed foods, you might need to grind them and add a little water to them for best results. Make a record of your results.

Material	Color After Adding Iodine	Has Starch	Does Not Have Starch
bread	purple	X	
milk	brown		X
rice			
orange			
cereal			
potato			
celery			
apple			

Some Important Chemical Changes

Burning is an important chemical change. When you burn paper, you see smoke. A black ash remains. Do you know what happens when something burns?

Fasten a candle to a baking pan. Have your teacher light the candle. Watch it burn. Now have your teacher place a jar over the candle. What happens? Air contains molecules of oxygen gas. As candle wax is heated, its atoms move apart. What kind of a change is this? Some of the atoms in the molecules of wax then join with the oxygen atoms from the air. What kind of a change is this? Are new compounds formed? How can you find out what these are?

FIND OUT

What compounds are formed when a candle burns?

EXPERIMENT

What You Need

2 candles, same size
limewater tablets
water
4 glasses
clean cloth
spoon
modeling clay
cup

What element is necessary for something to burn?

1. Set two drinking glasses in a cool place for half an hour.
2. Fasten a candle to the inside bottom of each of the other two glasses with modeling clay. Ask your teacher to light the candle in one glass.
3. Hold a cool drinking glass upside down over the mouth of each glass. Watch the inside of each glass for any change. What compound collects on the inside of the glass over the burning candle? Put the glasses down and blow out the flame.

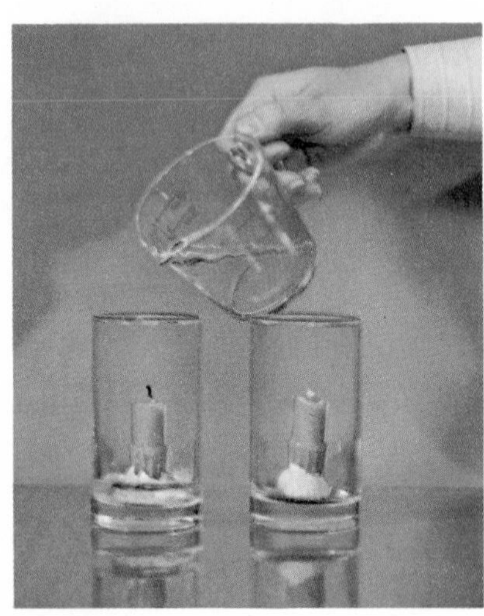

4. Have your teacher make some limewater in the cup, following the directions that come with the limewater tablets. Pour half an inch of limewater into each glass, being careful not to wet the wicks.
5. Light the candle in only one glass. Allow it to burn for two minutes before you cover the glass.
6. Place a cover on each glass. Wait for the candle to stop burning. Why do you think the candle goes out? Shake the test solution around in each glass. Hold both glasses up to the light.

What compound appeared on the cool glass held over the burning candle? What change took place in the limewater that was in the glass with the burning candle? Limewater becomes milky when it mixes with carbon dioxide. What two compounds are formed when a candle burns? Why did you use a glass with an unlighted candle for both parts of the experiment?

Materials such as paper, oil, wax, wood, and coal are made of compounds which have atoms of carbon, hydrogen, and oxygen. When these materials burn, some of the carbon joins with some oxygen in the air. What compound forms? At the same time, the hydrogen and oxygen atoms join. What compound do they form? Compounds containing carbon, which were not burned completely, formed the black soot. This black soot is the element carbon. Nothing can burn without a supply of oxygen.

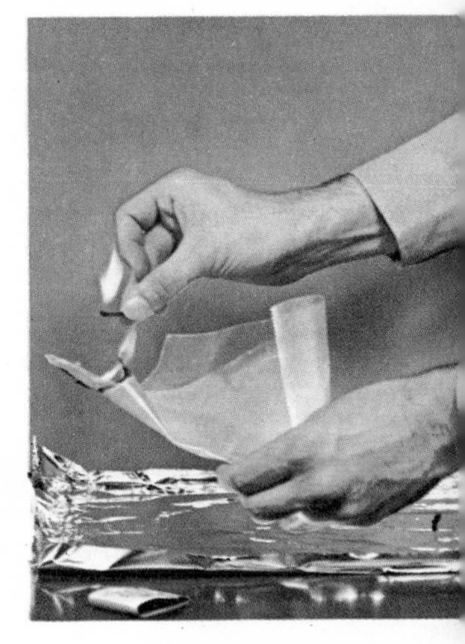

Burning is an important chemical change which produces heat and light. Heat from burning may be used to cook foods, to heat homes, to run factory machines, to power automobiles, trains, and airplanes, and to dispose of wastes. Heat from burning may be used to produce steam which runs electric generators in your community.

Whenever oxygen joins other atoms, the chemical change is called **oxidation** (ok′ sə dā′ shən). When a material joins quickly with oxygen, enough heat is produced to cause a flame. This quick oxidation is called **combustion** (kəm bus′ chən), or burning. Often, however, there is no combustion. Oxidation can take place with just a little heat and no light.

What is slow oxidation?

Flames can be used to provide both heat and light.

When materials join with oxygen slowly, the chemical change is called slow oxidation. Oxygen joins with many other kinds of atoms, including those in food materials.

Your body temperature is usually near 98 degrees Fahrenheit. Do you know why your body is warm?

Use a thermometer to find your body temperature.

DISCOVER

What causes body heat?

What You Need

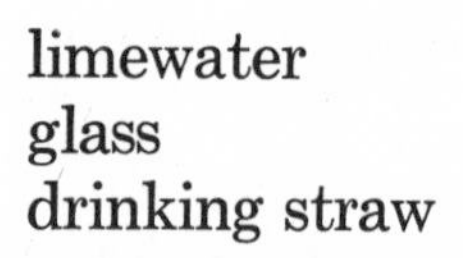

limewater
glass
drinking straw

1. Pour some clear limewater into a glass. Place a drinking straw into the liquid.
2. Take a deep breath and slowly blow through the straw into the limewater. Repeat until you notice a change. Explain what happened.

Where did the carbon dioxide come from? What compound was formed by your body? Where did the oxygen come from? Where did the carbon come from?

Oxygen in the air you breathe is carried to all parts of your body by your blood. Carbon is present in many of the foods you eat. What chemical change occurs? Is this oxidation? Is heat produced when carbon dioxide gas is formed? You breathe carbon dioxide and other gases out of your lungs. Is your body kept warm by oxidation of the foods you eat? Is carbon dioxide the only compound you breathe out? Do you know another compound that you breathe out?

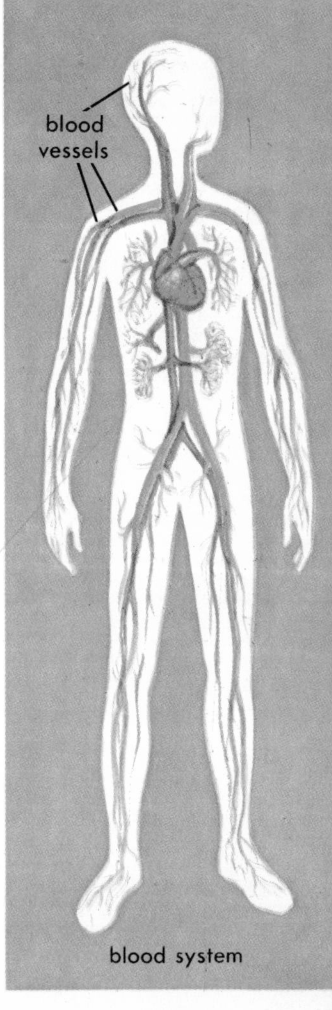

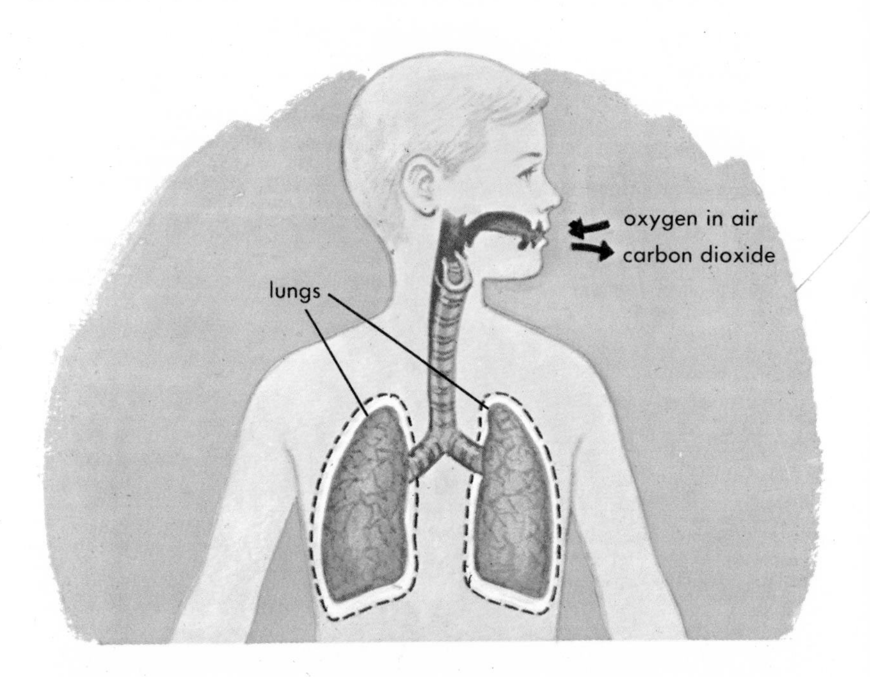

DISCOVER

What product of oxidation, other than carbon dioxide, do you breathe out?

What You Need

small mirror

What is one chemical change that takes place in your body?

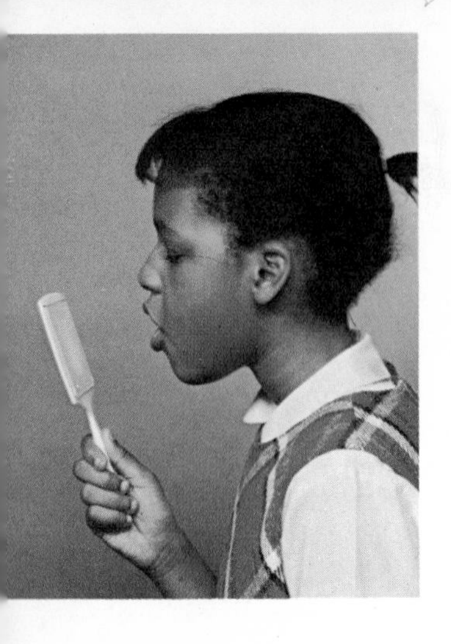

1. Cool the mirror. Then polish its surface.
2. Hold the mirror near your nose and breathe on it. What collects on the mirror?

Many of the foods that you eat contain hydrogen. Some of the hydrogen joins with oxygen in the air you breathe to form what compound? What two compounds you breathe out are formed by the oxidation of foods in your body? How are the results of these last two experiments like the results of the experiment in which you tested the compounds formed by a burning candle?

Oxidation is just one of the important chemical changes which takes place in living things. Plants as well as animals take in elements and compounds. As these elements and compounds change, plants and animals grow and change.

Drugs

Do you know what drugs are? Drugs are chemical compounds, other than food and water, that are taken into the body. Medicines and pills are drugs. Are drugs helpful or harmful?

Drugs are helpful when they are used to fight disease. When we are ill, a doctor may **prescribe** (prē skrīb′) medicine or pills. The doctor's **prescription** (prē skrip′-shən) tells exactly how much of a drug to take. It tells exactly when a drug should be taken. It is safe to take drugs prescribed by a doctor. It is safe if you follow the directions on the label. When are drugs not safe?

Taking drugs that are not prescribed by a doctor can be dangerous. Taking an amount of a drug other than that ordered by a doctor can be dangerous. Mixing drugs of different kinds can be very dangerous. Taking drugs in dangerous and unhealthful ways is called **drug abuse** (ə byūs′).

Drug abuse can affect both the minds and the bodies of people in harmful ways. Tobacco smoke and alcoholic drinks are drugs. They are both harmful to the body. What other drugs do you know which are often abused?

The doctor telephones the prescription to the druggist.

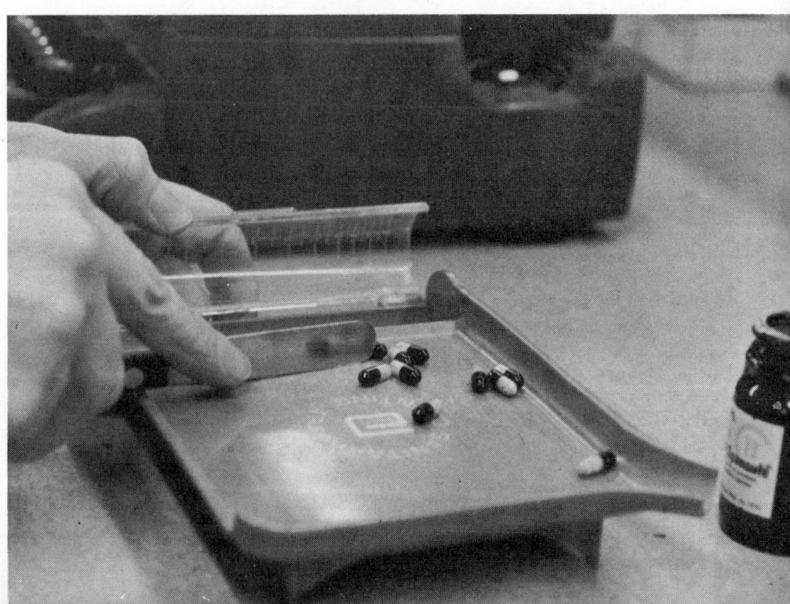

The druggist fills the prescription according to the doctor's order.

Exploring Your Learnings

Here are some ideas and vocabulary. What do these mean to you?

Words to Use

molecules (p. 2)
atoms (p. 3)
elements (p. 3)
compounds (p. 4)
physical change (p. 6)
chemical change (p. 7)
carbon (p. 10)
oxygen (p. 10)
carbon dioxide (p. 10)
chemical symbols (p. 10)
chemical formula (p. 12)
chemical equation (p. 13)
flame test (p. 20)
oxidation (p. 27)
combustion (p. 27)
prescription (p. 31)

Some valuable elements are stored in the form of bars.

Ideas to Use

1. All matter is made of atoms which combine in many ways to form molecules.
2. Materials with only one kind of atom are elements.
3. Molecules with more than one kind of atom are compounds.
4. Every kind of material has its own kind of molecules.
5. A physical change does not change the kind of molecules in a material.
6. A chemical change changes molecules in a material so that different molecules are formed.
7. There are more than one hundred different elements which join in many, many ways to form compounds.
8. Letter symbols may be used to represent the atoms of each element.

9. Formulas may be used to represent the molecules of a compound.
10. Symbols and formulas may be written together in a chemical sentence or equation.
11. An element may be identified by color, odor, weight, or the way it acts physically and chemically when mixed with known materials.
12. Drugs are compounds other than food and water that are taken into the body.

Using Your Ideas

(Do not write in this book.)

1. Find out if heat can cause chemical changes. Dip a clean pen or paintbrush into lemon juice ($C_6O_7H_8$). Write on white paper with the pen or brush. Allow the paper to dry. Can you read the writing? Have your teacher heat the paper carefully over an electric hot plate. What caused the change?
2. Why should some foods and drugs be stored in a refrigerator? Why should some foods and drugs be stored in tinted bottles?
3. Mix one teaspoon of baking soda ($NaHCO_3$) with one teaspoon of cream of tartar ($KHC_4H_4O_6$) in a dry cup. Is there a change? Add one teaspoonful of water to the cup. Is there a change? What do you think caused the change?
4. Many man-made elements were named for important scientists. Read about some of these elements such as curium, einsteinium, fermium, and mendelevium. Make a report on one of these elements.
5. Find out why some drug prescriptions cannot be refilled. Find out how drugs such as aspirin and cough medicine are often abused.

Sound and How It Travels

Do oceans make sounds? This picture may make you think of the roaring or booming of the ocean. Many people who have lived near the sea enjoy its different sounds. The sea is said to hiss, lap, splash, slap, and crash! The ocean is never quiet because its water is always moving.

Does sound seem to move? When you speak to someone, the sound of your voice must travel to reach the ears of that person. Sound must move very fast because it does not seem to take any time at all for words to travel between people. But men can travel in jets and rockets that move faster than the speed of sound.

Do you know how all sounds are like the ocean? The water of an ocean travels to the shore in waves. How do you think sound travels?

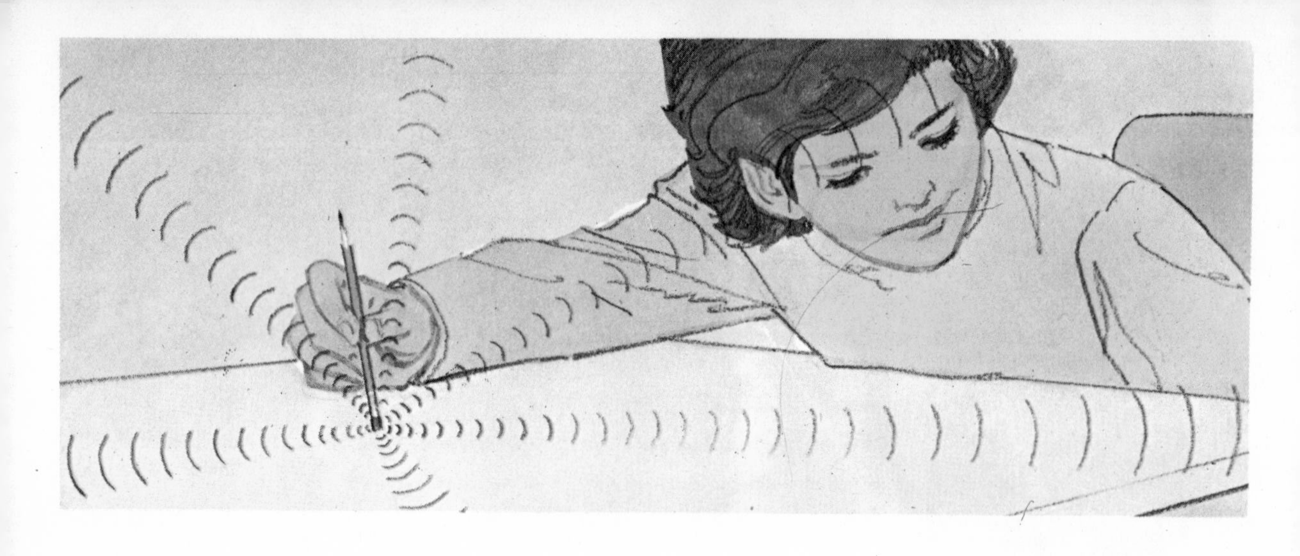

Sound Vibrations

Tap your desk with a pencil and listen to the sound. As the pencil hits the desk, molecules in the desk and pencil **vibrate** (vī′ brāt), or move back and forth many times. This movement causes the air molecules next to the pencil and desk to vibrate also. These air molecules bump into other air molecules and the movement is passed along until the vibrations reach your ears. If there were no air between the desk and your ears, would you hear any sound?

Have you ever seen a wave in an ocean, a lake, or a river? You cannot see sound waves, but they are something like water waves. Sound vibrations travel in waves that spread out in every direction.

Water waves

If you throw a stone into a lake, do water waves spread out from the spot where the stone hits the water? In the same way, when you hit the desk with a pencil, waves of vibrating molecules spread out from the spot where the desk was hit. You hear the sound, but do you think someone in the next room hears the sound?

Is air the only material that sound waves can travel through? Press one of your ears against the desk and cover your other ear with your hand. Tap the desk again with your pencil. Can sound waves travel through the desk? How can you find out if sound waves travel in all directions through wood? Do you think sound waves travel fastest through a solid, a liquid, or a gas? Explain your answer in terms of what you know about the distances between molecules in solids, liquids, and gases.

How does sound travel through materials?

The Speed of Sound

Sound travels through air at a speed of about 1,100 feet per second. Sound travels through water at a speed of about 4,800 feet per second. Sound travels through wood at about 12,000 feet per second. Sound travels through all materials in waves that spread out in every direction.

Porpoises send sound messages to each other through water.

Would the sound of the ax reach your ears faster through wood or through air?

Flying Faster Than Sound

Another way of saying how fast sound travels in air is to say it travels about 750 miles per hour. At one time, it was believed that airplanes would never be able to travel at this speed. Scientists thought that the vibrations would break the airplane. They called the speed of sound the "sound barrier."

Today, many airplanes fly at speeds greater than 750 miles per hour. Planes that travel faster than the speed of sound are said to be **supersonic** (su′ pər son′ ik). An airplane flying faster than 750 miles per hour may cause vibrations that sound like an explosion. Sometimes this sound is called a **sonic** (son′ik) **boom.** Air molecules are squeezed together at the front edges of the wings of the airplane. The tightly squeezed molecules make a large coneshaped sound wave. A sonic boom may be heard when the wave touches the ground.

People who live near places where high-speed jet airplanes fly hear many sonic booms. Sometimes these vibrations are strong enough to break windows.

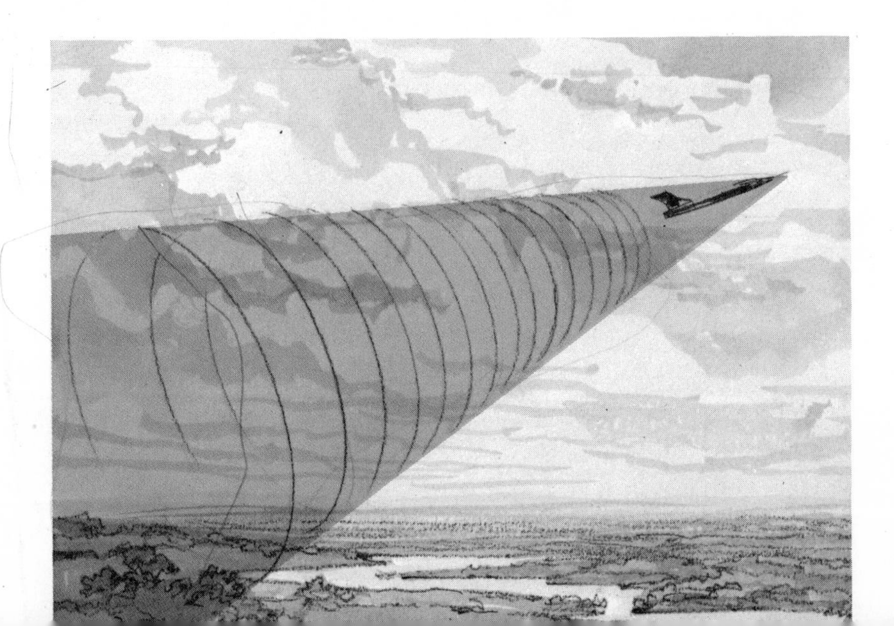

Controlling Sound Waves

Throw a ball against the side of a building. Does the ball bounce off the building and come back to you? Do you think sound waves bounce off surfaces?

Fill a large pan with water. Darken the room and hold a lighted flashlight so that it shines down into the water. Drop a stone into the water. Watch the pan carefully. What do you notice as the waves bump into the sides of the pan?

Sound waves act much like water waves. When the sound waves strike something, they bounce back, or are **reflected** (ri flek′ təd). You can hear reflected sound if you talk into a pail. How does your voice sound when you talk into a pail? Do you hear reflected words almost as soon as you speak them?

Reflected sounds are called **echoes** (ek′ ōz). To hear a sound reflected as a true echo, you would need to shout toward a stone building or cliff at least fifty-five feet away. Sound waves travel very quickly. If you wish to hear a true echo, a certain amount of time must pass between the start of the sound waves and their return to your ears. You cannot hear sounds clearly if they are reflected a short distance. Does the picture at left below show a good place to hear echoes? Why?

Making echoes may be fun, but can reflected sounds sometimes be a problem? Have you ever found it hard to understand someone speaking in a large room? Was it because of echoes? Maybe you have a room in your school in which ordinary sounds seem very loud. What do you think causes this? What can be done to stop echoes?

What are some materials that do not reflect sound well?

FIND OUT

Do all materials reflect sound equally well?

EXPERIMENT

What You Need

2 cardboard tubes
label marked "A"
label marked "B"
label marked "C"
wristwatch
materials to test, such as flat pieces of cardboard, wood, metal, glass, rubber, styrofoam, carpeting

1. Place the cardboard tubes and labels as shown in the picture.
2. Have someone hold a wristwatch at point A.
3. Have another person hold one of the materials to be tested at point B.
4. Listen at point C. Do you hear the ticking?
5. Try the same thing with each of the other materials to be tested.

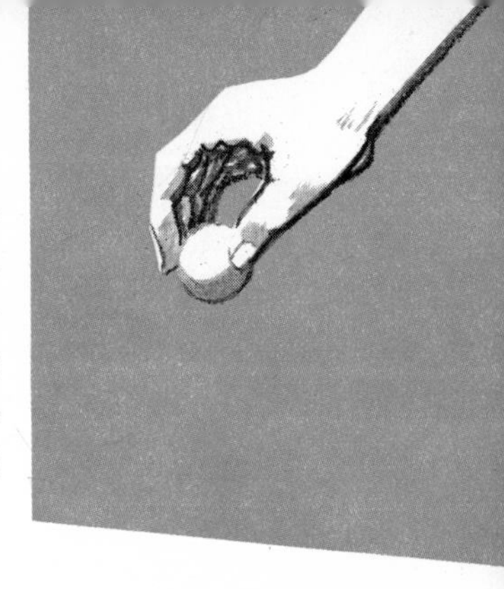

Which of the materials reflect sound the best? Which of the materials would you use if you did not want sound to be reflected? Drop a Ping-Pong ball on each of the materials from the same height to find out which materials are harder or softer than the others. Compare these results with the way in which soft and hard materials reflect sound.

Perhaps you had your ear closer to the tube for one experiment than for another. How might that affect the results? Perhaps you can use a tape recorder to record the results. Why might this way be better?

Do both hard and soft materials control sound? In a radio or television studio, how could too many reflected sounds affect broadcasts? Why are the walls sometimes hung with soft curtains? Would soft curtains reflect sound? Often both the ceiling and walls are covered with tile or plaster which has tiny holes or slits. Would such materials reflect sound well? Would the same materials be used where you wanted sound to reflect?

How can you use your hands to reflect sound waves?

How does the way this bandshell is built and the way the audience is seated help the sound to be heard?

A bandshell is built to reflect sounds toward the audience. The curved wall behind the band is made of wood, metal, or plaster. Are these materials good sound reflectors? Do you think there is a reason for the particular shape of this building?

Have someone across the room listen to your voice while you talk softly, cupping your hands around your mouth. Then say the same words softly without using your hands. Which way makes it easier for the person to hear the sound? Can you explain why?

Sound waves travel in all directions. When you speak, some sound waves move upward, some downward, some to either side, and some straight forward. Which sound waves will be heard by the person across the room? When you cup your hands, sound waves are reflected from them. Many of these sound waves are reflected straight forward. Why would this help the person to hear you better? Why does a bandshell enable the audience to hear more of the sound of an orchestra?

Your Hearing

Have you ever thought of how many different sounds you hear each day? The sounds of voices, music, and machines are part of the world around you.

How does the shape of your ear help you to hear?

Some sounds are soft like the hum of an electric refrigerator or the quiet breathing of a sleeping baby. Are there loud sounds, too? Have you ever been to a ball game and heard people shouting? At games, people sometimes shout through a cone-shaped object called a **megaphone** (meg′ ə fōn). A megaphone reflects sound waves forward, just as your hands did when you cupped them around your mouth. Do you think a megaphone works better than your hands? Why, or why not?

At one time, cone-shaped earphones were used by people who could not hear well. The wide end of the cone reflected sound waves down into the ear. Because the earphone was wide, more sound waves collected in it than would normally reach the ear. Why would sounds seem louder with this kind of earphone?

The outside part of the ear is wide, but inside the head it is narrow. Is your ear shaped like a small cone? The wide part "catches" sound waves and reflects them into the inner ear.

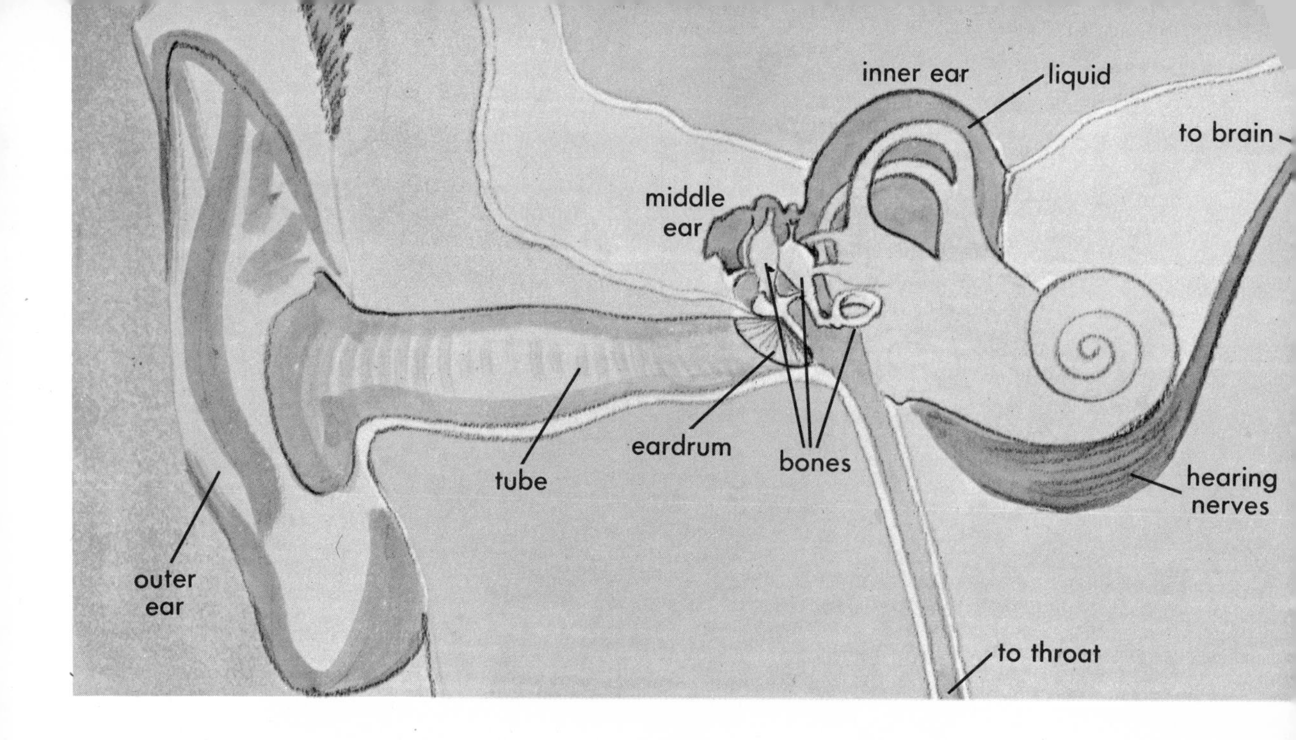

Look at the ear of a person near you. Compare it with the picture. Which parts can you see?

All you can see is the outer ear. Your outer ear helps to collect sound waves which travel through the air. Vibrations enter the outer ear and then travel through a tube. Molecules of air in the tube pass on the vibrations to a thin piece of stretched skin called the **eardrum** (ir′ drum′). From there, the vibrations travel along three tiny bones. How are these bones useful?

The tiny bones carry the vibrations from the eardrum to the inner part of the ear. The last bone touches a chamber filled with liquid. In the liquid are many tiny nerves. As the liquid vibrates, the nerves send messages to the brain, and you hear sound.

If the eardrum or bones of the ear are damaged, what may happen to your hearing? Why is it never wise to put anything smaller than your finger into the ear tube?

Can you usually tell the direction from which a sound is coming? Do you know why?

How is monaural sound different from stereophonic sound?

FIND OUT

How can you tell from which direction a sound is coming?

EXPERIMENT

What You Need

cardboard tube, at least 12 inches long
ruler
pencil
scissors
glass

1. Cut a cardboard tube to make one tube four inches long and another tube eight inches long.
2. Place one tube by each ear. Have someone stand in front of you and tap a glass with a pencil.

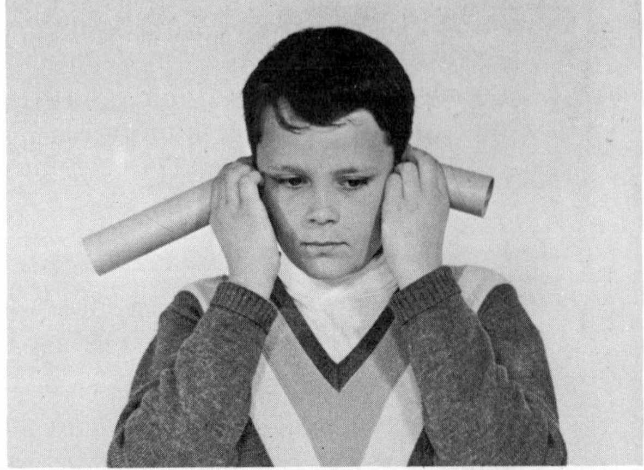

From which direction does the sound seem to come? Is the long or the short tube on that side?

A sound that comes from a direction other than directly in front of or in back of you may reach both your ears at slightly different times. Which ear will it reach first? This is how you usually tell the direction. Through which tube did sound reach your ear first? Did the sound seem to come from that side?

When you are listening to an orchestra in front of you, do your ears enable you to tell where certain instruments are located? The sounds of instruments on your left reach your left ear first. Sounds on your right reach your right ear first.

When you listen to a **monaural** (mä nôr′ əl) **record,** an orchestra sounds as if all of the instruments are crowded into the small space of the speaker. Such records are made by using one microphone. The records are played through only one speaker.

Most long playing records are **stereophonic** (ster′ ē ə fän′ ik) **records.** Stereophonic records enable you to hear music as if the orchestra were actually in the room. The sound is recorded by using two or more microphones. Where do you think the microphones are placed? By using a stereophonic record player, you can hear the sounds from each side of the orchestra on a different speaker. How should the speakers be placed? Where should you sit to hear the sounds as if the orchestra were in the room?

What is the difference between subsonic vibrations and ultrasonic vibrations?

Recording stereophonic music in a studio

Silent Sounds

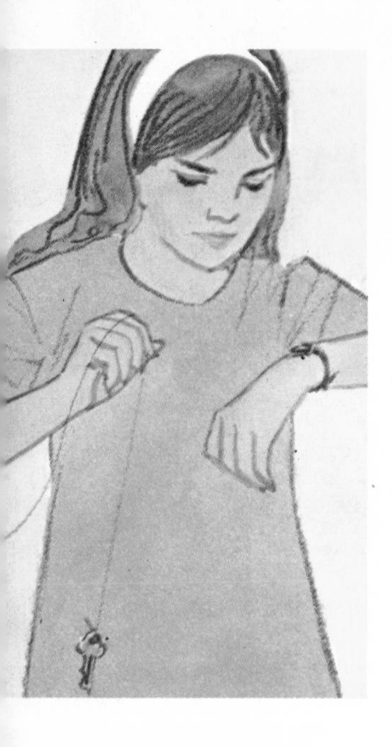

Can you hear everything that vibrates? Some things vibrate too slowly for you to hear the sound.

Tie a key to a string and swing it so that it changes direction two times each second. To get this result, you may have to hold the string closer or farther from the key. Can you hear a sound?

The key is vibrating once each second. Is the key vibrating too slowly for you to hear the vibration? Does this mean you have poor hearing? Most persons cannot hear vibrations that occur less than twenty times per second. Vibrations that are too slow to be heard are **subsonic** (sub son′ ik) vibrations. Most people cannot hear vibrations that occur more than 20,000 times per second. These fast vibrations are called **ultrasonic** (ul′ trə son′ ik) vibrations.

Have you ever seen a person using a "noiseless" whistle to call his dog? Dogs, bats, and some other animals can hear ultrasonic vibrations.

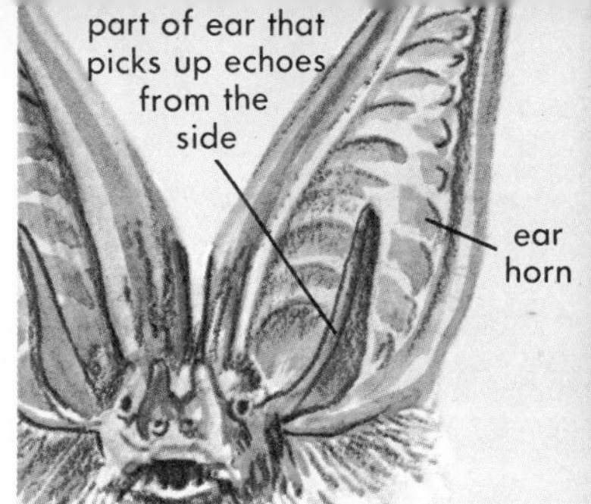

A bat has sensitive ears which pick up the echoes of its ultrasonic vibrations.

Why can bats fly in complete darkness without bumping into anything? Bats can make ultrasonic vibrations with their throats. Ultrasonic vibrations, like ordinary sounds, are reflected as echoes. Bats send out such vibrations and listen for the echoes. They can tell their distance from objects by knowing the time it takes for the echoes to reach their ears.

Echoes of ultrasonic vibrations can be used by persons aboard ships to locate underwater objects. Instruments measure the time that passes between the sending and receiving of the "silent" sound. The instrument which produces and detects the "silent" sound is called **sonar** (sō′ när′). How can sonar be used to make travel by ship safer? How can sonar be useful to fishermen?

Ultrasonic vibrations can even be used for washing dishes or clothing. Vibrations can clean clothing and dishes without soap by shaking the dirt and grease from them. Ultrasonic vibrations have been used to kill germs, to mix paints, and to clear the air of smoke and fog. Scientists are still experimenting to find new uses for these "sounds" you cannot hear.

A. Sonar being used on a ship

B. Parts of an ultrasonic instrument

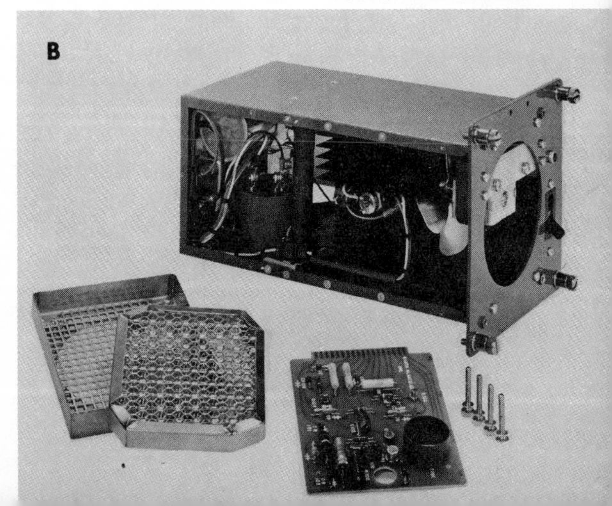

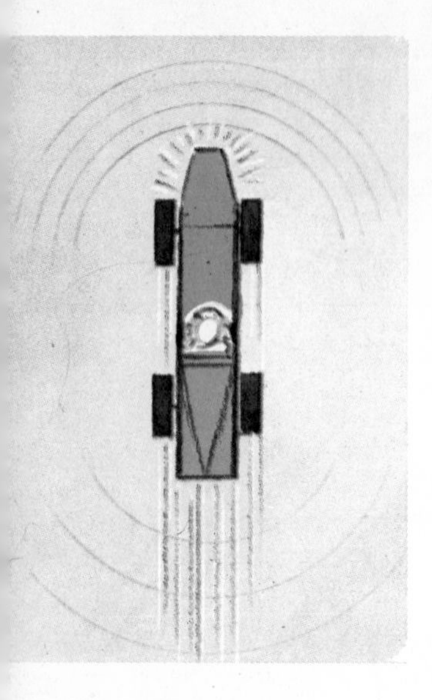

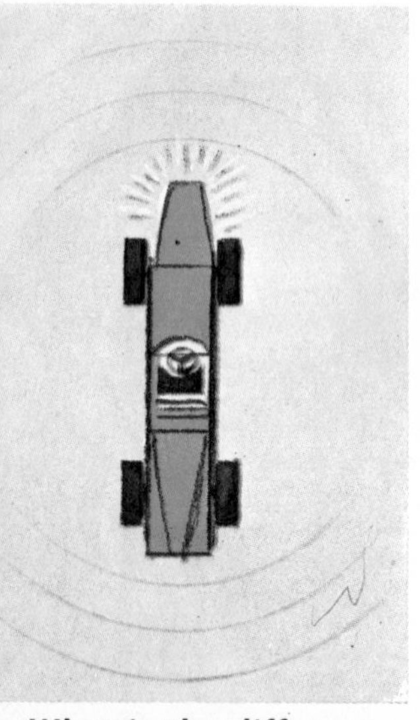

What is the difference between sound waves produced by a moving racing car and a racing car that is standing still?

Exploring Your Learnings

Here are some ideas and vocabulary. What do these mean to you?

Words to Use

vibrate (p. 36)	eardrum (p. 47)
supersonic (p. 39)	monaural record (p. 49)
sonic boom (p. 39)	stereophonic records (p. 49)
reflected (p. 40)	subsonic (p. 50)
echoes (p. 41)	ultrasonic (p. 50)
megaphone (p. 46)	sonar (p. 51)

Ideas to Use

1. Vibrating molecules make sound waves that you may hear as sounds.
2. Sound waves traveling in a solid, a liquid, or a gas spread out in every direction.
3. Sound travels faster through some materials than through others.
4. Sound waves may be reflected from some surfaces as echoes.
5. Curved surfaces such as bandshells, and cones such as megaphones or earphones may direct sound waves so that they can be heard more easily.
6. The ear is made of an outer part which collects sound vibrations, and an inner part which passes on the vibrations.
7. You can often tell what direction a sound is coming from if it does not reach both ears at the same time.
8. Most people cannot hear vibrations which are either subsonic or ultrasonic.

9. The reflection of ultrasonic vibrations can be used to measure distances between objects.

Using Your Ideas

(Do not write in this book.)

1. Plan an experiment to find out what materials can be used on or inside of a wall to prevent sound from passing through it.
2. Find out what a stethoscope is. Make a stethoscope by using funnels, rubber tubing, and a "Y"-shaped glass tube.
3. Demonstrate how an ultrasonic washer might work. Connect an electric bell to an electric cell and a switch. Hang the bell in a jar of water so it is not touching the jar. Make the bell vibrate by closing the switch. Touch the water. What do you notice?
4. Is there a place near your home where you can hear an echo? If so, you can learn to measure distances by listening to echoes. Use a stopwatch or watch with a second hand. Record the time that passes between the time you shout and the time you hear an echo. This length of time multiplied by 550 feet will give the distance to the reflecting surface in feet. If sound travels about 1,100 feet per second, why should you multiply by 550 feet? Try measuring from several places.
5. Do some reading to discover how sounds are recorded on records and tapes so that they can be stored and played back later.

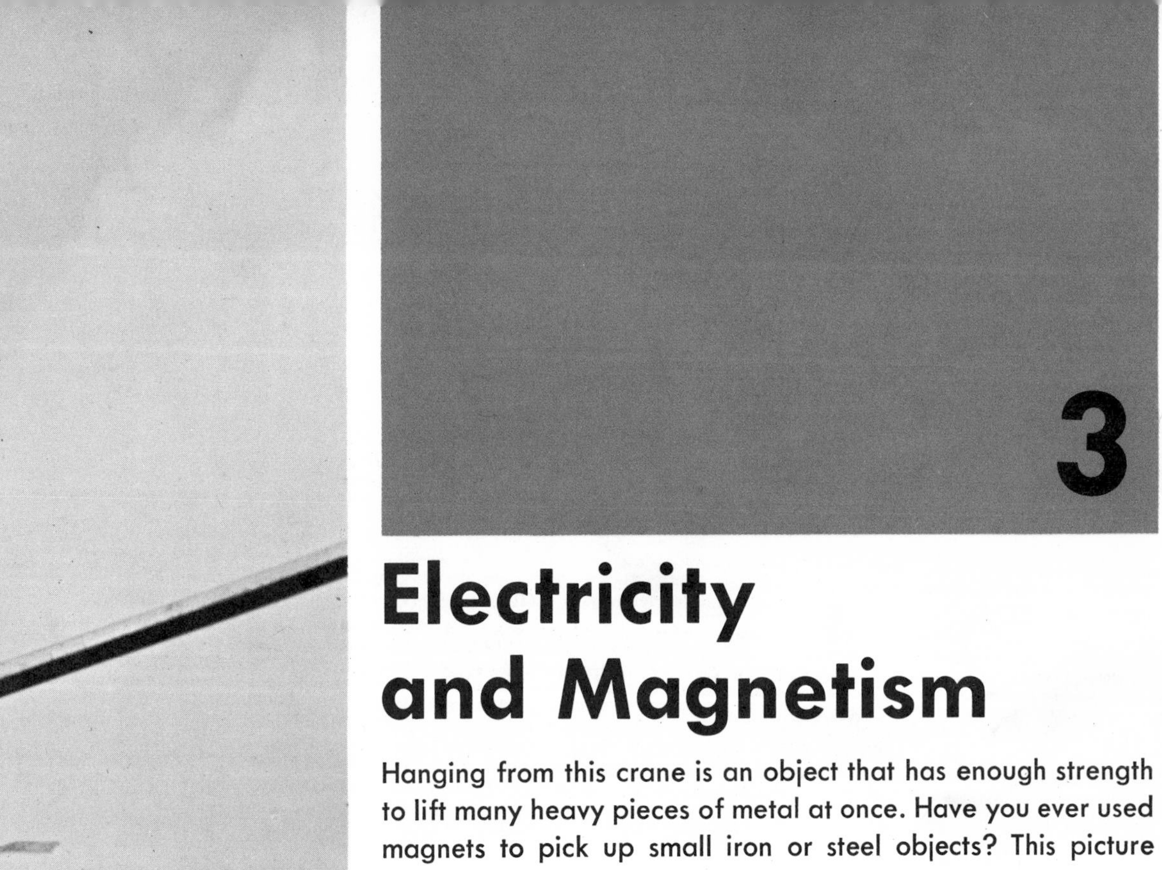

3

Electricity and Magnetism

Hanging from this crane is an object that has enough strength to lift many heavy pieces of metal at once. Have you ever used magnets to pick up small iron or steel objects? This picture shows one kind of magnet.

The next time you use a telephone, you will be putting a magnet operated by electricity into use. Some doorbells and motors use this kind of magnet. Do you know how electricity can be used to make a magnet? Powerful magnets like the one in this picture use electricity to help do some of the work for modern industry. How can you discover how electricity can be used to change a piece of iron into a kind of magnet? You can learn how to use electricity to give an ordinary nail the strength to pick up small pieces of iron!

What Can Magnets Do?

Get a bar magnet and touch it to different materials. Does it attract any of the materials? Use different kinds of magnets. What kinds of materials do all magnets attract?

How can you find out if an object is a magnet? Look at the objects on the table in the picture below. Suppose one object is a magnet. What would you do with each object to find out if it is a magnet?

Can electricity be used to make a magnet? Do you know how?

DISCOVER

Does electric current flowing along a wire have an effect on iron filings?

What You Need

insulated wire, 3 feet long
insulated wire, 5 feet long
electric cell
iron filings
gloves or pliers with insulated handles
dish
cardboard
tiny nails
iron or steel bolt
knife switch

1. Remove the insulation from the ends of the wires. Connect them to the knife switch and electric cell as shown in the picture. What do electric cells supply? When the switch is down, does electricity have a complete path along which it can travel? Follow the path with your finger showing that electricity travels from the cell, along the wires and the switch, and back to the cell again. This path is called a **circuit** (sėr′ kit). When the switch is down, or closed, is the circuit closed? When the switch is up, or open, is the circuit open? Is the flow of electricity stopped?

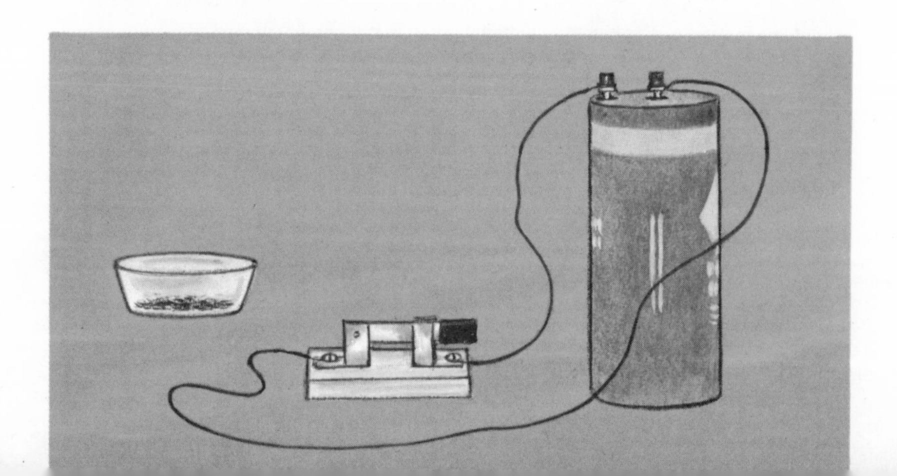

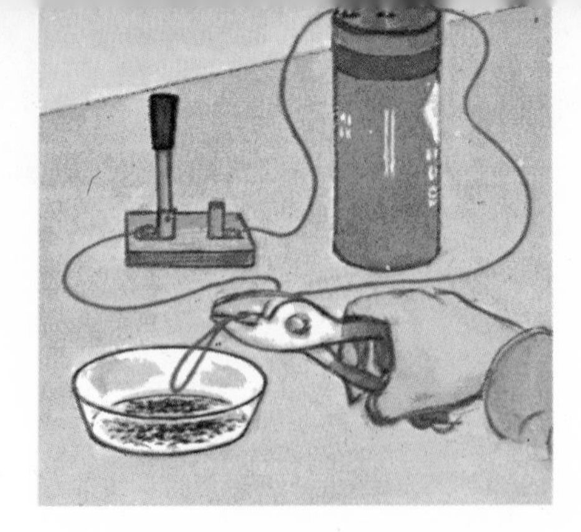

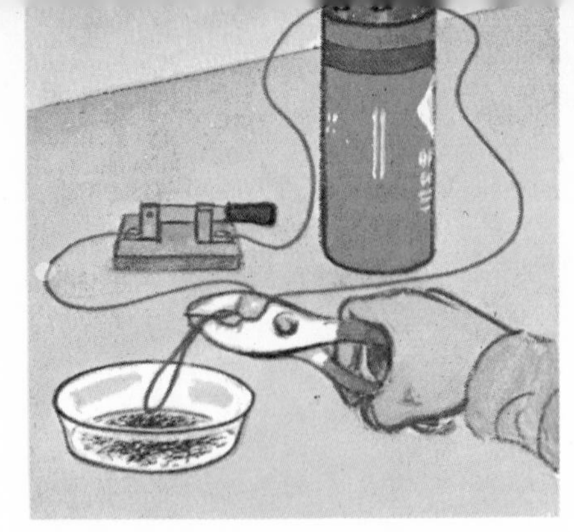

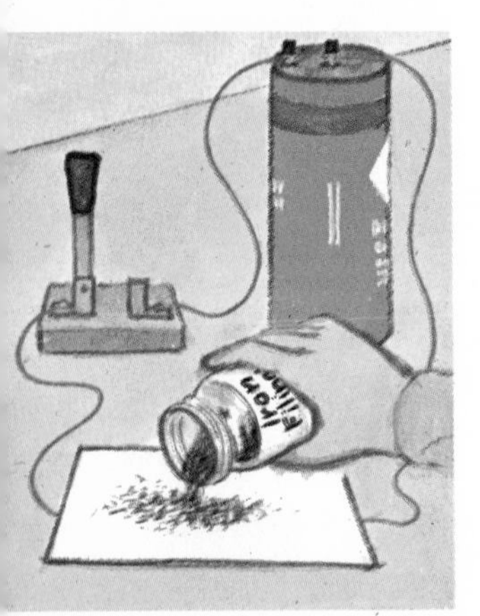

2. Open the circuit. Bend the three-foot wire at its center. Using the pliers or gloves, touch the bent wire to iron filings in a dish. Does anything happen? Record the results.
3. Close the circuit. Touch the wire to the filings again. What happens? Record the results.
4. Open the circuit. Unbend the wire. Lay a piece of smooth cardboard over the wire. Sprinkle iron filings on the cardboard over the wire. Does anything happen? Record the results.
5. Close the circuit. Tap the cardboard lightly. What do you notice? Record the results.
6. Open the circuit. Bend the wire as before. Touch the wire to the tiny nails. Does anything happen? Record the results.
7. Close the circuit. With the pliers or gloves, touch the wire to the tiny nails. What happens? Record the results.

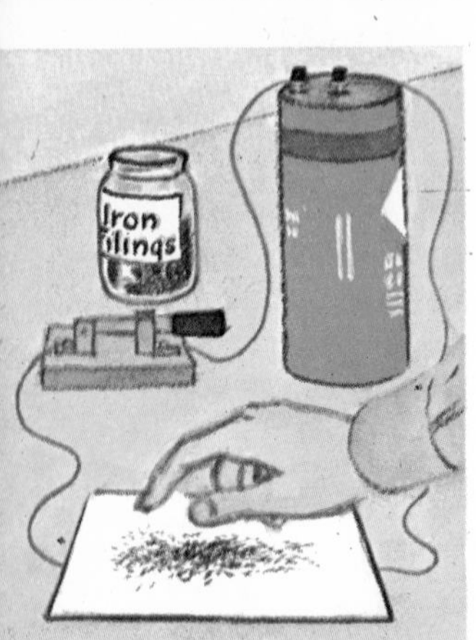

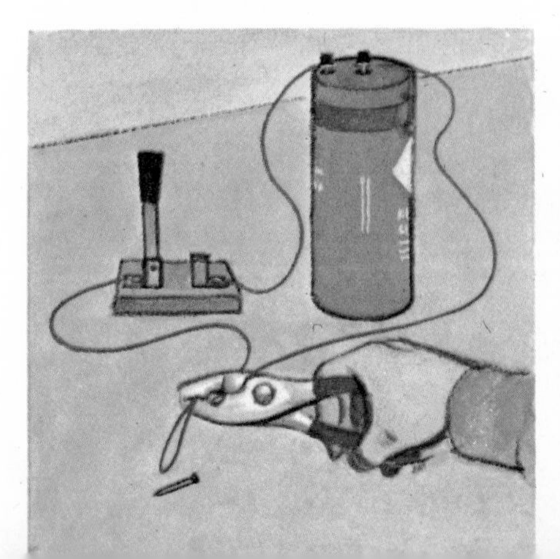

8. Test an iron or steel bolt to see if it is a magnet by touching it to some iron filings. Is the bolt a magnet?
9. Open the circuit. Wind a section of the long wire around the bolt ten times. Touch the bolt to the tiny nails. Does anything happen? Record the results.

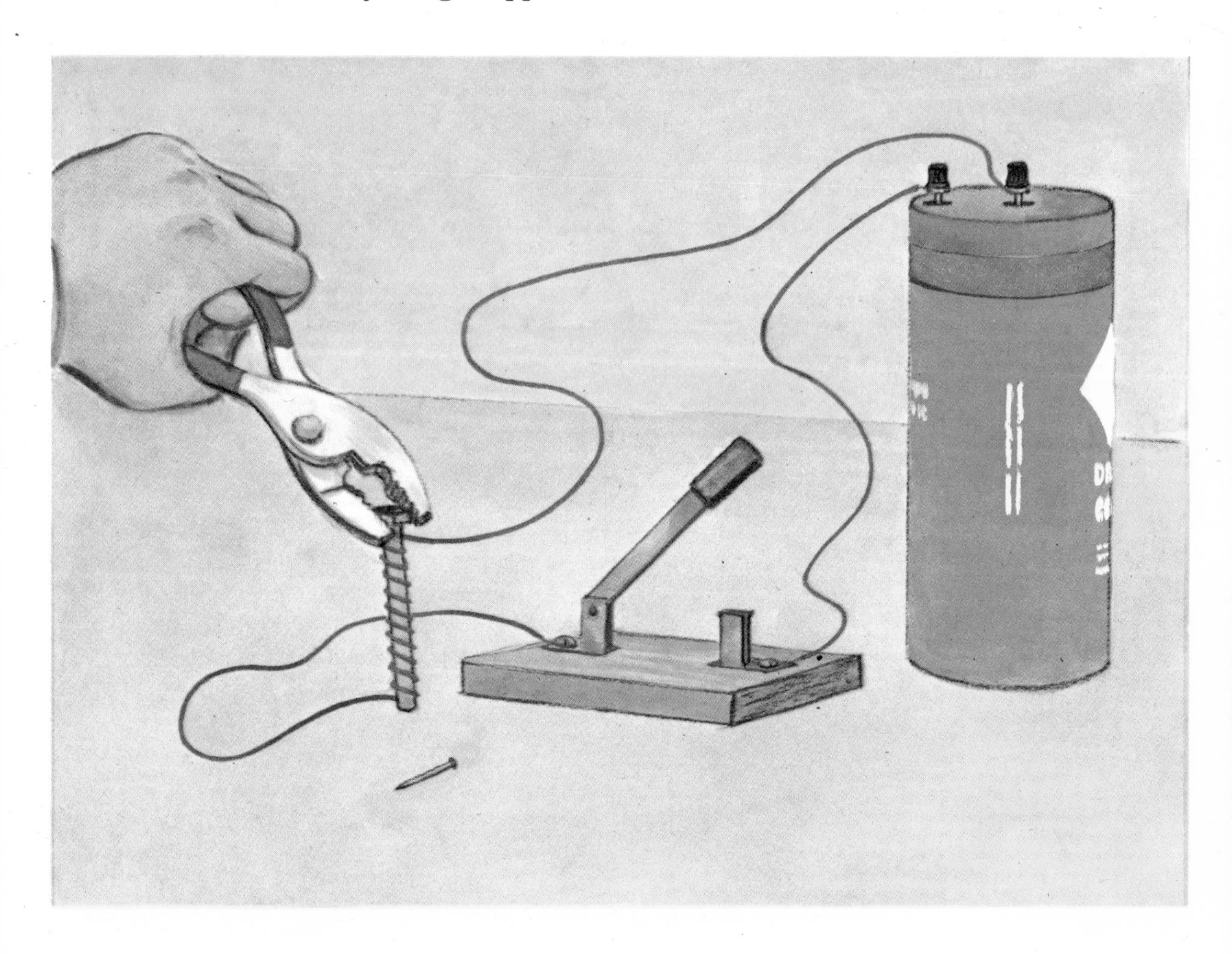

10. Now close the switch and use the pliers or gloves to touch the bolt to the nails. What happens? Open the switch and wait to see what happens. What do you observe? Record the results.

What is an electromagnet?

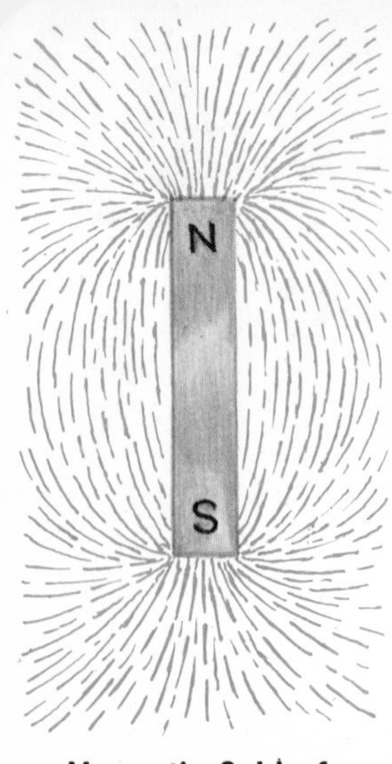

Magnetic field of a bar magnet

When the circuit was closed, did the wire attract bits of iron? What else will attract iron filings? While electricity is flowing through it, is the wire like a magnet?

A magnet has a field of force, or a **magnetic** (mag net′ ik) **field,** around it. Do you think that a wire with electricity flowing through it has a magnetic field around it? You may wish to test other parts of the wire to see if they have a magnetic field, too.

Is the wire magnet strong enough to attract tiny iron filings? Can it attract small nails? How did you make a stronger magnet?

Electromagnets

When electricity flows along the wire, the magnetic field of the wire causes the iron bolt to become a magnet. Is the bolt a magnet only while electricity is flowing along the wire? When electricity is flowing along the wire, the bolt and wire are called an **electromagnet** (i lek′ trō mag′ nit).

An electromagnet usually has a soft iron center called a **core** (kôr). The wires around the core are called a **coil** (koil). When electricity flows through the coil, there is magnetism in the core. Together the core and coil are an electromagnet.

Electromagnet

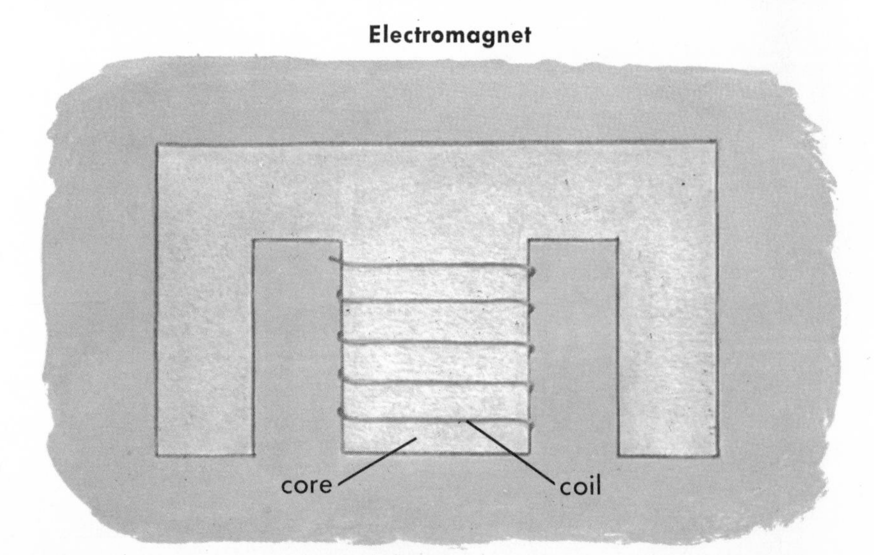

The electromagnet you made was weak. But was it stronger than the wire magnet? Can you think of a way to make your electromagnet stronger? What parts of an electromagnet might you change?

FIND OUT

Can you make an electromagnet stronger by winding more wire around the core?

EXPERIMENT

What You Need

circuit you made
large iron bolt
gloves or pliers with insulated handles
several tiny nails
small dish

1. Use the circuit you made. Wind three turns of wire around the bolt near its head.

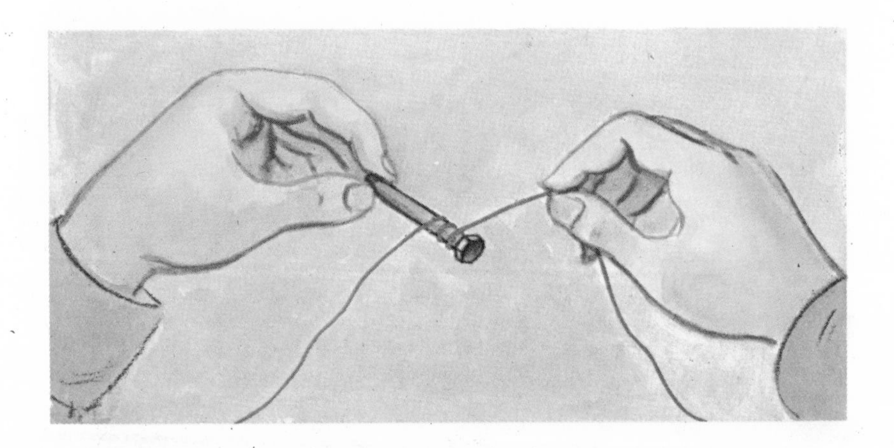

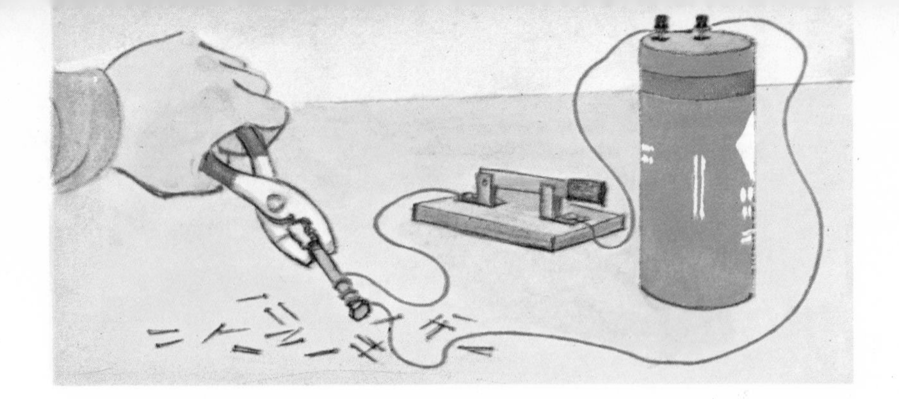

2. Close the circuit and use the pliers or gloves to touch the head of the bolt to the paper clips. Attract as many as you can by moving the head of the bolt around. *Remember to always handle the electromagnet with the pliers or gloves.* It may get hot.
3. Drop the nails into the small dish by opening the circuit.
4. Count the number of nails that were attracted. Record the results.
5. Repeat steps 2, 3, and 4, using six turns of wire. Repeat these steps seven times using three more turns of wire each time.

Number of Turns of Wire	Number of Nails Attracted
3	
6	

What was the only thing you changed each time you attracted more paper clips? As you added more turns to the coil, did the number of paper clips which were attracted change? With how many turns of wire were the most paper clips attracted? What have you discovered about the strength of an electromagnet and the number of turns in the coil?

FIND OUT

Can you make an electromagnet stronger by adding more electric cells to the circuit?

EXPERIMENT

What You Need

circuit and electromagnet you made
3 electric cells
several tiny nails
gloves or pliers with insulated handles
small dish

1. Have ten turns of wire on the bolt.
2. Close the circuit. Using the pliers or gloves, place the electromagnet on the nails. Attract as many nails as you can.
3. Drop the nails into the small dish by opening the circuit. Count the number of nails. Record the results.
4. Repeat the experiment using two electric cells. Connect the cells as shown in the picture. What happens? Record the results.
5. Try the experiment two more times, adding one more cell each time. What do you observe?

How may strong electromagnets be used?

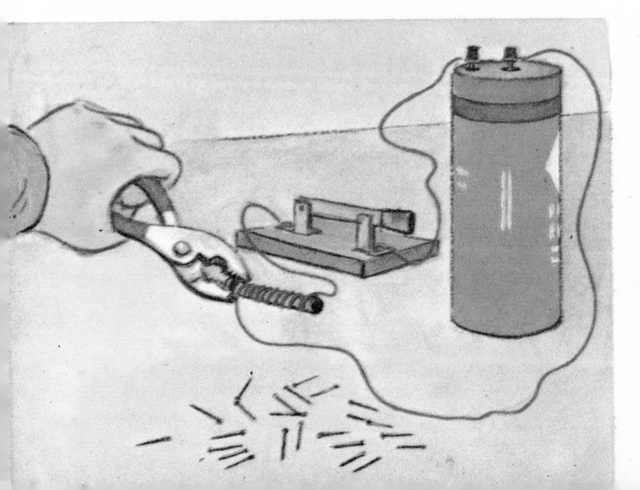

Number of Cells	Number of Turns of Wire	Number of Nails Attracted
1	10	
2	10	
3	10	
4	10	

Did adding cells change the strength of the electromagnet?

When you connect cells as shown in the pictures, you increase the amount of electricity in the circuit. With how many cells was the greatest number of nails attracted? What have you discovered about electricity and the strength of an electromagnet?

The electromagnets you have made, work in the same way as large electromagnets used in industry. Huge coils of wire, large iron cores, and much electricity are important in these electromagnets. They are so strong that they can lift things as heavy as an automobile. Have you ever seen one in use? Are small electromagnets useful? Where might they be found in a home?

Industrial electromagnet

Electromagnets and Sound

When you use a doorbell or buzzer, you are using small electromagnets. Remove the cover of a doorbell that is not connected to wires and observe the electromagnets in it.

What are some other things that use electromagnets?

How many coils can you see? Do you have any ideas about how they make the bell ring?

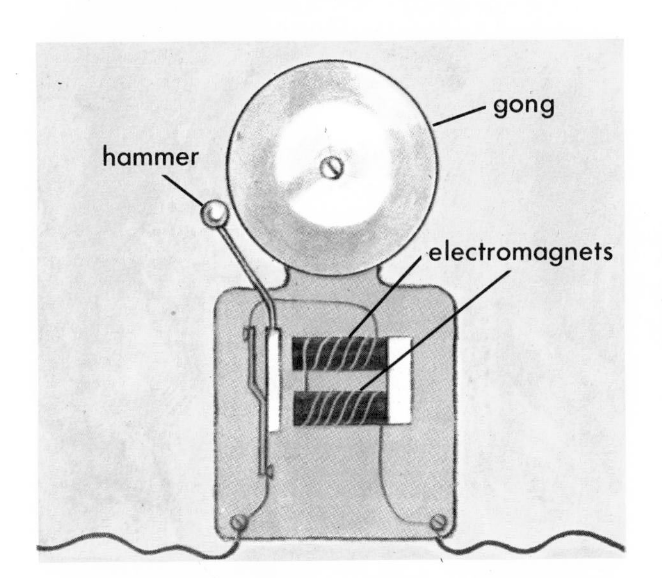

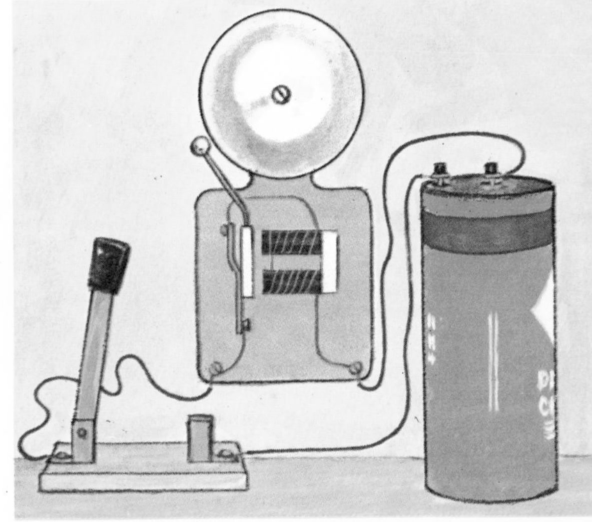

Wire a circuit with an electric cell, a knife switch, and a doorbell, as shown in the picture. You now have one circuit that can be opened and closed in two places. One place is at the knife switch. The other place where the circuit can be opened and closed is at the end of the hammer near the electromagnets. Move the bell hammer back and forth gently with your finger. Does the hammer connect with the rest of the circuit when the hammer is at rest? This is the other place where the circuit can be opened and closed.

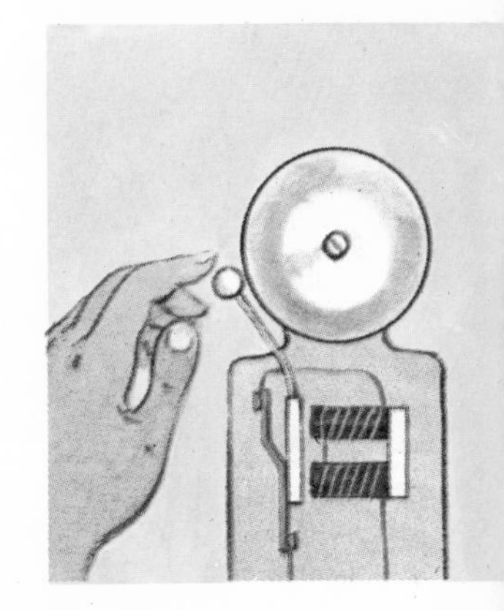

Now close the circuit with the knife switch and watch the bell. What pulls the hammer?

Telegraph operator sending a message many years ago

When the hammer is pulled toward the gong, it opens the circuit at the end of the hammer. What happens to the electromagnets when the circuit is opened?

The hammer is pulled back in place by a small spring. When the hammer is back in place, is the circuit open or closed? What happens to the electromagnets? This happens very quickly, over and over again, when you close the circuit with the knife switch.

Doorbells are only one of the ways in which electromagnets are useful. Without electromagnets, radio speakers, telephones, and the telegraph would probably not have been invented.

The telegraph was once used regularly to send messages quickly from one place to another. Working a switch, or **key,** an operator could send a message to another operator far away. This second operator listened to a **sounder** which tapped out the message.

DISCOVER

How does an electromagnet work in a telegraph sounder?

What You Need

3 pieces of insulated copper wire, each 2 feet long
small wooden drawer knob with screw
hinge, 4 inches long
hinge, 6 inches long
screwdriver
hammer
5 pieces of wood, about 2 inches wide and 1 inch thick, cut into the following lengths:
 2 pieces, 5 inches long
 2 pieces, 4½ inches long
 1 piece, 3 inches long
7 screws, ½ inch long
screw, 1½ inches long
all-purpose cement
rubber faucet washer, ½ inch wide
6 nails, 1½ inches long
adhesive tape

1. Remove one inch of insulation from both ends of each wire. Bend the wire ends as shown in the picture.

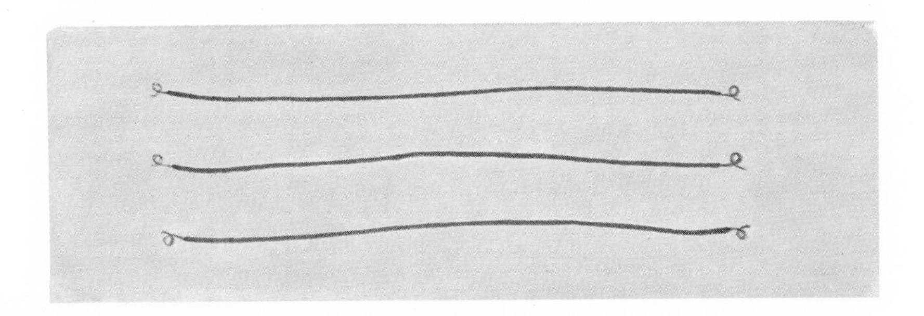

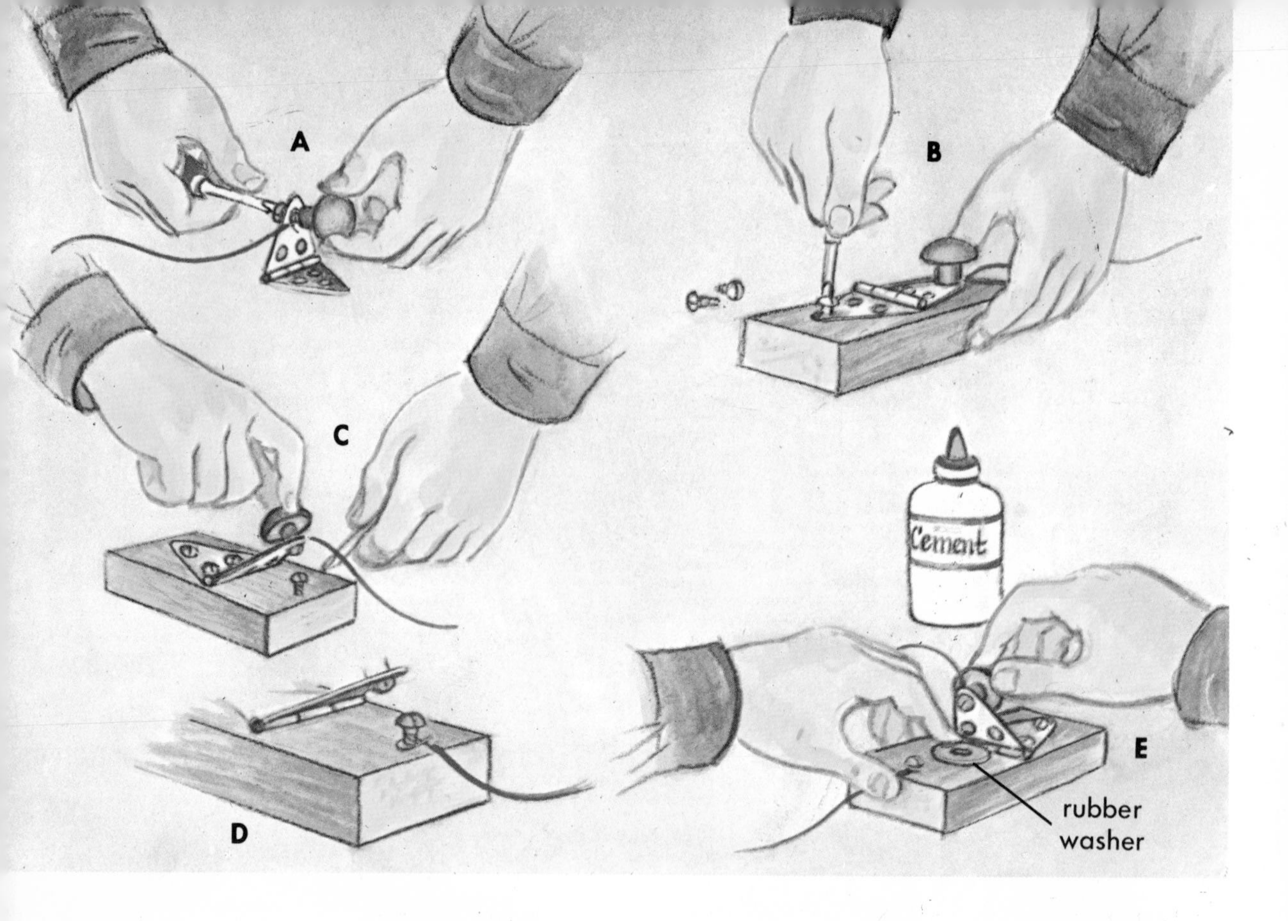

2. Screw the wooden knob to the end of one part of the 4-inch hinge, catching a loop of bare wire between the knob and the hinge (**A**).
3. Fasten the other part of the hinge to a 4½-inch piece of wood with three ½-inch screws (**B**).
4. Into the other end of this piece of wood, place a ½-inch screw so that its head will touch the screw which holds the wooden knob on the hinge (**C**). Fasten the bare loop of another piece of wire under this screw and tighten it against the board (**D**).
5. Glue the rubber washer under the free end of the hinge (**E**). Make only a small space between the screw of the knob and the screw holding the wire to the board. You have made a telegraph key.

6. Place a $1\frac{1}{2}$-inch screw into the center of one end of a piece of wood that is 5 inches long. Screw it into the wood so that an inch remains sticking out of the board.
7. Beginning twelve inches from the end of the third piece of wire, wind ten loops next to each other near the head of the screw. Wind another layer of ten loops over this layer. Do not cut the wire, but start each layer near the head of the screw **(A)**.
8. Using the $4\frac{1}{2}$-inch piece of wood, join the two 5-inch pieces as shown. Use two $1\frac{1}{2}$-inch nails at each end of the $4\frac{1}{2}$-inch piece of wood **(B)**.
9. Attach the 6-inch hinge as shown, using three $\frac{1}{2}$-inch screws **(C)**.
10. Put a $\frac{1}{2}$-inch screw into the center of the end of the 3-inch piece of wood. Turn in the screw until the head is just above the wood.
11. Attach the 3-inch piece of wood **(D)**. Use two $1\frac{1}{2}$-inch nails, so that the screw is just under the free end of the hinge. You have just made a telegraph sounder.

What does a telegraph message consist of?

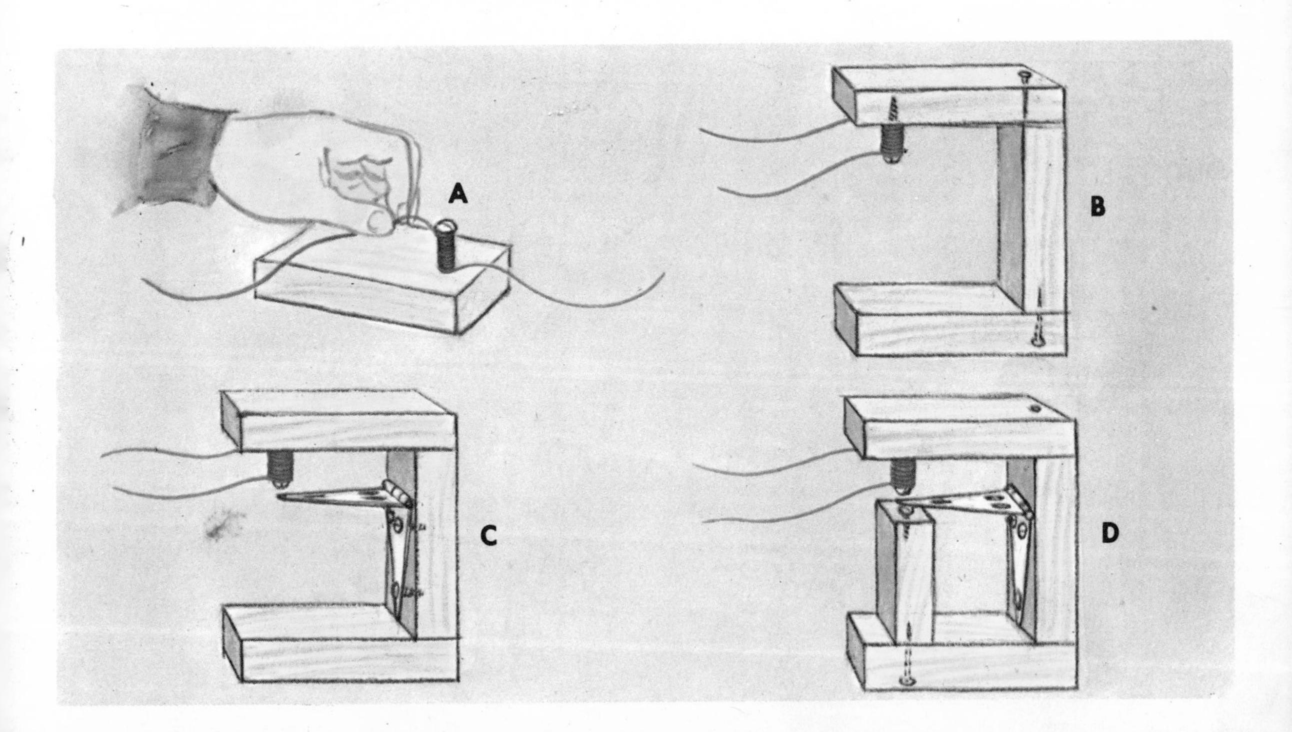

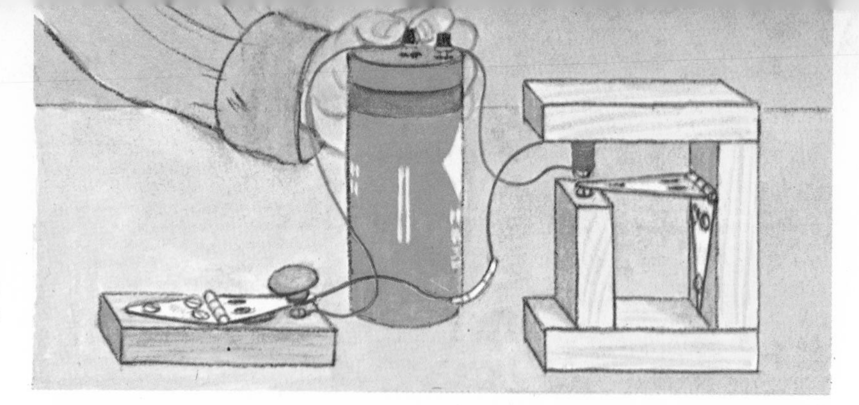

This Morse code is often used to send messages on a telegraph.

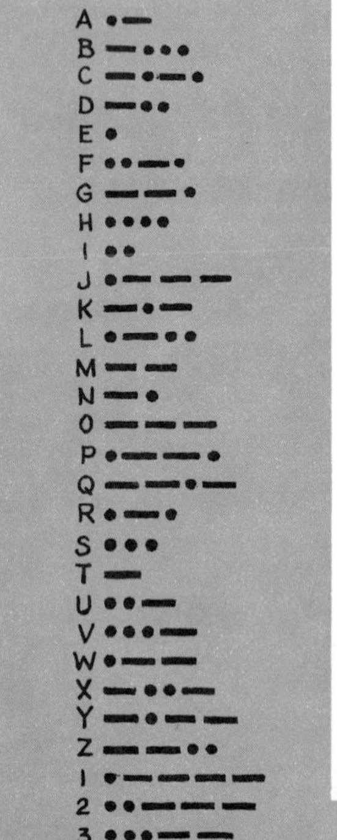

12. Connect one end of the wire forming the coil to the wire attached to the knob. Twist them tightly together. Wrap the twisted wires with adhesive tape. You have connected the key to the sounder.
13. Connect the other end of the wire forming the coil to the dry cell. Connect the wire attached to the bottom screw on the sender to the dry cell as shown.
14. Push the key down. What happens? Why?

Which part of the sounder is an electromagnet? Does one of the parts you made act as a switch, opening and closing the circuit? Explain why part of the sounder moves when you push down on the key. A message can be sent as a series of different amounts of electricity.

Today, the telegraph is seldom used. Most messages are sent by teletypewriter. As a certain typewriter key is pressed by an operator in one city, the teletypewriter in another city types the same letter. Teletypewriters have electromagnets which operate the keys. A teletypewriter is like a long-distance typewriter which uses electromagnets.

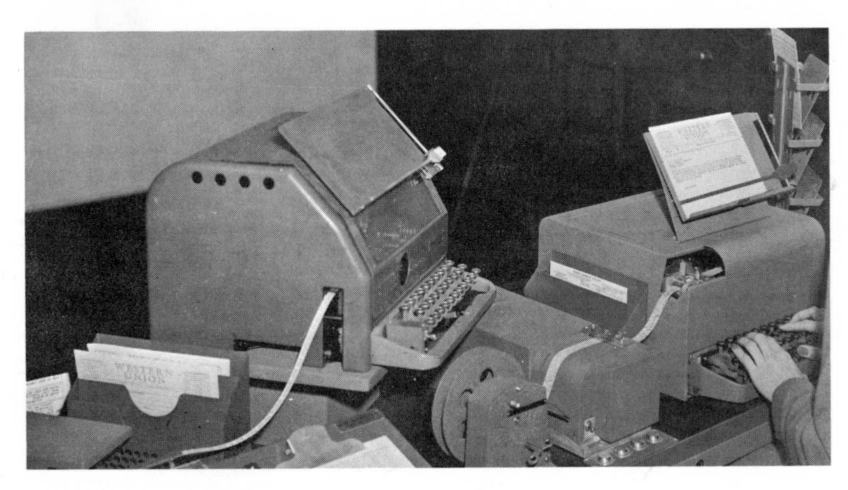

Sending a telegram by teletypewriter

Telephones

Electromagnets are important parts of telephone receivers, too. Can you find the electromagnet in the picture? Find out how telephone receivers produce sound.

What causes the metal in an earphone to vibrate?

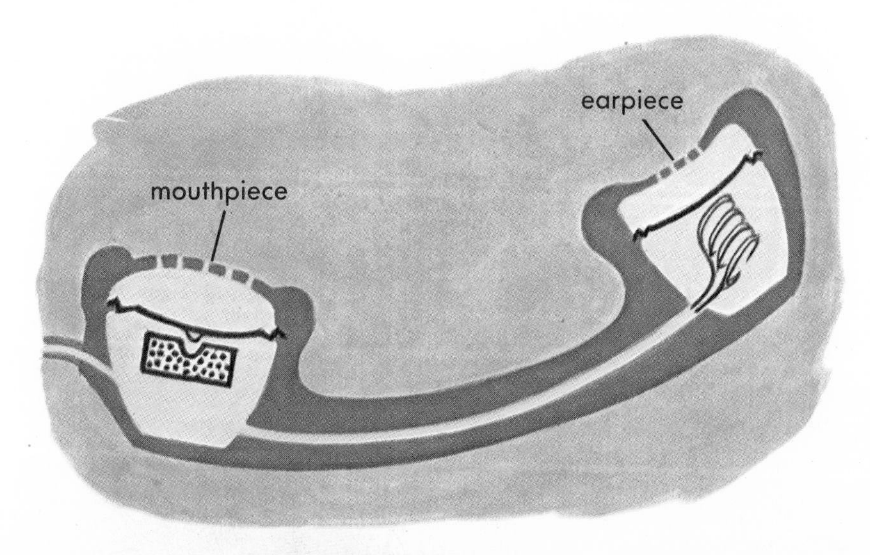

Earphones work much like the earpiece of a telephone. Get a set of earphones. Touch the plug across the posts of an electric cell as shown in the picture. Do you hear a crackling sound? If you cannot hear the sound, put on the earphones and repeat the activity.

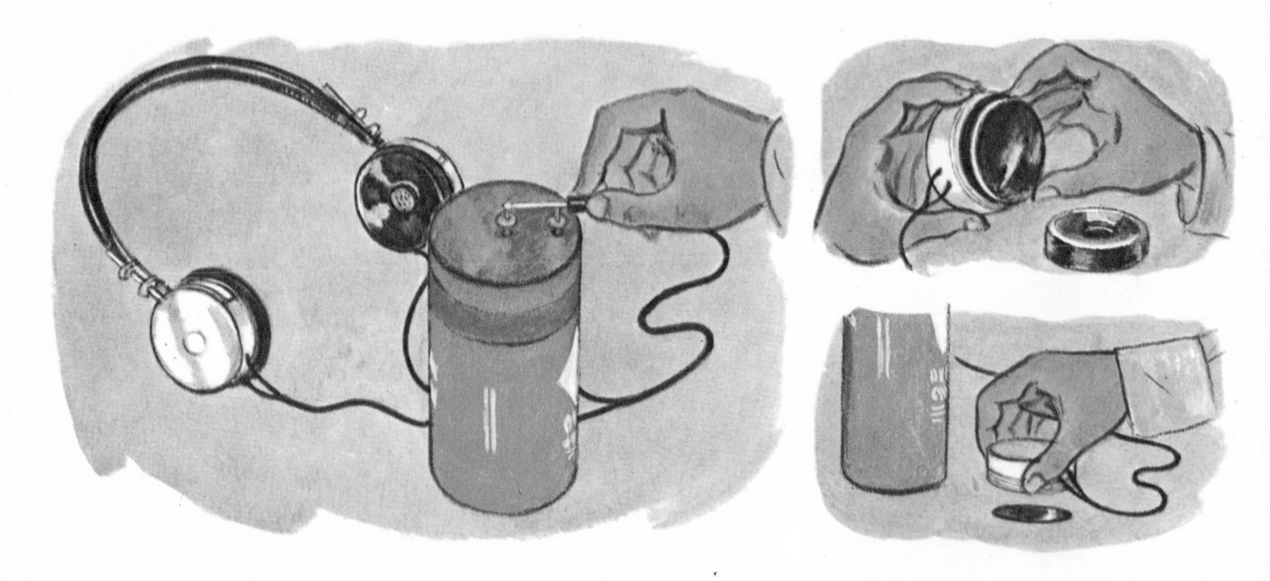

Disconnect the earphones from the electric cell. Unscrew the cover from one earphone. Pull up on the round metal circle. The metal circle has iron in it. Can you find the coils of two electromagnets underneath? Try to pick up the round piece of metal with the electromagnets.

Iron is attracted to the earphone even if the electromagnets are not connected to the electric cell. The core of each electromagnet is a magnet. It attracts iron even when electricity is not flowing through the coil. When electricity flows through the coils, the magnet becomes stronger. As different amounts of electricity are sent through the coil, the piece of metal moves back and forth. The vibrations of the metal set up vibrations in the air which are passed on to your ear.

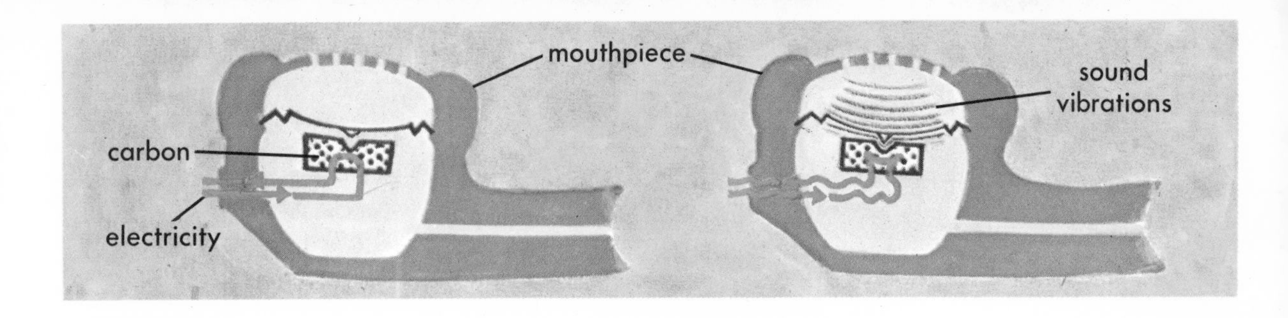

The mouthpiece of a telephone has a small container filled with bits of carbon. These are used to change the amount of electricity that travels through the coil.

What does the flow of electricity depend upon?

FIND OUT

How is carbon used to change the amount of electricity in a circuit?

EXPERIMENT

What You Need

3 insulated wires, each 1 foot long
2 small washers
small pill bottle
2 or 3 old electric cells
newspaper
hammer
small porcelain lamp socket
bulb for socket
electric cell
pencil

1. Remove the insulation from both ends of each wire.
2. Wrap the bare end of one wire around a washer. Put this washer into the pill bottle.

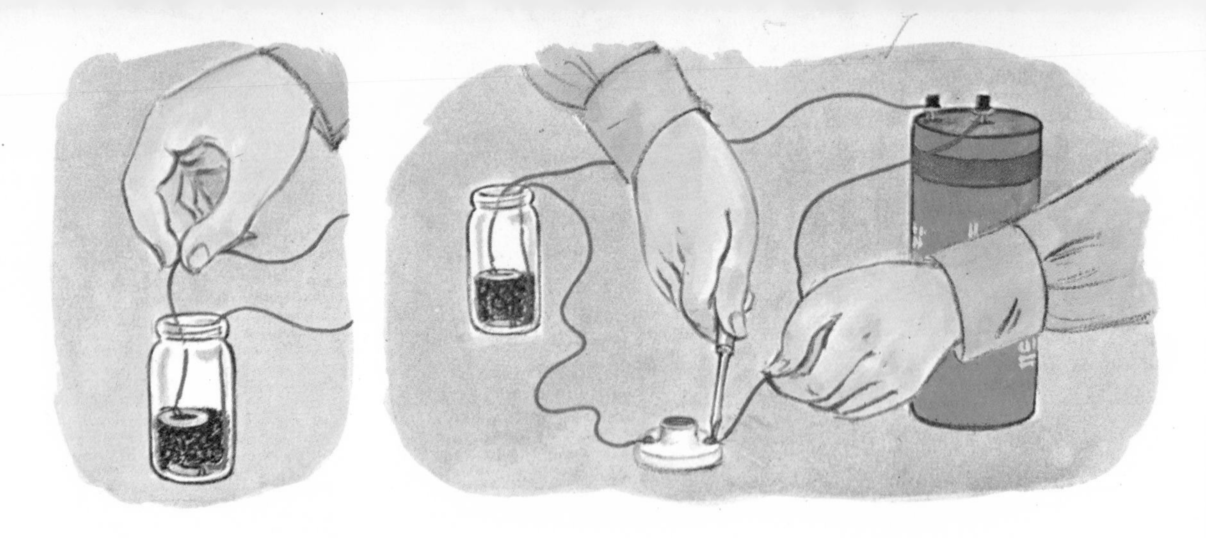

3. Remove the carbon rod from an old electric cell. Put the carbon between layers of newspaper. Use the hammer to crush the carbon into small pieces. Put the carbon pieces into the pill bottle on top of the washer.
4. Wrap the bare end of a second wire around the other washer. Lay this washer on top of the carbon in the bottle.
5. Connect the wire from one washer to the socket. Attach the wire from the other washer to the cell. Use the third wire to connect the socket to the cell.
6. Twist the bulb into the socket. Does the bulb light? Is the light bright?
7. Press the top washer gently with a pencil. Then, press as hard as you can. What difference do you notice in the lamp?

Electricity from the electric cell can flow from one washer to the other through pieces of carbon. The amount of electricity that flows depends upon how hard the pieces of carbon are pressed together. Does more electricity flow when you press hard on the top washer? How do you know? You may want to repeat the experiment with more carbon to see what differences you can observe.

Inside the mouthpiece of a telephone, there is a thin piece of aluminum. This metal vibrates when the sound waves of your voice strike it. As it vibrates, the piece of aluminum presses on carbon, just as the washer did in your experiment. The amount of electricity which passes through the carbon changes with the way the aluminum vibrates. In this way, sound waves create a pattern of electric current through telephone lines.

During a telephone conversation, a little electricity is always flowing from the mouthpiece of one telephone to the receiver of the other. Sound vibrations at the mouthpiece of one telephone change the amount of electricity traveling to the receiver of the other telephone.

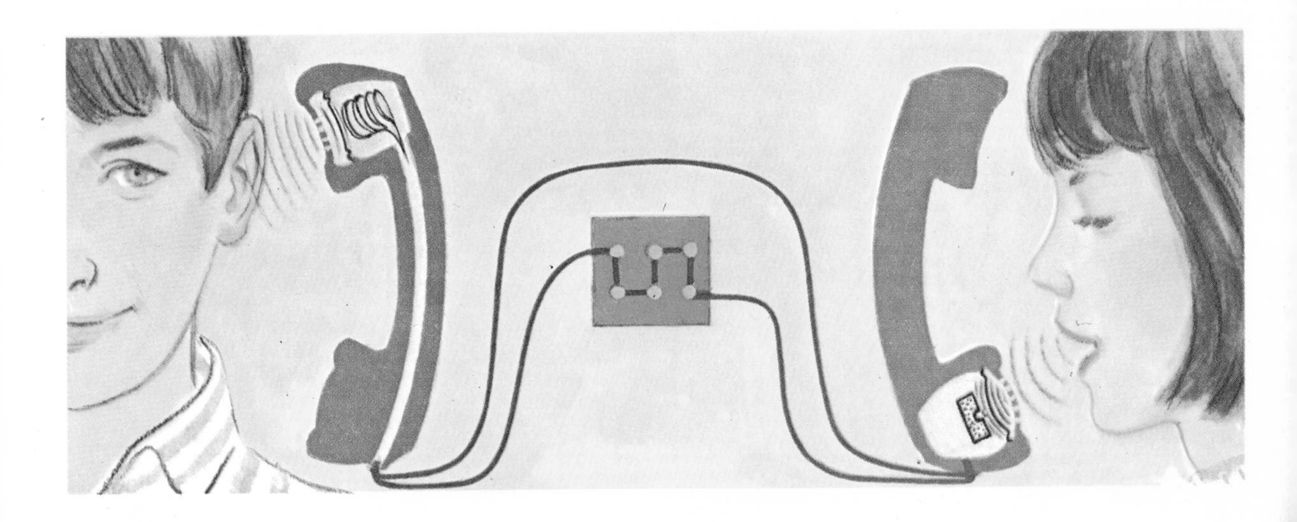

Telephone receivers have electromagnets and a thin piece of metal in them. As different amounts of electricity flow through the coil, what happens to the core? When more electricity is received, is the electromagnet stronger than when less electricity is received? The electromagnet attracts the piece of metal which vibrates in the same way that the mouthpiece vibrated.

Can electromagnets make parts of a machine turn?

When you speak into the mouthpiece of a telephone, the sound waves are changed to different amounts of electricity. The electricity reaches your telephone receiver and makes sound wave vibrations that you hear.

Loudspeakers on radio and television sets work in somewhat the same way as telephone receivers, but the sounds are much louder. If you have a smaller speaker that is no longer used, test it as you did the earphones. Can you see where the coils and magnet are located?

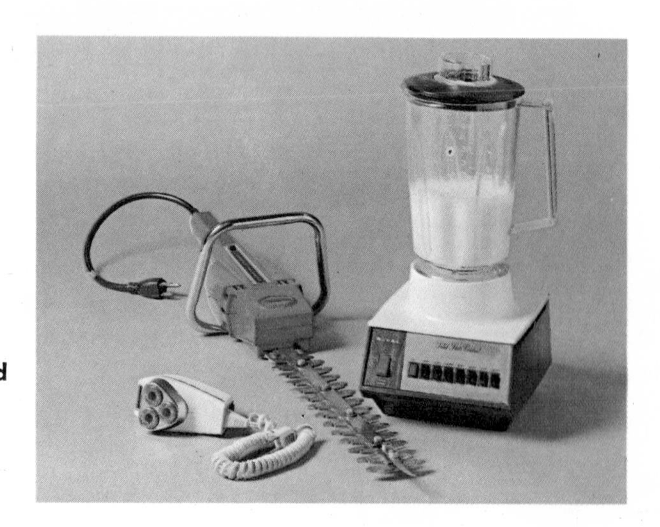

Electromagnets are used in these machines.

How Do Motors Work?

Electromagnets can attract iron and a few other metals. As a result, doorbells ring, telegraph sounders click, and sound comes from a radio speaker. Making sounds is only one of the important uses of electromagnets.

When you press the switch of a vacuum cleaner or a mixer, you expect more than sound. You expect the machine to do some type of work. Electromagnets can make things vibrate, but electromagnets can also make parts of a machine turn.

The ends of a magnet are called **poles.** A magnet has a north-pointing pole and a south-pointing pole.

Poles that are alike push each other apart. Poles that are unlike pull each other together. When poles push apart, they **repel** (ri pel′) each other. When poles pull together, they **attract** (ə trakt′) each other. Does an electromagnet have poles, too?

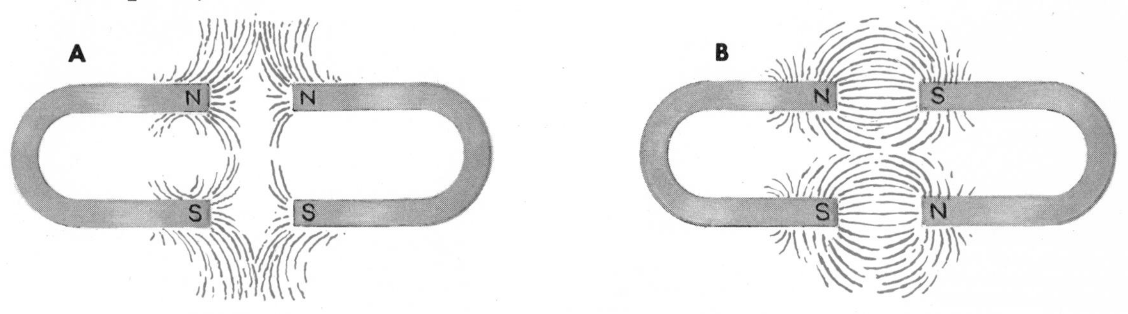

In which picture are the poles of the magnets attracting each other? In which picture are they repelling each other?

FIND OUT

How can you tell which pole of an electromagnet is north-pointing and which is south-pointing?

EXPERIMENT

What You Need

insulated wire, 3 feet long
insulated wire, 1 foot long
electric cell
string
bar magnet
iron bolt
knife switch
gloves or pliers with insulated handles
red crayon

How can you make an electromagnet?

1. Remove the insulation from both ends of each wire. Use the short wire to attach the switch to the cell.
2. Make an electromagnet by winding fifty turns of the long wire around an iron bolt. Begin winding three inches from one end of the long wire. Connect one end of this wire to the switch. Connect the other end of this wire to the cell.
3. Tie a piece of string around the middle of a bar magnet. Ask a person to hold the string so that the magnet is about two inches above the table. The magnet should be able to turn freely.
4. Use the gloves or pliers to hold the electromagnet. Bring one end of the electromagnet toward the north-pointing pole of the hanging magnet. Close the circuit with the switch. Do the poles repel or attract? Is that end of the electromagnet north-pointing or south-pointing? Test the other end of the electromagnet. Is that end of the electromagnet a north-pointing or a south-pointing pole?
5. Open the circuit. Mark the north-pointing pole of the electromagnet with red crayon.

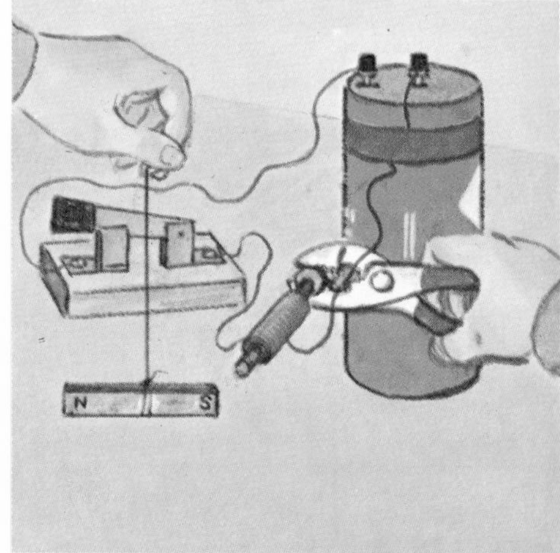

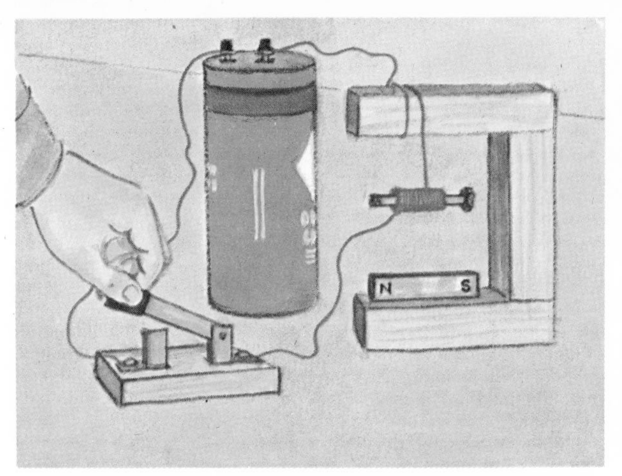

An electromagnet is used in this motor.

Does an electromagnet have a north-pointing pole and a south-pointing pole? How can you tell?

In an electric motor, does the electromagnet turn because its poles are attracted and repelled by the poles of another magnet?

Hang the electromagnet just above the poles of a bar magnet as shown. Close the circuit. What happens? Why does it happen? Remember in which direction the head of the bolt turned.

Why does the electromagnet stop turning? Do the unlike poles of the two magnets remain together?

Can the poles of the electromagnet be changed by changing the way the electricity flows through the coil? With clay or tape, prop a U-shaped magnet on a table so that its poles are pointing straight up. Hang and center the electromagnet above the U-shaped magnet. Exchange the two connections on the cell as shown in the picture. Close the circuit. What happens? In which direction does the head of the bolt turn?

What are the parts of a simple motor?

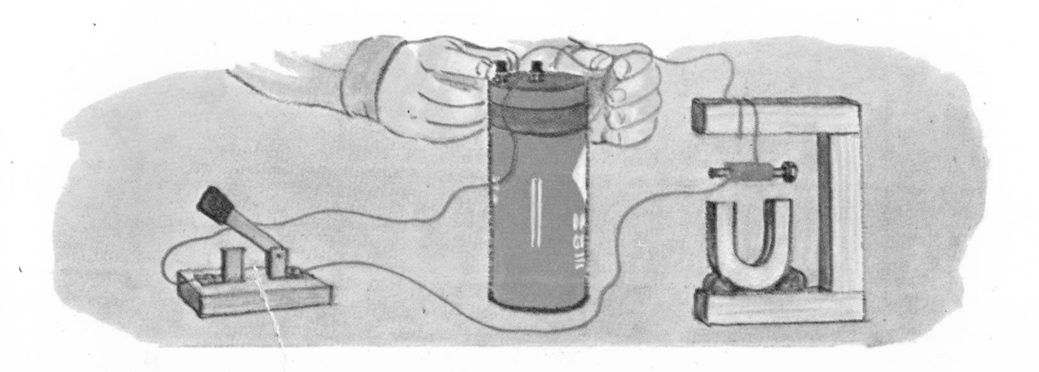

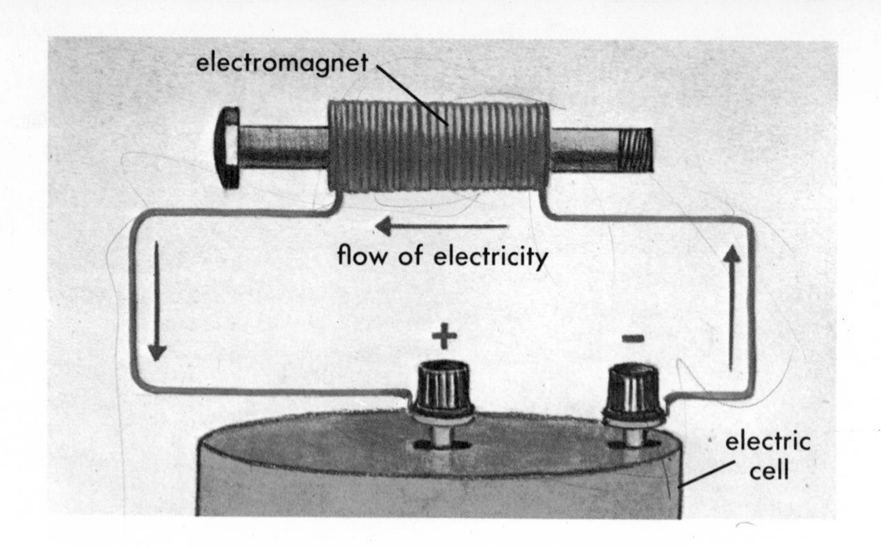

Electricity flows from the electric cell, around the coil, and back to the cell. When you first connect the coil, electricity flows in one direction. When the wires to the cell are changed, electricity flows in the opposite direction. Do the poles of an electromagnet change when the direction of the electric current in the coil is changed?

Have you discovered that changing the direction of electricity changes the poles of the electromagnet? Is this idea used with electric motors? Look at how a simple electric motor is made and try to find out how the electromagnet turns.

Explain how an electric motor, such as this one, works.

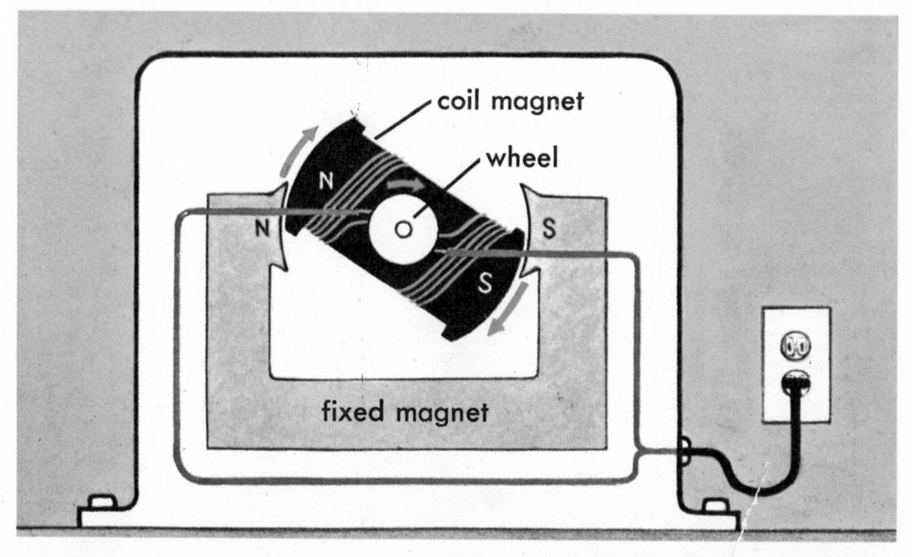

The coil of most motors is an electromagnet that can turn. On each side of the electromagnet is a pole of a U-shaped magnet that does not turn.

The electricity in the electromagnet does not always travel in the same direction. As the electricity changes direction, the poles of the electromagnet change.

At one instant, the poles of the electromagnet are attracted to the U-shaped magnet. The electromagnet turns halfway around.

Then, the current travels in the other direction through the coil, and the poles of the electromagnet change. The poles of the coil and the poles of the U-shaped magnet repel each other. The electromagnet turns halfway around again.

As the electromagnetism changes, the axle turns. The spinning axle can be made to do many kinds of work. Electric motors used in homes and factories are much larger and more powerful than the one you have just read about. All electric motors are made with electromagnets.

Electric motor

Exploring Your Learnings

Here are some ideas and vocabulary. What do these mean to you?

Words to Use

circuit (p. 57)	key (p. 66)
magnetic field (p. 60)	sounder (p. 66)
electromagnet (p. 60)	poles (p. 77)
core (p. 60)	repel (p. 77)
coil (p. 60)	attract (p. 77)

Ideas to Use

1. A wire along which electricity is flowing has a magnetic field around it.
2. An electromagnet has a center core with a coil of wire around it.
3. The strength of an electromagnet is affected by the length of wire in the coil and by the amount of electricity flowing through the wire.
4. Doorbells, radios, telephones, and telegraphs are examples of the ways that electromagnets are used.
5. Both the key and the sounder of a telegraph have electromagnets which send messages by electricity.
6. In the mouthpiece of a telephone, sound vibrations are changed to different amounts of electricity which are sent along the wires.
7. Earphones and a telephone receiver work much the same way; each changes different amounts of electricity into vibrations which are heard as sound.
8. In motors, electricity is used to turn parts by attracting and repelling them with an electromagnet.

9. In electromagnets, as in other magnets, like poles repel and unlike poles attract.
10. The electromagnet in an electric motor is fastened near a U-shaped magnet. The electromagnet turns as electricity traveling along the coil changes direction.

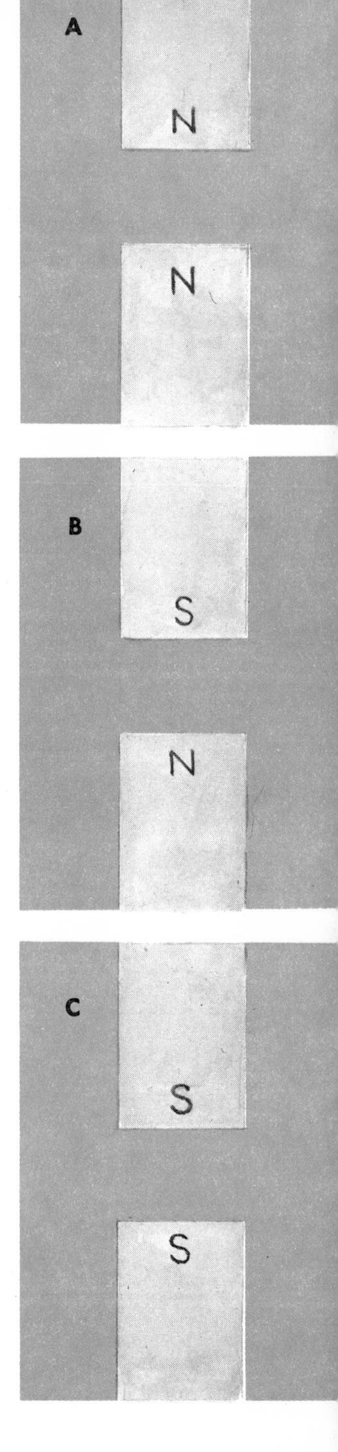

Using Your Ideas

(Do not write in this book.)

1. Tell what will happen to the magnets in each picture at the right.

   Use iron filings sprinkled on cardboard to find out about the magnetic fields of magnets placed as they are in these pictures.
2. Wind fifty turns of wire around a *steel* nail. Using pliers, connect the wires to an electric cell for a few seconds. Remove the nail from the coil. Use the nail magnet to attract iron filings or small nails. How is this magnet different from the core of an electromagnet?
3. Read about the inventions of Alexander Graham Bell, Samuel F. B. Morse, and Guglielmo Marconi. Report on one of these inventions.
4. Invent a new kind of telegraph sounder.
5. The parts of an electric motor have special names. Find out where these parts are located in a motor:

armature	magnetic field
commutator	brushes

6. Take apart a worn-out motor. Identify the parts.
7. Plan and make a bulletin board display that shows different uses for electromagnetism.
8. Find out about the use of electromagnetism in solenoids which operate door chimes.

4

Gravity

This huge balloon carrying a girl in a basket is floating in air! You may wonder why the balloon does not fall to earth. Most objects, including some balloons, cannot float in the air. Have you ever thought about why most things cannot float in air? Unless there is a force to attract objects to each other, they remain apart. The earth must possess a powerful force that keeps things attracted to it. Do you know what that force is called?

The earth does not attract this balloon strongly enough to pull it from the air to the ground. Do you want to discover how the molecules of air help this balloon float?

Gravity

What happens when you jump from a chair? What happens when you drop a book or a ball?

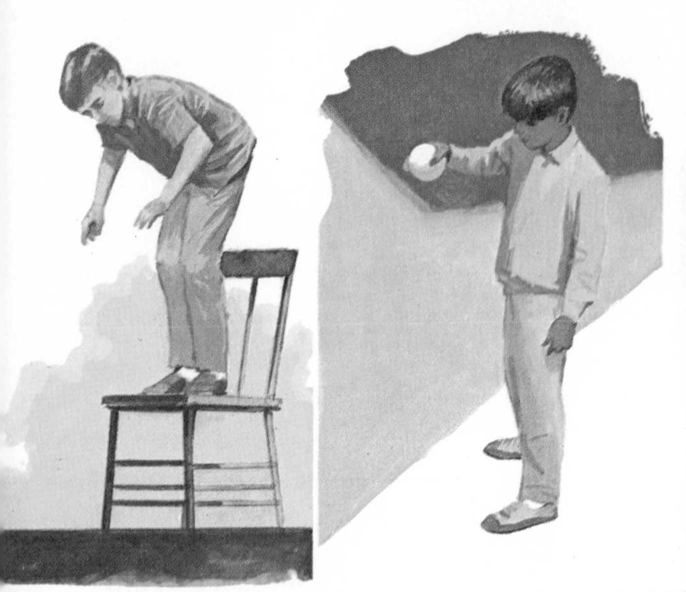

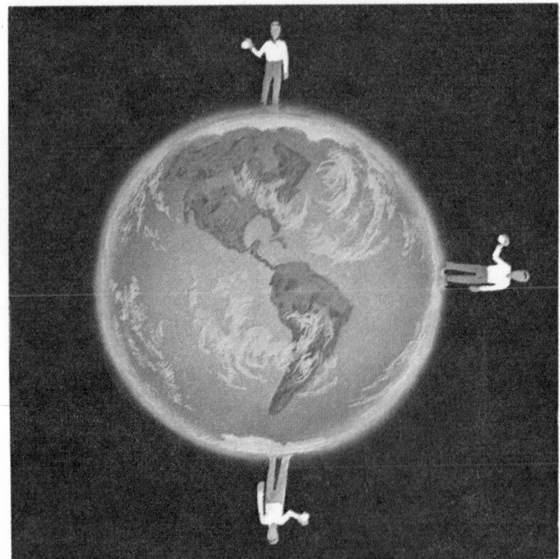

Suppose, at the north pole, you were to drop a rock. In which direction would it fall? Suppose you stood at a place along the equator and dropped a rock. In which direction would it fall? What do you think would happen if you were to drop a rock at the south pole? In which direction would it fall?

When something falls, do you think it moves toward the center of the earth?

Objects are pulled toward the center of the earth by an attraction called **gravity** (grav′ ə tē). Do you think that all objects are affected by gravity with the same amount of force? What do you think makes the difference in the amount of force with which the earth attracts objects? One reason for this difference is that objects do not have the same mass.

DISCOVER

What is meant by the mass of an object?

What You Need

modeling clay
ruler
knife

1. Cut a cube of clay that is one inch long, one inch wide, and one inch thick. Is the cube of clay a definite amount of material, or matter? All the matter in the cube of clay is its mass.
2. Cut the cube of clay in half, leaving the halves together. Have you changed the mass of the clay?
3. Pull the cube of clay into many small bits and place them together in a pile. Do you still have the same amount of mass that you started with?
4. Roll the bits of clay into a ball. Has the mass of the clay changed?

Mass is the total amount of matter in an object. Does the mass of the clay change by dividing it? Does the mass of the clay change if you change its shape?

FIND OUT

How does the effect of gravity on an object depend upon the object's mass?

EXPERIMENT

What You Need

- sharp knife
- milk carton
- ruler, 12 inches long
- pencil
- scissors
- tape
- straight pin
- 2 pieces of florist's wire, each 6 inches long
- 2 small paper cups
- all-purpose cement
- marker or grease pencil
- modeling clay

1. Ask your teacher to use a knife to remove the top of a milk carton. Use a ruler to measure down two inches from the top on one side of the milk carton. Draw a straight line, and with the scissors, cut off the side so that it is two inches below the other sides as in the center picture. Cut off the opposite side in the same way. Save both pieces of milk carton to use later.
2. Use the ruler to find the center along the top edge of a tall side. Cut a V-shaped notch at this point. The notch should be one-half inch wide at the top and one-half inch deep. Do the same to the other tall side.

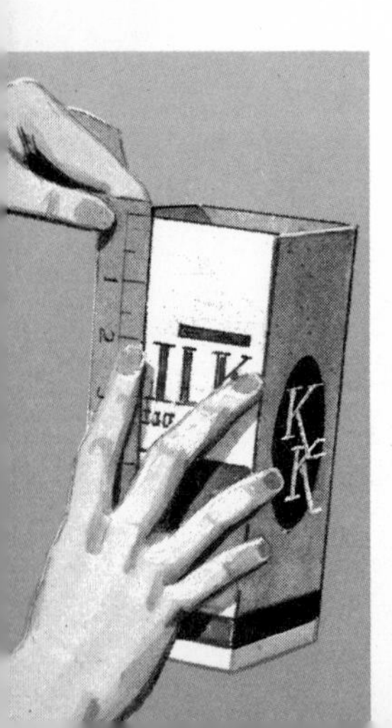

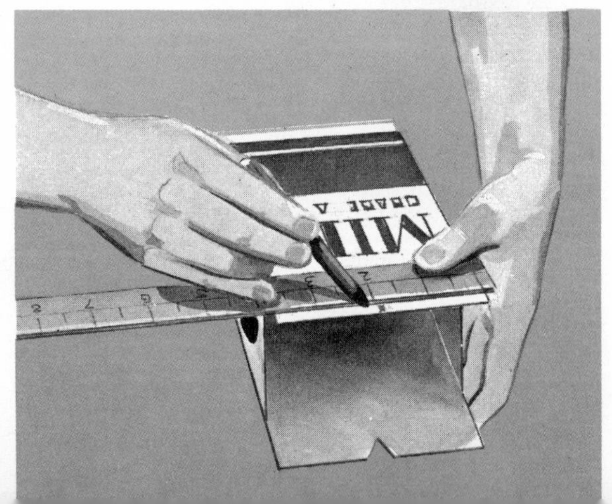

3. Use tape to fasten a pencil across a ruler under the six-inch mark. Set the pencil in the notches of the milk carton. If the ruler does not balance, move the pencil slightly to one side or the other of the six-inch mark. Re-tape the pencil so that the ruler balances in the milk carton.

4. Use a piece of florist's wire to make a handle on each paper cup as shown in the picture. Hang one cup over the ruler at the one-inch mark. Hang the second cup over the ruler at the eleven-inch mark. The ruler should balance. If the ruler does not balance, move the cups until it does. Mark the ruler to show where each cup must hang for the ruler to balance.

5. Use the pieces of milk carton you cut off earlier. Cut two strips one-half inch wide and three-fourths inch long. Mark one-fourth inch and one-half inch along the length of each strip. Fold the strips on these marks to make a U-shape. Cement one U-shaped piece over the center of each mark you made for the cups. These are cup holders.

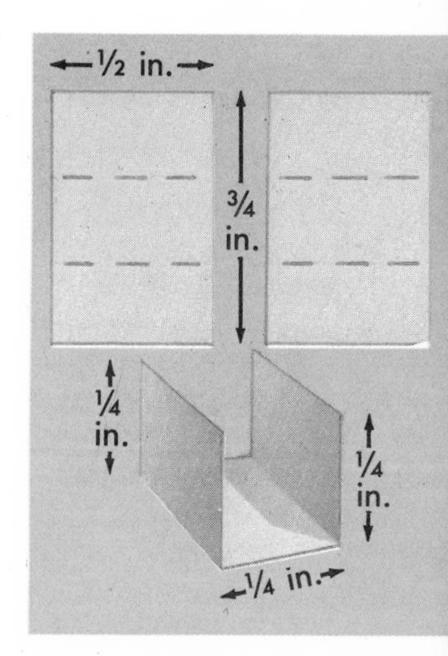

6. Push a straight pin through the eraser of the pencil. When the ruler is balanced, the pin should point straight down. This is a pointer.

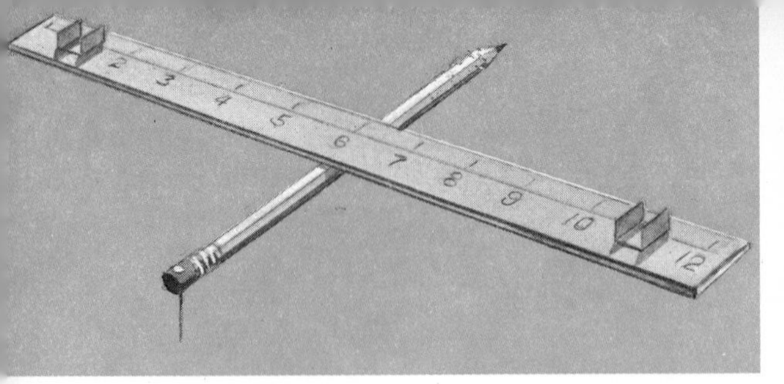

7. Hang the cups in the holders. The ruler should balance. Use the marker or grease pencil to make a line on the carton below the pointer. In your experiments, when the pointer points to this line, the ruler will be balanced. You have now made a balance scale.
8. Cut three cubes of clay, each one inch long, one inch wide, and one inch thick.
9. Put one cube of clay into each cup of the balance. What happens?
10. Put a second cube of clay into one of the cups. What happens?

When equal masses are placed opposite each other on the balance, what happens? Does gravity affect equal masses with the same force? What happens when the balance has twice as much mass on one side as on the other? Does gravity have greater effect on greater mass?

DISCOVER

How can the effect of gravity on a mass be measured?

What You Need

3 one-inch cubes of clay
large paper cup
spring scale that measures weight in grams or ounces

1. Make a container to hang from the scale by fastening wire to the cup as shown below.

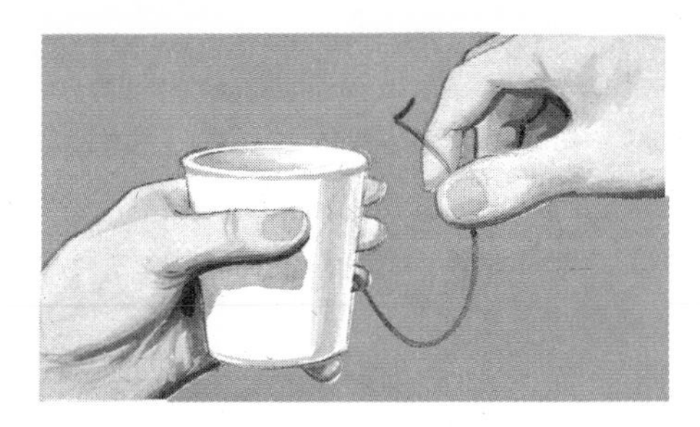

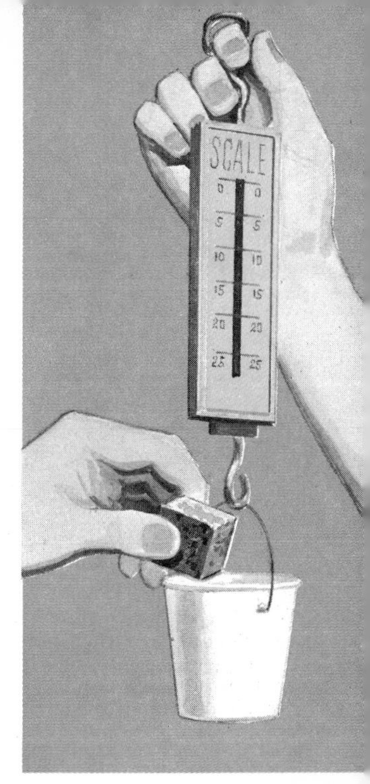

What is a gravimeter?

2. Place the cup on the scale. Put one cube of clay into the cup.
3. Measure the attraction of gravity for one cube of clay by reading the scale. Record the results.
4. Put another cube into the cup. Read the scale. Record the results.
5. Put a third cube into the cup. Read the scale. Record the results.

Mass	Weight
1 cube of clay	
2 cubes of clay	
3 cubes of clay	

What happened to the effect of gravity when the mass was doubled? What happened when it was tripled? Do you think a certain mass is attracted by the same amount of force everywhere on the earth's surface?

The spring scale shows how strongly gravity pulls on mass. When you weigh an object, are you measuring the pull of gravity on the object's mass? **Weight** (wāt) is the effect of gravity on a certain mass. Do you think mass changes by moving an object? Do you think weight changes by moving an object?

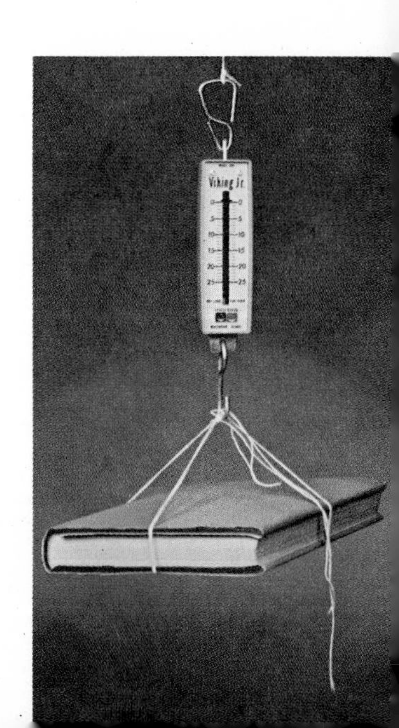

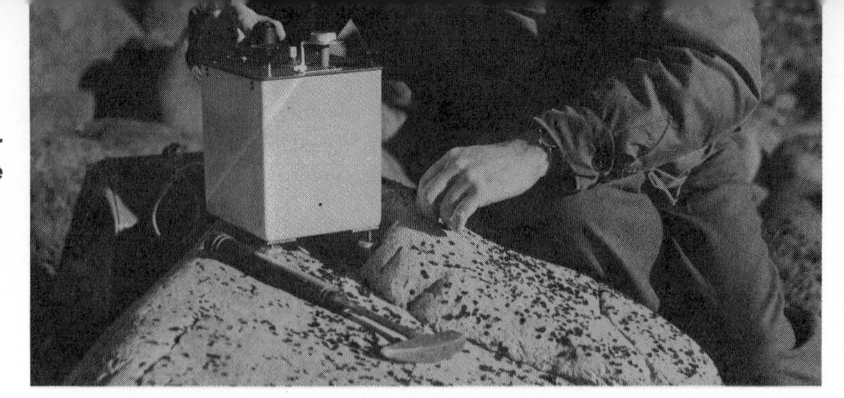

Scientist using a gravimeter to study the earth's gravity

Scientists have measured the effect of gravity at many different places on the earth. Some scientists have worked in submarines to measure the pull of gravity below the surface of the ocean.

One of the instruments used to measure the effect of gravity is called a **gravimeter** (gra vim′ ə tər). The gravimeter shows different readings for the same mass at different places on the earth. The pull of gravity at the north and south poles is greater than the pull of gravity at the equator! Can you think of a reason for this difference?

The earth bulges at the equator and is flattened at the poles. Is the surface of the earth closer to the center of the earth at the poles or at the equator? In which place would the earth's gravity pull you with greater force, at the equator or at the north pole? In which place would you weigh more?

Mass and Volume

Did each cube of clay you cut have the same measurements for each side? Each cube was one inch long, one inch wide, and one inch thick. Multiplying these three measurements together will give you the **volume** (vol′ yəm) of the cube.

$$1 \text{ inch} \times 1 \text{ inch} \times 1 \text{ inch} = 1 \text{ cubic inch}$$

The volume of the cube is one cubic inch. Volume is the measure of an amount of space. The cube of clay has a volume of one cubic inch. This means that the clay takes up one cubic inch of space. Do you remember that gravity had the same force of attraction for two cubes of clay when each had the same volume?

DISCOVER

Does gravity affect two masses that have the same volume with the same amount of force?

What You Need

balance scale used before
cubic inch of clay
cubic inch of wax
cubic inch of lead

What is density?

1. Place the cubic inch of clay and the cubic inch of wax on opposite sides of the balance scale. Which does gravity attract more?
2. Compare clay and lead in the same way. Observe what happens.
3. Compare lead and wax in the same way. Observe what happens.

You used a simple balance scale to compare equal volumes of two different materials. Did gravity affect one cubic inch of wax with as much force as it affected one cubic inch of clay? Which did gravity affect with more force, a cubic inch of clay or a cubic inch of lead? Which did gravity affect with more force, a cubic inch of wax or a cubic inch of lead?

Whenever the masses of different materials are compared, it is necessary to compare equal volumes. By comparing equal volumes, you found that clay had a greater mass than an equal volume of wax. Which had a greater mass, lead or wax?

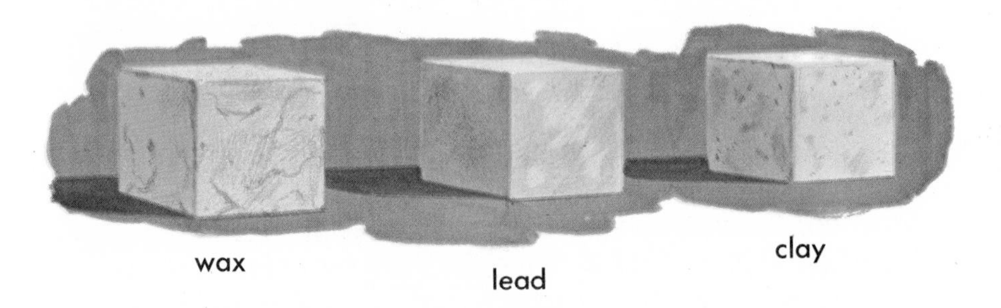

When you talk about the mass of a certain volume of a material, you talk about its **density** (den′ sə tē). The denser a material is, the more it is affected by gravity. Clay is denser than wax. Is clay denser than lead? Which has the greater density, wax or lead?

Can you also compare the densities of liquids? To compare the densities of two liquids, what must be the same? How can you make a container for liquids that will hold a volume of one cubic inch?

Get a measuring cup with a small spout and fill it with water until it overflows. When the water is no longer overflowing, hold a small paper cup of the same size you used for the balance scale beneath the measuring cup spout. Carefully put a cubic inch of clay completely into the water. The water should overflow into the paper cup. Is the volume of the water which overflowed the same as the volume of the clay cube? Mark the height of the water on the side of the cup with a pencil. Now you have a mark on a container with which you can measure one cubic inch of liquid. Mark two other paper cups of the same size at exactly the same height.

How is a hydrometer used?

These cups should fit inside the cups of your balance scale. Fill one cup to the mark with water. Fill another cup to the mark with cooking oil. Fill a third cup to the mark with some other liquid. Compare the liquids. Which liquid is the densest? How can you tell?

Some paints and pastes are liquids that are much denser than water. What will happen if you place a cubic inch of paint or paste opposite the cubic inch of oil on the balance scale?

When a scientist wants to find the density of a liquid, he does not need to weigh the liquid. Instead, he may use an instrument called a **hydrometer** (hī dräm′ ə tər). The hydrometer floats in the liquid. In a denser liquid, the hydrometer will float higher. The denser the liquid is, the better it is able to hold up the mass of the hydrometer against the effect of gravity.

One kind of hydrometer floating in a liquid

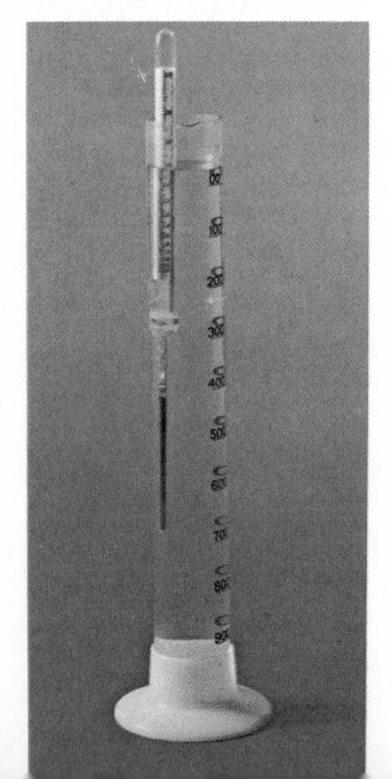

FIND OUT

Which is denser, plain water or water with salt dissolved in it?

EXPERIMENT

What You Need

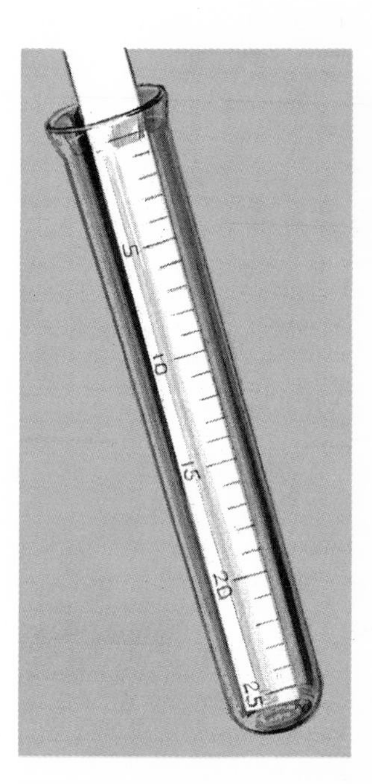

- paper
- scissors
- test tube
- ruler
- pencil
- tall drinking glass
- water
- paper clips
- table salt
- tablespoon

1. Cut a strip of paper as long as the test tube and about one-half inch wide. Use your ruler to mark off quarter inches on the strip. Make a scale by numbering every fifth quarter-inch from the top to the bottom of the strip as shown in the picture. Put the strip into the test tube. This is your hydrometer.
2. Fill the drinking glass half full with water. Put the test tube hydrometer you just made into the water. One by one, slowly drop paper clips into the test tube until the bottom of the test tube nearly touches the bottom of the drinking glass.
3. Read the scale. Record the results.

4. Add one tablespoon of salt to the water in the glass and stir until the salt is dissolved. Push the hydrometer to the bottom of the glass. Slowly let go. When the test tube is still, read the scale. Record the results.
5. Add more salt, one tablespoon at a time. Read the hydrometer after each tablespoon of salt has been added.

Material	Hydrometer Reading
water	
water, 1 tablespoon salt	
water, 2 tablespoons salt	

A hydrometer floats higher in a denser liquid than in a less dense liquid. Was the salt water denser or less dense than plain water? What evidence do you have? To check your results, try this. Put equal volumes of plain water and salt water into cups and place them in the balance scale cups. Which is denser? Is syrup denser or less dense than water? How can you use the hydrometer to find out?

Floating and Sinking

Have you ever wondered why some things float in water and why other things sink? Do you think density and mass might make a difference in whether an object floats or sinks?

Put the cup with one cubic inch of water into the balance scale cup. Put the one-inch cube of clay into another cup the same size and put it into the balance scale cup opposite the water. Which way does the pointer move and how far? Try the same thing again, but this time use the cube of wax instead of the clay. Which way does the pointer move and how far? Both cubes are the same size. Which cube would you say is denser than water? Which cube is less dense than water?

How can you discover if something is less dense than water?

Put the wax and clay cubes into a cup of water. What happens to each? Pour some salad oil into a cup of water. What happens?

Whether something will float or sink in water depends upon its density. Wax and oil are less dense than water. Do both materials float when you put them into water? The molecules of water apply enough force on these materials to hold up their mass against the effect of gravity. Is granite less dense than water? Is wood less dense than water? How might you find out?

What happens when things that are denser than water are put into water? What happens when you put a nail into water? A nail sinks because its mass is affected by gravity and because it is denser than water. Yet, a huge steel ship floats. Would you like to find out why?

Place a quart measuring pitcher on a tray. Fill it with as much water as possible. Carefully put a large apple into the water. Water will overflow into the tray. Carefully pour the water from the tray into a paper cup which you can then fit into the balance cup.

Place the apple on the opposite balance cup. What do you notice?

When you put the apple into the water, did it float? Did it sink into the water enough to push out some of the water? How does the mass of the water pushed out compare to the mass of the apple?

The apple floats because it is pushed upward by the force of the water molecules around and under it. This upward force of the water is equal to the downward pull of gravity on the mass of the apple.

FIND OUT

How can the upward force of water keep a ship afloat?

EXPERIMENT

What You Need

aluminum foil	3 pennies
scissors	deep pan of water
ruler	

Can some things float in air?

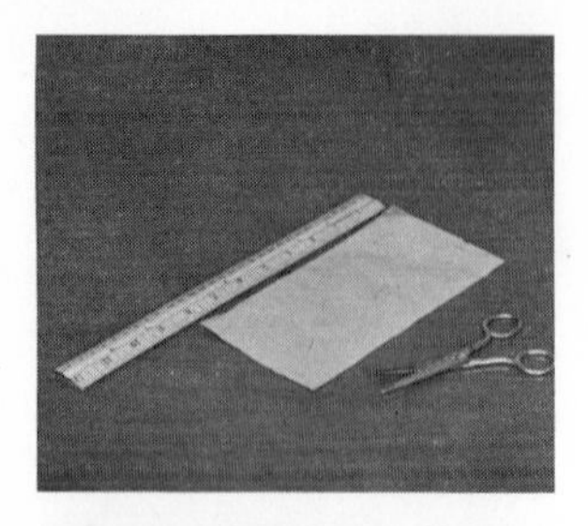

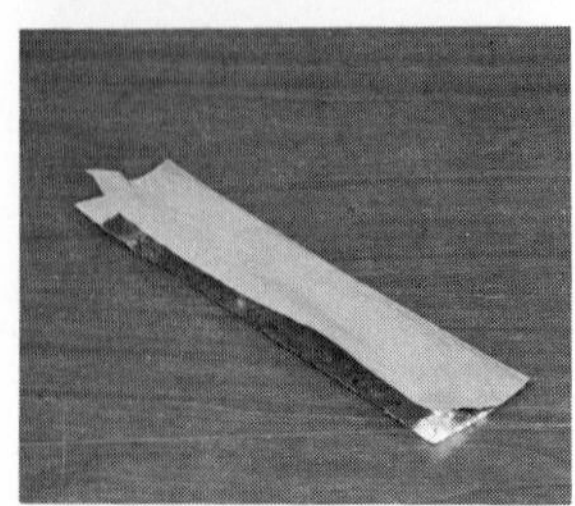

1. Cut a piece of aluminum foil eight inches long and four inches wide. Fold it in the center, then fold the ends over tightly. To make a boat, spread the foil as shown in the picture.
2. Put three pennies into the boat. Put the boat into a deep pan of water. Does the boat float?
3. Take the boat from the water. Crumple the foil tightly around the pennies. Put it into the water. What happens?

Why does the same weight float when it is spread out in the shape of a boat, and sink when it is crumpled? When the foil was crumpled, did it push aside much water? Did the foil and pennies have more mass than the water they pushed aside? Why did they sink?

When the foil was spread out, more water was holding it up. When the foil was crumpled, less water was holding it up. When the foil was spread out, how much water did it push aside? Was the mass of the water pushed aside equal to the mass of the foil and pennies? Why did the boat float?

Certain kinds of balloons that are sold as toys must be held tightly by a string because they float in the air. These balloons are usually filled with the gas called helium. Is helium denser or less dense than air? How can you tell?

Some gases, such as carbon dioxide, do not "float" in air; they settle to the ground. Is carbon dioxide denser or less dense than air?

Gravity and Balance

Suppose you and a friend wanted to use a seesaw. One thing you might want to do is to balance. What do you think the word "balance" means?

Place a yardstick across a chalkboard eraser so that neither end touches the table. Where is the mass of the stick pressing against the table?

What is the center of gravity?

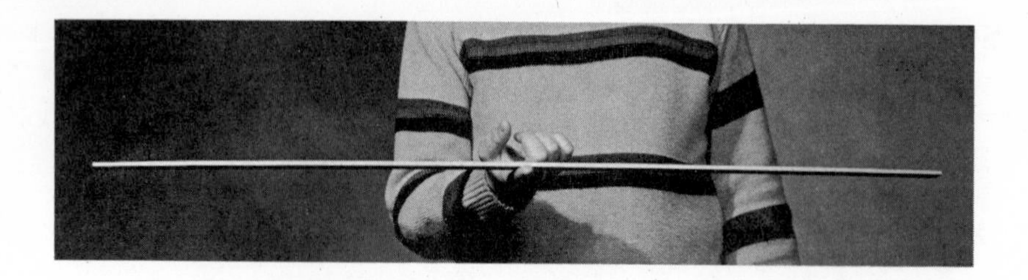

When something is balanced, it looks as if all its mass is balanced around one spot. Although gravity is pulling at both ends of the stick, it seems as if the stick is being pulled only at the center. This place on the stick is called the **center of gravity.**

Can you balance the yardstick by placing your finger under it at its center of gravity? Where is the center of gravity of the yardstick? If you were to place a small weight at one end of the yardstick, how might you find the new center of gravity?

Now, what do you think the word "balance" means?

It is often easy to balance an object if you know where its center of gravity is located. Do you think knowing about the center of gravity can help you explain why some objects fall over more easily than others? Can you tell which lamp in the picture could be knocked over more easily?

FIND OUT

How do the center of gravity and the size of the base it rests on affect balance?

EXPERIMENT

What You Need

empty soft drink bottle

1. Turn the bottle upside down and set it on a flat surface. Give it a slight push. Does the bottle tip easily?
2. Now set the bottle right side up on a flat surface. Give it the same kind of push. Does the bottle tip as easily?
3. Turn the bottle on its side. Try to push it into an upright position.

In which of the three positions is the center of gravity the lowest? In which of the three positions is the bottle hardest to tip?

Where is the center of gravity in an object?

Which of these vases would be knocked over more easily?

The center of gravity is located where most of the mass is. The lower the center of gravity, the more difficult the object is to tip over. You may also have noticed that it is resting on a larger base when the bottle is right side up. Both the position of the center of gravity and the size of the object's base affect balance. Does a lamp that has most of its mass near the bottom tip as easily as one that has most of its mass higher up? If the center of gravity is located at the same place in two objects, will the one resting on the narrower base be more or less easily tipped? Of course, you can make almost any object tip if you push it over far enough. What happens to the center of gravity when something tips?

FIND OUT

How does the position of the center of gravity affect balance when something is tipped?

EXPERIMENT

What You Need

pencil	string
ruler	small weight
shoe box	

1. Use a pencil and a ruler to draw two lines across the bottom of the box, one from each corner to the opposite corner as shown in the bottom pictures.
2. Punch a small hole into the box where the lines cross. The hole marks the center of gravity of the box.
3. Put one end of a string through the hole and knot the end inside the box. Tie a small weight to the other end. Set the box near the edge of the table so that the string hangs over the edge.
4. Tip the box up on one corner as shown in the picture. The string should not hang past the bottom corner of the box. Let go. Does the box fall over?
5. Now tip the box up on one corner again. This time, the string should hang past the bottom corner of the box. Let go. What happens to the box?

The string shows the direction in which the mass is attracted. The mass of an object is attracted straight down from its center of gravity. As long as this force is directed through the lowest part of the box, does it tip? When the direction of force is not through the lowest part of the box, what happens?

Does matter on the moon have an attraction for other matter?

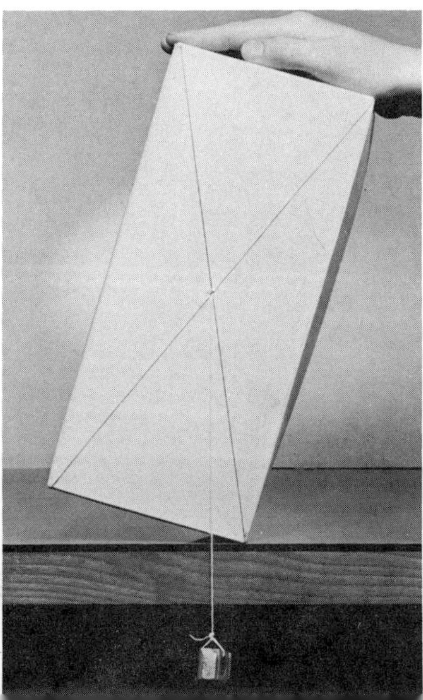

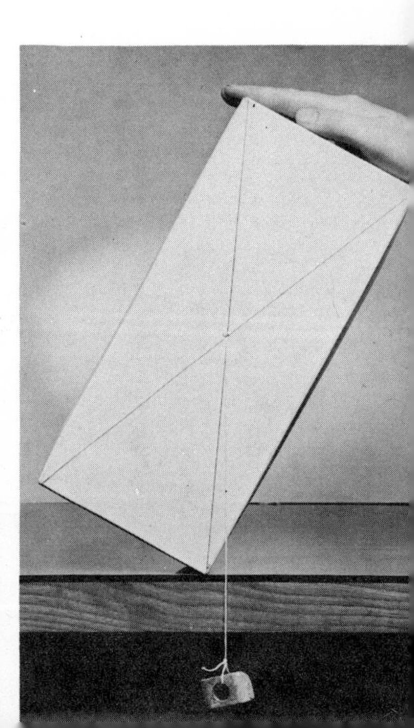

Objects fall toward the center of the earth. What force pulls them in that direction? Gravity is the attraction of the earth for objects near its surface. Learning about gravity may help you to understand why objects balance and why objects either float or sink. But there is more to gravity than the way that it affects things on the earth.

All matter has an attraction for other matter. The attraction between all matter is called **gravitation** (grav′ ə tā′ shən). Even the smallest bits of dust have gravitation. Molecules and atoms have gravitation. All objects do not have the same amount of gravitation. A large mass has a greater gravitation than a small mass.

The sun has a larger mass than the earth. The sun has a gravitational effect which is stronger than the gravitational pull of the earth. Compare the mass of the earth with the mass of its moon. Which do you think has a stronger gravitation? Would you weigh more on the earth or on the moon?

Think about the ways that gravity is important on the earth. Think about why gravitation is important in space. Both the word gravity and the word gravitation describe the same kind of attraction. What is the difference in the ways these words are used?

Why is gravity important to a satellite traveling around the earth?

Exploring Your Learnings

Here are some ideas and vocabulary. What do these mean to you?

Words to Use

gravity (p. 86)	density (p. 94)
mass (p. 87)	hydrometer (p. 96)
weight (p. 91)	center of gravity (p. 104)
gravimeter (p. 92)	gravitation (p. 108)
volume (p. 93)	

Ideas to Use

1. The earth's attraction for objects is called gravity.
2. Mass is the amount of material in an object.
3. Masses can be compared on a balance scale.
4. The amount of space an object takes up is its volume.
5. Density is the mass of a certain volume of material.
6. An object floats because it is less dense than the material in which it is floating.
7. The place in an object on which the mass of the object seems to be resting is its center of gravity.
8. Gravitation is the attraction all matter has for all other matter.

Why does this boat float?

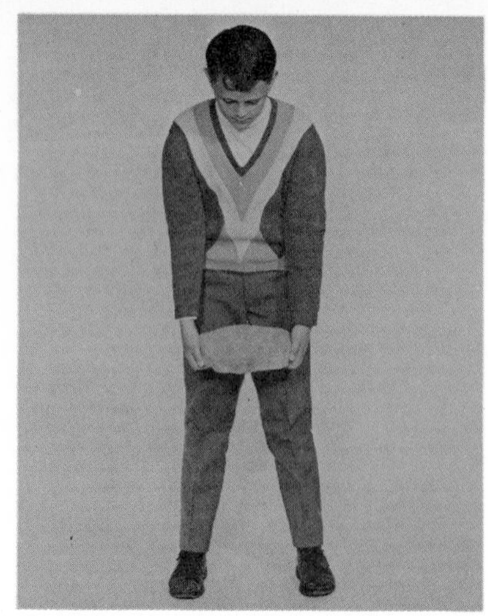

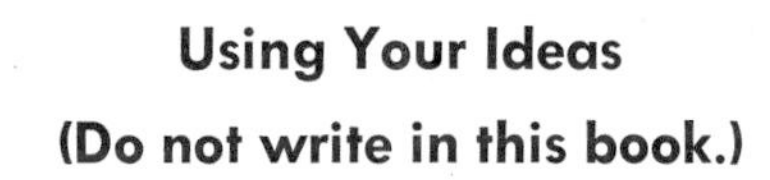

Using Your Ideas

(Do not write in this book.)

1. In what ways is gravity important? Write a story about what the world would be like without gravity.
2. Explain how gravity is at work in each picture above.
3. Find out why a hoop weighted with clay will roll uphill.
4. Try to make a pencil balance over the edge of a table by using wire and clay.
5. Tell why a cube of lead will float in a dish of mercury.
6. Read to find out how submarines can be made to rise and sink. Use the idea of density in your explanation.

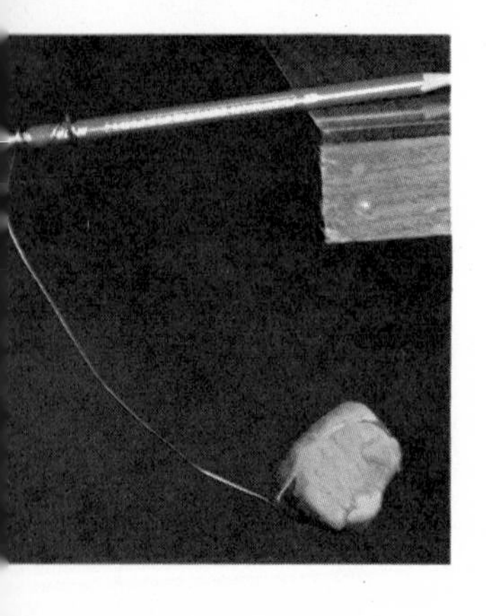

7. Compare the ways the boy is standing. In which way would the boy lose his balance more easily? Why?
8. Add one tablespoon of vinegar and one tablespoon of baking soda to a glass of water. Put in five mothballs. Explain why you think they rise and sink.
9. Find out how and why hydrometers are used in gasoline stations to test water in a radiator or in a car battery.
10. Make another kind of hydrometer using a small bottle and filling it half full of water and capping it. Test densities of different liquids with your hydrometer.

Station attendant using a hydrometer

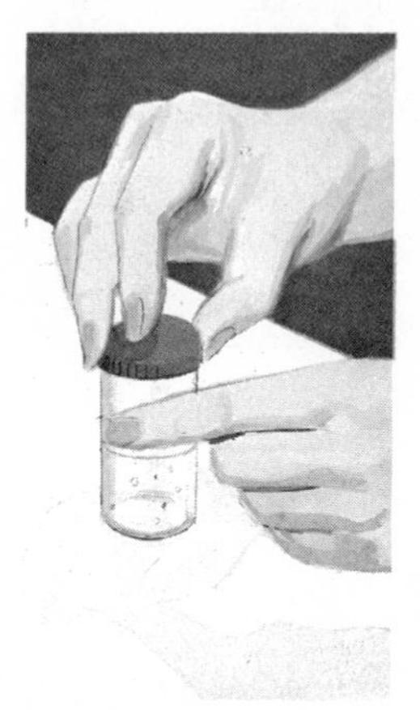

5

Understanding Heat

Hot and cold. You may think of these words as equally important, but scientists think of cold as simply the absence of heat. Heat can be used to change matter. In what ways is heat important to you?

Some of the most exciting questions that scientists are trying to answer concern heat. Molecules make up all matter. All molecules are constantly moving. Adding heat makes them move faster. Removing heat makes them move slower. If all the heat could be removed from matter, would the molecules still be moving? Would they still be molecules? Would there still be matter?

Temperature

Do you use the words hot, cold, warm, and cool? These words are used to describe an object or the weather conditions. But are these words exact enough in meaning for scientists to use in their work?

FIND OUT

How hot is hot? How cold is cold?

EXPERIMENT

What You Need

3 large plastic bowls
very warm water
very cold water

1. Fill one bowl with very cold water. Fill another bowl with very warm water.
2. Add equal amounts of warm and cold water to the third bowl.
3. Put one hand into the cold water, the other into the warm water.

4. After a few minutes, put both hands into the bowl which has both warm and cold water in it. How does the water in this bowl feel to each hand?

To which hand does the water in the third bowl feel cool? To which hand does the water in the third bowl feel warm? The water into which both hands are placed seems warm and cool at the same time. Is feeling an exact way to decide what is warm or cool? Words such as *warm* and *cool* are not always useful in science.

Scientists do not usually depend upon touch to decide whether a material is hot or cold. To be more accurate, they measure the **temperature** (tem′ pər ə chər) of a material, that is, how hot or cold the material is on a scale. What instrument may be used to measure temperature?

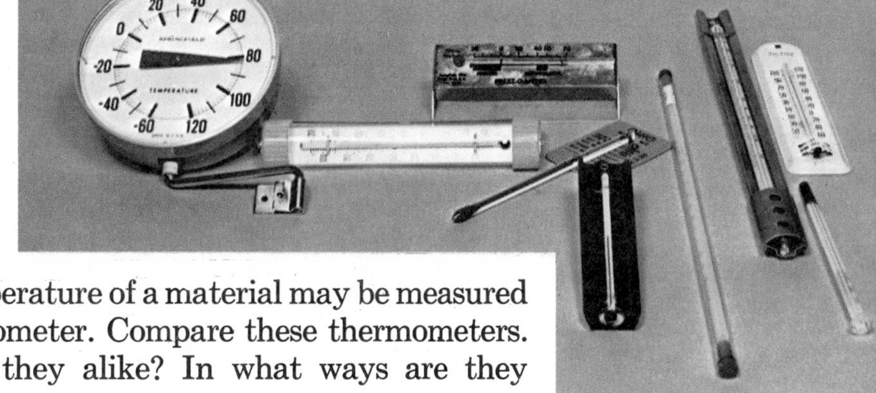

What are two kinds of thermometers?

Thermometers

One way the temperature of a material may be measured is by using a thermometer. Compare these thermometers. In what ways are they alike? In what ways are they different?

All thermometers have scales along which the temperature can be read in units called **degrees** (di grēz′). Most thermometers contain a thin tube of liquid. The length of the liquid changes when the temperature changes. When does the liquid become longer? When does the liquid become shorter?

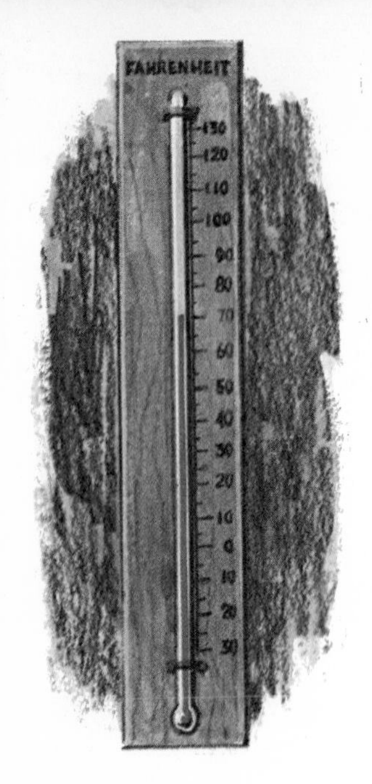

Can you read this thermometer? The length of the liquid in the thermometer tube shows the temperature as 70 degrees. This temperature can also be written as 70°.

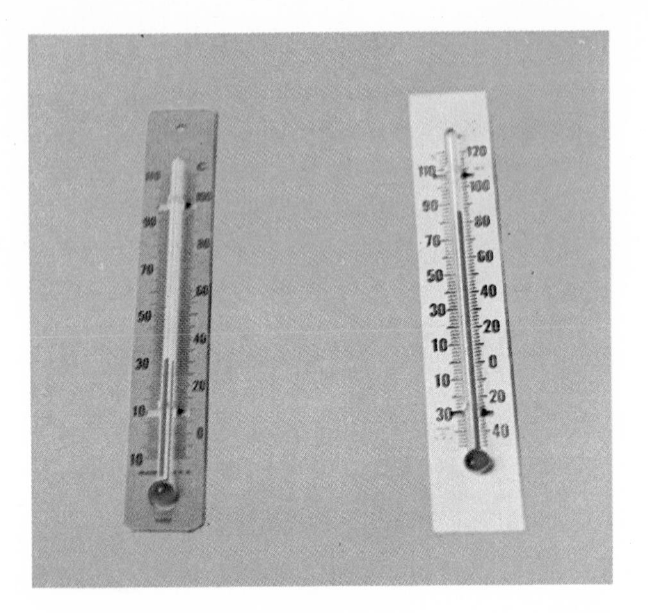

Compare the readings on these two thermometers. One is a **Fahrenheit** (far′ ən hīt) thermometer and the other is a **Celsius** (sel′ sē əs) thermometer. What temperature does each show? Would they both read the same when placed in a container of boiling water?

Boil some water in a pan. While the water is boiling, place both thermometers in the pan. Read the thermometers. What temperature does each thermometer show? How do you explain the difference in the readings?

Perhaps it is because the scale on one thermometer is different from the scale on the other thermometer. At what temperature on the Fahrenheit thermometer scale does water boil? On the Fahrenheit thermometer scale, water freezes at 32° Fahrenheit. This temperature can be written as 32° F.

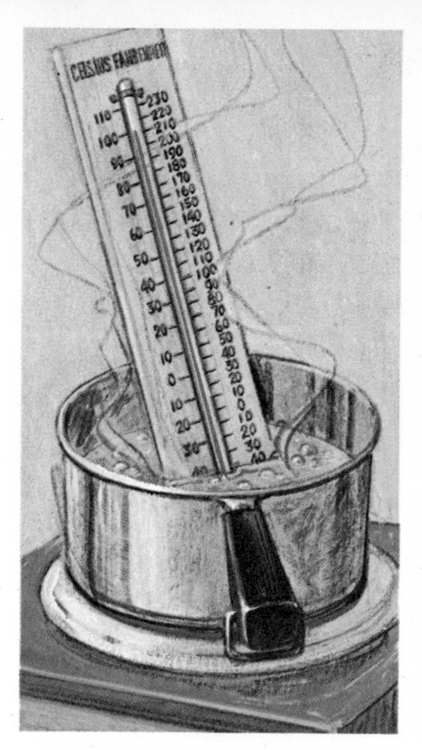

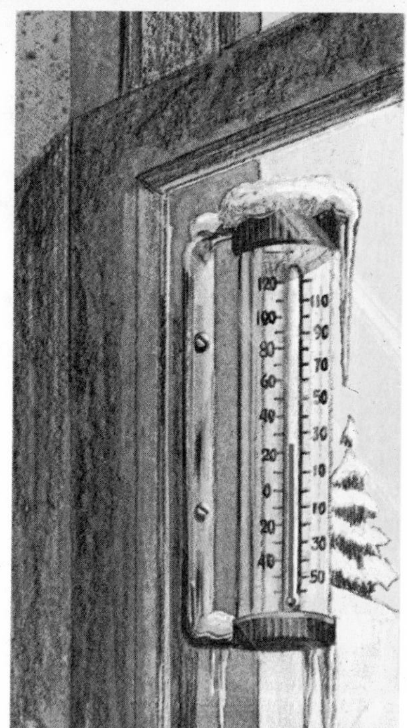

How many degrees are on the Fahrenheit scale between the temperature at which water boils and the temperature at which water freezes? Do you have a weather thermometer at home? It is probably marked in Fahrenheit degrees. Most wall thermometers and oven controls are also marked in the Fahrenheit degree scale.

Scientists commonly use the Celsius, or centigrade, scale. At what temperature does water boil on the Celsius thermometer scale? On a thermometer marked in the Celsius scale, water freezes at 0° C.

How many degrees are on the Celsius scale between the temperature at which water boils and the temperature at which water freezes? Does a Fahrenheit degree or a Celsius degree measure a greater difference in temperature? Why might a thermometer marked in the Celsius degree scale be easy for a scientist to use?

When you measure a temperature, why is it important to tell in which degree scale it was measured?

In the summer, it may be as hot as 100° F or even hotter. On a Fahrenheit scale thermometer, 100° may be uncomfortable, but you can live at that temperature. On a Celsius scale thermometer, 100° is the temperature at which water boils. Would you be able to live at 100° C? Normally a room is comfortable if it is around 72° F. This temperature is only 22° C.

What do you think causes differences in temperature? How do scientists explain heat and temperature?

Molecules in Motion

All matter is made of atoms. Molecules are groups of atoms bound together. Scientists have discovered that both atoms and molecules are always in motion.

FIND OUT

Do molecules of warm water or of cold water move faster?

EXPERIMENT

What You Need

2 glasses	thermometer
water	measuring cup
food coloring	
stopwatch or timepiece with a second hand	

1. Fill each glass with one cup of water. Place one where it will remain overnight at room temperature.
2. Place the second glass of water in a refrigerator overnight.
3. The next day, set both glasses side by side. Measure the temperature of each glass of water.
4. When the water in both glasses has stopped moving, put a drop of food coloring into each glass. Observe how long the molecules of food coloring take to mix with the molecules of water in each glass. Do you think the food coloring will mix more rapidly with the warmer or cooler water?

What happens when an object gains heat?

Did you see evidence of moving molecules? Why did the food coloring mix with the water? In which glass did the molecules of water mix with the molecules of food coloring more quickly? Which has a higher temperature, a material in which the molecules are moving slowly or the same material in which the molecules are moving quickly?

Expansion and Contraction

When an object gains heat, its molecules move faster and its temperature rises. When an object loses heat, its molecules move slower and its temperature falls. Something else happens to the object also. Do you know what this might be?

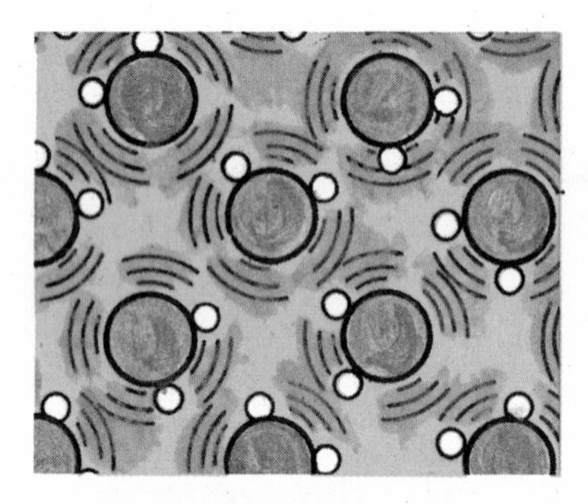

Molecules of hot water

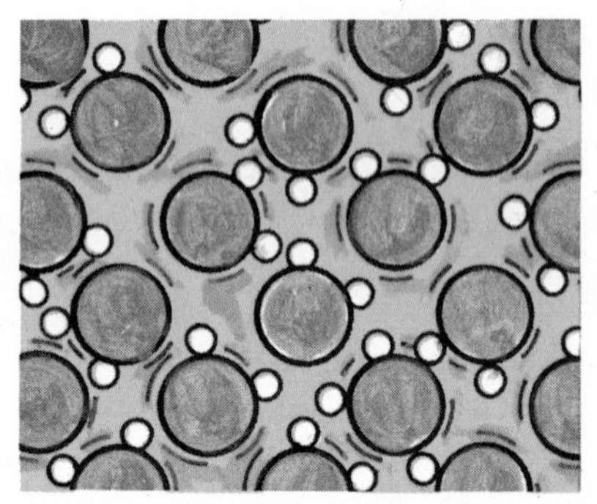

Molecules of cold water

One way to show what happens when a solid gains or loses heat is to use a brass ball and ring. Brass ball and ring sets are made especially to use to study heat. Both the brass ball and brass ring are fastened to wooden handles.

If you can obtain a brass ball and ring set, try the next experiment to learn what else happens when a solid is heated.

FIND OUT

What happens to the size of a solid when the solid is heated?

EXPERIMENT

What You Need

ball and ring	hot plate
2 pans	ice cubes
water	

1. Try to push the ball through the ring. Can it pass through at room temperature? Record the results.
2. Put a pan of water on the hot plate. When the water is boiling, put the ball into it for a few minutes. Take the ball out of the water and try to fit the ball through the ring. What do you observe? Record the results.
3. Let the ball cool to room temperature. Try to pass the ball through the ring. What do you observe? Record the results.

Why does an object expand and contract?

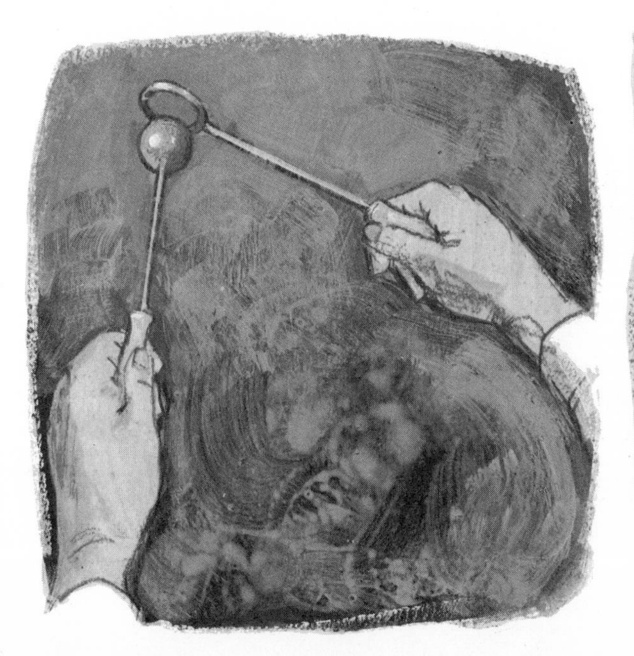

4. Fill another pan with ice and water. Put the ring into this pan for a few minutes. Now try to pass the ball through the ring. What do you observe? Record the results.
5. Let the ring warm to room temperature. Try passing the ball through the ring again. What do you observe? Record the results.
6. Try passing the ball through the ring after both have been heated. Then try it again after cooling both. Record your observations.

Temperature of Ball	Temperature of Ring	Observation
room	room	
hot	room	
room	room	
room	cool	
room	room	
hot	hot	
cool	cool	

As an object gains heat, its molecules vibrate more quickly and move farther apart. Does it seem as though the object's mass increases? Or does the object's volume increase? When an object's volume increases as it gains heat, the object **expands** (eks pandz′). As an object loses heat, its molecules vibrate more slowly and move closer together. Does the object seem to have less mass? Do you think the object's mass changes? Does the object's volume change? When an object's volume decreases as it loses heat, the object **contracts** (kən trakts′). You cannot see the change in distance between two molecules. But when there are many molecules in an object, you can notice the total change in distance between all its molecules. Does the ball get larger or smaller as it is heated? Does it get larger or smaller as it cools?

Most solids expand as their molecules move faster. Most solids contract as their molecules move slower. Does concrete of streets and sidewalks take up more room on hot days? When streets or sidewalks are built, why are the large pieces of concrete laid with other material between them? Can you see these separations in the picture of the bridge roadway? Look for the separations in streets and sidewalks near your school and home.

When does the temperature of a substance change?

FIND OUT

Do molecules of liquids also move apart as they gain heat?

EXPERIMENT

What You Need

Pyrex bottle
one-hole stopper that fits bottle opening
strong plastic tubing, 8 inches long
water
food coloring or ink
tape
pan
hot plate

1. Wet the end of the plastic tubing and put it into the hole in the stopper.
2. Fill the bottle with water. Color the water with a little food coloring or ink.

3. Put the stopper tightly on the bottle. Some of the water will be forced up into the tube. Mark the height of the water in the tube with a piece of tape.
4. Heat the bottle by putting it into a pan of water on a hot plate. What happens to the liquid in the tube?
5. Allow the bottle to cool. What happens to the liquid now?

When the temperature of a liquid rises, what do you observe? When the liquid cools, what do you observe? What happens to molecules of a liquid when they gain heat? When a substance loses or gains heat, its temperature changes. What happens to molecules of a liquid when they lose heat? Why can liquids be used in thermometers to indicate temperature changes?

Do gases contract and expand?

Have you ever noticed a change in the tires of a bicycle after it has been standing in the sun? Do they become larger? Does heat change the temperature of gases such as air?

FIND OUT

What happens when molecules of air are heated?

EXPERIMENT

What You Need

balloon	water
Pyrex bottle	hot plate
pan	

1. Place a balloon over the top of a clean, empty bottle as shown in the picture.
2. Put the bottle into a pan of water on a hot plate. Heat the water.
3. As the water in the pan warms the air in the bottle, what happens to the balloon?
4. Remove the bottle from the warm water. Allow the bottle to cool. What happens to the balloon now?

As you heated the air in the bottle, did it take up more room? Do you think the molecules moved farther apart? Can you explain why air molecules moved from the bottle into the balloon? As the air cooled, what did you observe? Explain what happens to gas molecules as they are heated and as they are cooled.

Three Kinds of Water

With changes in temperature, molecules of solids, liquids, and gases move farther apart or closer together. These materials expand and contract. Adding heat to a liquid can cause a slight increase in the volume of the liquid. What will happen if you continue to add heat to a liquid? How much will a liquid expand?

Put a small amount of water into a pan. Heat the pan on a hot plate with low heat until the water disappears. Explain what happened to the molecules of water.

As more heat is added, the molecules of water move faster and faster. The molecules continue to move farther and farther apart. Some molecules of water break away from the liquid. When molecules of a liquid move far enough apart that they cannot be seen as a liquid, they are a gas. Water molecules as a gas are water vapor. When any liquid changes to a gas, it **evaporates** (i vap′ ə rāts). When does a liquid evaporate very quickly?

At what temperature does mercury boil?

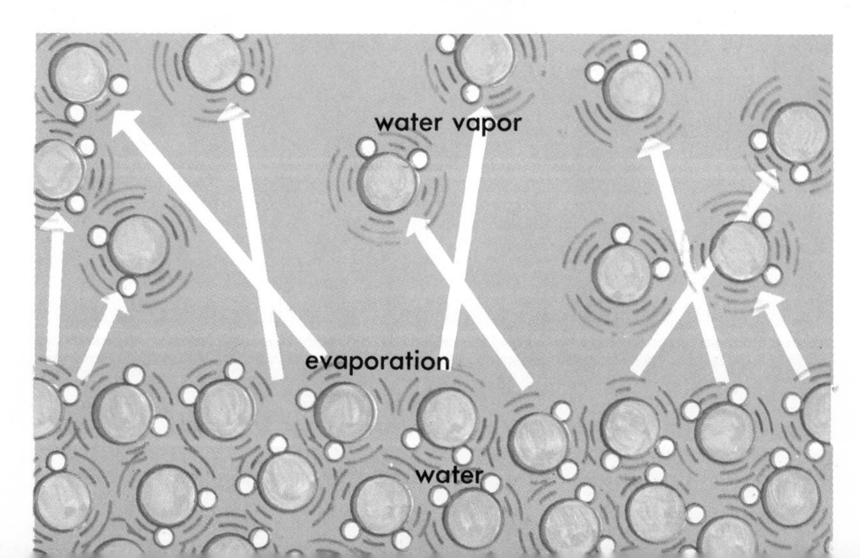

The temperature at which a liquid boils is its **boiling point.** The chart shows the boiling points of some liquids. Do all liquids boil at the same temperature? Which have a higher boiling point than water? Which have a lower boiling point?

BOILING POINTS

Liquid	Temperature	
water	212° F	100° C
alcohol	173° F	78° C
mercury	674° F	357° C
turpentine	318° F	159° C
gasoline	158° to 194° F	70° to 90° C
ether	95° F	35° C

Do some liquids need a higher temperature than others to change rapidly to a gas? Do you think the boiling point temperature will tell you anything about how fast a liquid evaporates?

FIND OUT

Does a liquid with a low boiling point or a liquid with a high boiling point evaporate faster?

EXPERIMENT

What You Need

aluminum foil
2 medicine droppers
alcohol
water

1. Place a small piece of aluminum foil in a place where it will remain undisturbed.
2. Using one medicine dropper, put a drop of alcohol onto the piece of foil.
3. Using the second medicine dropper, put a drop of water onto the foil near the drop of alcohol. Be sure the two drops do not touch each other.
4. Use the chart on page 128 to find out which of the two liquids has the lower boiling point. Predict which of the drops will evaporate faster.
5. Observe the drops every ten minutes until one of the drops is completely evaporated.

Which liquid evaporates faster, the liquid with the lower boiling point or the liquid with the higher boiling point? Would water or gasoline evaporate faster? Would gasoline or ether evaporate faster?

As a liquid gains heat, molecule by molecule the molecules escape and the liquid changes to a gas. As both the alcohol and the water gained heat, they gradually changed to gases. Where did the heat come from to evaporate these liquids? Do you have any ideas how the gases might be changed back to liquids?

What is condensation?

DISCOVER

How do the molecules of a gas become a liquid?

What You Need

ice cubes
towel
hammer
shiny metal can
magnifying glass

1. Put ice cubes into a towel. Use a hammer to crush the ice cubes.
2. Fill the metal can with the crushed ice. With the magnifying glass, observe the sides of the can as it cools. What happens?
3. Touch the outside of the can with your finger. What is on your finger?

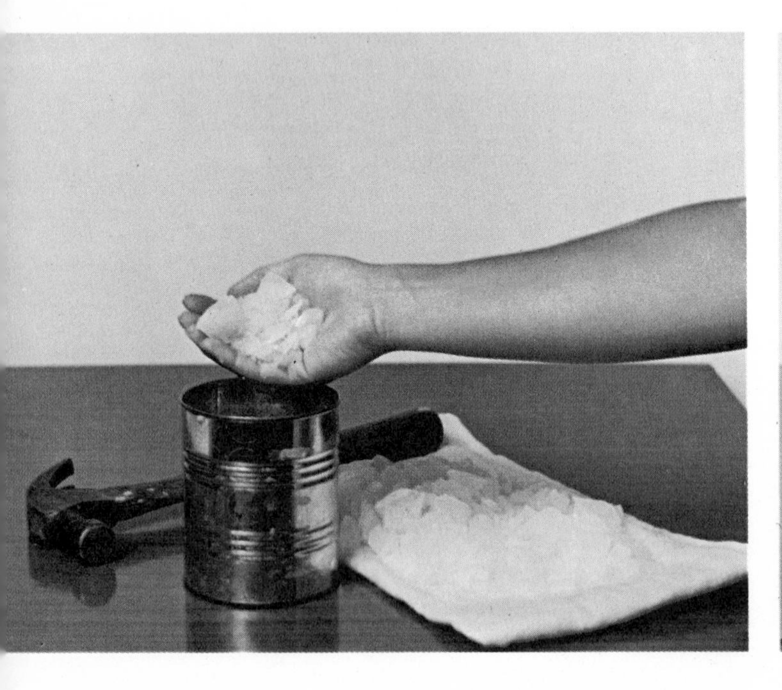

What do you think causes frost and water to collect on a window?

Can you use the idea about moving molecules to explain why the water molecules in the air formed liquid water on the outside of the can? Did molecules of water vapor in the air near the can lose some heat?

As the molecules of water vapor began to move more slowly, what happened to the gas? Did some of the molecules of water vapor in the air move close enough together to form tiny drops of water? The changing of a gas into a liquid is **condensation** (kon′ den sā′ shən). The water vapor condensed to liquid water.

What do you suppose would happen if you were to place a dry, shiny metal can into a freezer overnight, then remove it on the next day and place it on a table?

What is the difference between freezing and melting?

FIND OUT

What happens if you continue to remove heat from water?

EXPERIMENT

What You Need

hammer	coarse salt
ice cubes	spoon
towel	2 thermometers
large can	water
measuring cup	test tube

1. With the hammer, crush some ice in a towel.
2. Put three cupfuls of crushed ice into the can. Add a cup of salt and stir the mixture well. Put one thermometer into this mixture. Record the temperature.
3. Put about one-half inch of water into a test tube. Put another thermometer into the test tube. Put the test tube into the can. Record the temperature of the water in the test tube. Turn the test tube slowly.

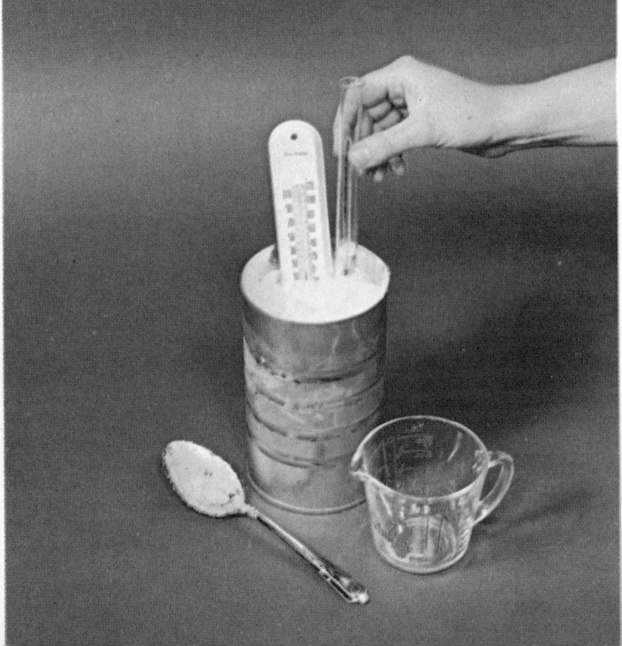

4. After about ten minutes, remove the test tube from the can. What is the temperature of the water in the test tube? What is the temperature of the salt and ice?

Material	Beginning Temperature	Temperature After Ten Minutes
salt and ice mixture		
water in test tube		

What change took place? When you mixed ice and salt, what happened to the ice? Did the ice lose heat or gain heat? From where did the mixture of ice, salt, and water take heat? Did the water in the test tube lose heat or gain heat? What gained the heat from the water in the test tube? What happened to the speed of the water molecules in the test tube? What formed in the test tube? **Freezing** (frēz′ ing) takes place when a liquid changes into a solid. How can you change ice to water? **Melting** (melt′ ing) takes place when a solid changes into a liquid. What happens to the molecules of a solid which melts?

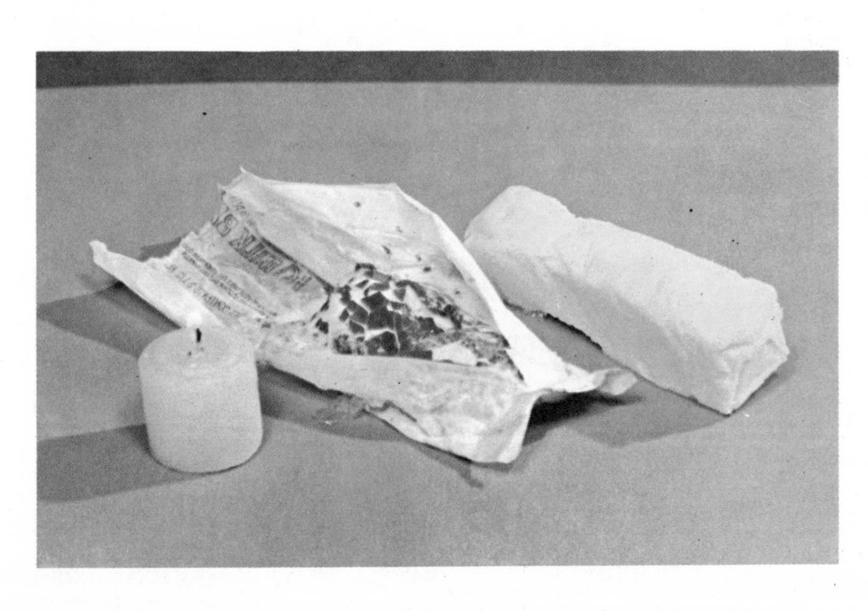

Traveling Heat

Your experiments showed expansion, contraction, evaporation, boiling, cooling, condensation, freezing, and melting. Are all of these changes evidence that heat can travel?

Does heat travel from a hotter area to a colder area, or from a colder area to a hotter area? When something evaporates, it gains heat. When a liquid freezes, it loses some of its heat. Will it give up heat to something cooler than it is or to something warmer than it is?

When you remove a hot metal pan from the stove, the handle may be hot. Only the bottom of the pan is touching the stove. How did the handle get hot?

DISCOVER

How does heat travel through a solid?

What You Need

paraffin wax	long metal spoon
small metal can	nails
hot plate	glass

1. Put some wax into the can. Heat the can on the hot plate just enough to melt the wax. Dip the head of each nail into the melted wax and hold each nail against the spoon until the wax hardens. Place the nails as shown in the picture. Turn off the hot plate.
2. Place the bowl-end of the spoon onto the edge of a hot plate. Support the other end of the spoon with a glass.
3. Turn on the hot plate. Which nail falls from the handle first? Which nail falls last? Turn off the hot plate.

Where did the heat come from to make the molecules of wax on the handle of the spoon move more quickly? Did heat travel along the handle of the spoon? What do you think happened to the molecules in the handle of the spoon? Does this explain how the heat traveled?

Molecules do not move from one end of the handle to the other. The molecules at the bowl-end of the spoon on the hot plate absorb heat. When these molecules gain heat, how are they different from other molecules in the spoon? Molecules may bump into other molecules when they are moving. As fast moving molecules bump other molecules, these slower molecules begin to move more quickly. As many of the molecules move more rapidly, will the temperature of the spoon handle increase?

Molecules may bump into other molecules, increasing their speed.

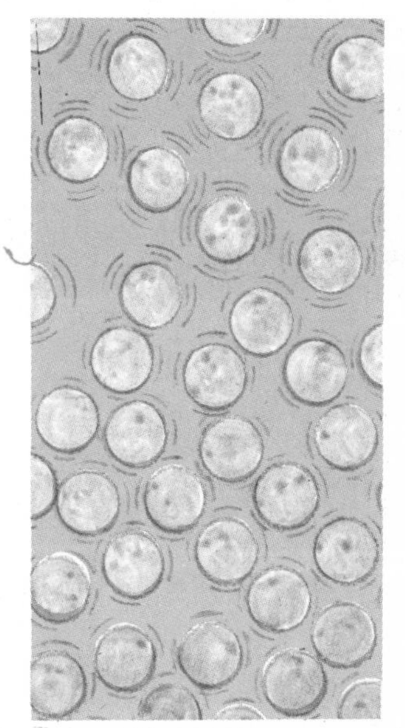

Imagine several baseballs on the top of a table. If you were to throw a baseball at the group of baseballs on the table, what would happen? The ball you threw would be moving fast. As the moving ball bumped into several other balls, how would they be affected? Is this like the faster moving molecules at the heated end of the spoon bumping into other, slower-moving molecules?

Conduction

Heat can travel through a substance from molecule to molecule. This way of heating is called **conduction** (kən duk′ shən). Do all solids conduct heat? Does everything conduct heat as well as the metal spoon does?

FIND OUT

Which common materials conduct heat well and which do not?

EXPERIMENT

What You Need

- shallow pan
- hot plate
- penny
- dime
- bit of wool from sweater
- thin wood
- bit of fur
- thin cardboard
- hard plastic
- glass
- hard rubber
- birthday candles

1. Place a shallow pan on the hot plate and turn the heat on low.
2. Put the materials listed into the pan.
3. After five minutes, touch the end of a small candle to each material, one at a time. *Do not touch the materials as you may burn yourself.*

What is an insulator?

Which materials are the best conductors of heat? How can you tell? Which materials do not conduct heat well? Materials which are poor conductors of heat are called **insulators** (in′ sə lā′ tərz).

Were wool and fur insulators or conductors? Put the wool and fur into a pan and weight them down with some stones. Carefully pour water into the pan until these materials are covered. What substance is trapped in the wool and fur?

Heat travels by conduction when molecules bump into each other. Molecules of air are far apart. Will molecules of air bump into other air molecules very often? Is air a heat insulator or a heat conductor?

Why doesn't heat from your body escape easily when you wear woolen clothing? Why does the fur of some animals and the feathers of birds help keep them warm?

Can trapped air help to keep a home warm?

Why are storm windows often used in winter? Why are materials that are very loosely packed often placed between the walls and above the ceilings of homes and other buildings? Why are these materials called insulation? How is insulation helpful in summer and winter?

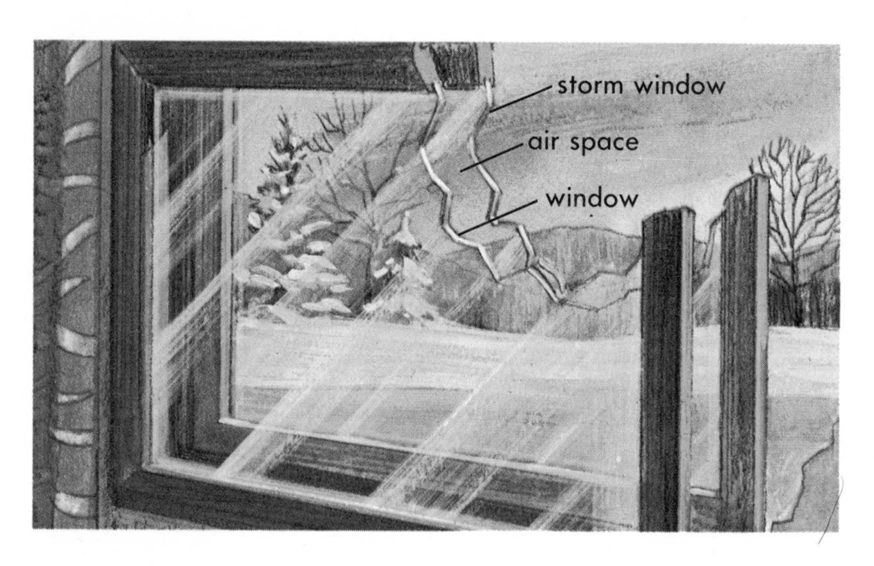

Molecules in a gas

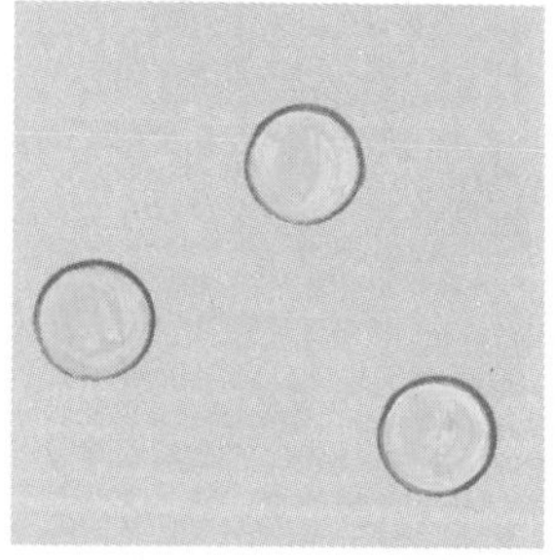

Molecules in a liquid

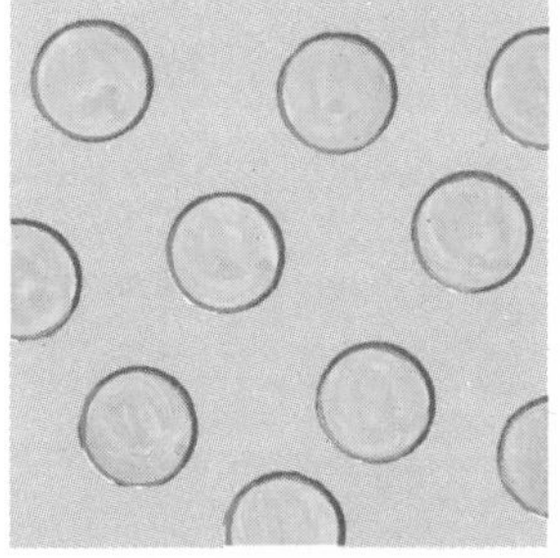

Molecules in a solid

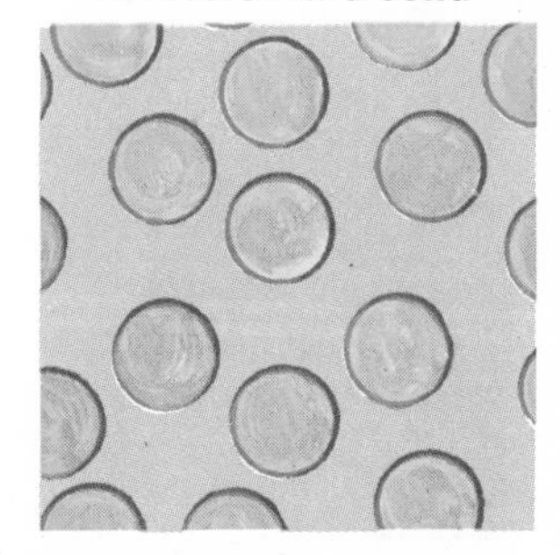

Convection

Heat can travel by conduction. Can heat travel in other ways?

How are the molecules of a liquid different from the same molecules when they are in a solid? How are gas molecules different from those in a liquid?

A solid has a definite shape and the molecules are not free to move around much. When the molecules of a solid are heated, they move more rapidly; the solid may even expand slightly. As long as the material does not change to a liquid or to a gas, the molecules will vibrate in the same space. Heat travels from one molecule to another when molecules bump together.

What two things happen to molecules of a liquid as they are heated? Since a liquid does not have a definite shape, the molecules can move easily from one part of the liquid to another. When the temperature of a liquid rises, the molecules move about more rapidly.

DISCOVER

What is another way in which heat can travel?

What You Need

pencil shavings	water
large Pyrex container	hot plate

1. Put water into the container within an inch of the top.
2. Soak the pencil shavings in the container until they sink.
3. Place the container on a hot plate so that only a small part of one side of the bottom is heated. Watch what happens to the pencil shavings.

Why is the water on the warm side of the container less dense than the water on the cool side? What happens when one material is put into a denser material? In this experiment, what is happening to the water which is heated? In a liquid, do faster moving molecules travel away from the heat? Do they lose heat to parts of the liquid that are cooler? As they lose heat, what happens to these water molecules? This way of heating is called **convection** (kən vek′ shən). Explain how convection heats a teakettle of water.

The molecules in a gas are much farther apart than the molecules in a liquid. Do molecules in a gas or molecules in a liquid move about more freely? A gas does not have a definite shape. A gas is an insulator because it does not conduct heat well. But can heat travel in a gas in some other way?

DISCOVER

How can heat travel in a gas?

What You Need

black poster paint
paint brush
shoe box
knife
3 corks
light bulb, 25 watts or less
light bulb socket on extension cord
transparent plastic wrap
tape
tongs
incense or damp paper
matches

1. Paint the entire inside of a shoe box with black poster paint.

2. Cut three holes into a shoe box into which the corks can be fitted as shown in the picture. Mark the openings 1, 2, and 3 as shown in the picture. Fit a cork into each hole.
3. Make an opening in the bottom of the box near one end into which you can place the narrow part of the light bulb from inside the box. Screw the light bulb into the socket.
4. Cover the open part of the box with transparent plastic wrap.
5. Remove the cork from opening 3. Ask your teacher to use tongs to place a piece of smoking damp paper or smoking incense into the box through opening 3. Replace the cork. Do not remove this cork again.
6. When the box is filled with smoke, darken the room and turn on the light. How does the smoke travel in the box?
7. Remove the cork from opening 1. What happens to the smoke? Why?
8. Keeping the first cork out, remove the cork from opening 2. What happens to the smoke? Why?

How does your observation of convection in a liquid compare with your observations of convection in a gas? In what ways are they similar? Does the idea that molecules of warmer materials move a bit farther apart apply to warm air? How does heat travel in air?

How does heat from the sun reach the earth?

Where does most of the heat go from an open fire? Can you feel heat by sitting next to a fire? Does heat from a fire reach you by conduction? Does heat from a fire reach you by convection? Is there another way that heat can travel?

Radiation

When you hold your hand above a light bulb that is on, why does your hand feel warm? When you hold your hand to the side of the bulb, why does your hand feel warm? Does the light bulb give off both heat and light in every direction?

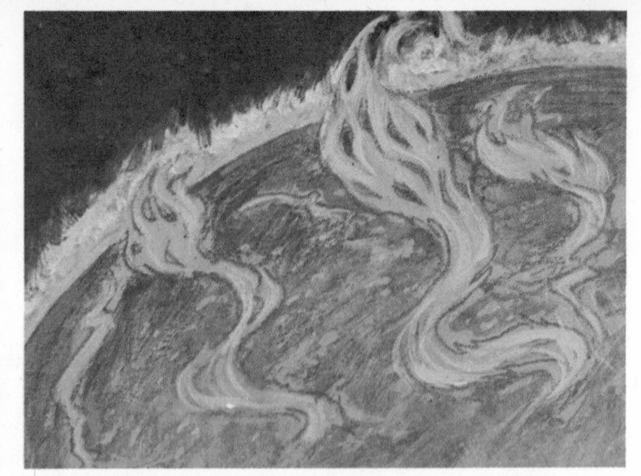

Heat from coals is given off by radiation just as heat from the sun is.

Anything that is warm gives off heat rays, called **infra-red** (in′ frə red′) **rays.** Heat rays travel in every direction from something that is warm. The traveling of heat in this way is called **radiation** (rā′ dē ā′ shən).

Radiation from the sun travels millions of miles through space before it reaches the earth. There are too few molecules in space for heat to travel by conduction or convection. Does heat traveling as radiation depend upon moving molecules?

FIND OUT

How do heat rays affect the temperature of a material?

EXPERIMENT

What You Need

2 metal cans	paraffin wax
can opener	2 nails
black paint	light bulb socket
paint brush	small light bulb
hot plate	extension cord

1. Remove both ends from one can. Paint half of the inside black from top to bottom. Stand the can on end.
2. Melt some wax in the other can on the hot plate. Dip the head of each nail into the wax. Put a nail on each side of the painted can as shown in the picture.
3. Screw the light bulb into the socket and put it inside the painted can. Turn the bulb on and watch carefully.

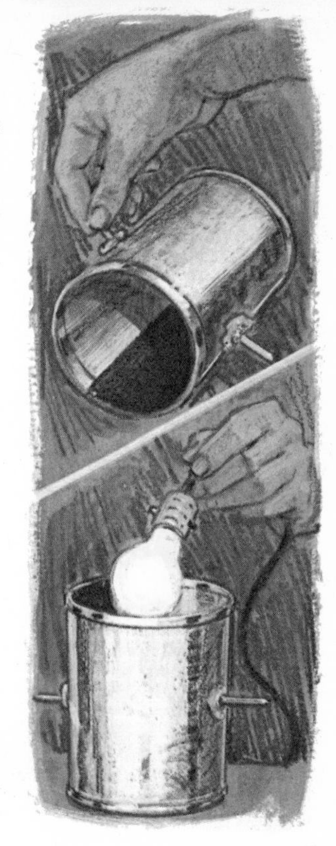

Which nail falls first? Look inside the can. How are the two halves of the can different? Which side of the can becomes warm enough to melt the wax first?

Heat rays can be reflected or absorbed when they reach a material. Which side of the can reflected heat rays? Which side of the can absorbed heat rays? When molecules absorb heat, how does their temperature change?

Some temperatures may be high enough to make you uncomfortable. Is it just as important to know how to keep cool when it is warm as it is to know how to keep warm when it is cold?

When it is very warm outside, it is a good idea to wear clothing that reflects radiation from the sun. Would light-colored or dark-colored clothing reflect radiation better? If you lived in a place that was very warm, would you choose a light-colored roof or a dark-colored roof for your home?

How can heat be removed from an object?

Removing Heat

An air conditioner removes heat from air in a room; a refrigerator removes heat from food. Do you know how they remove heat?

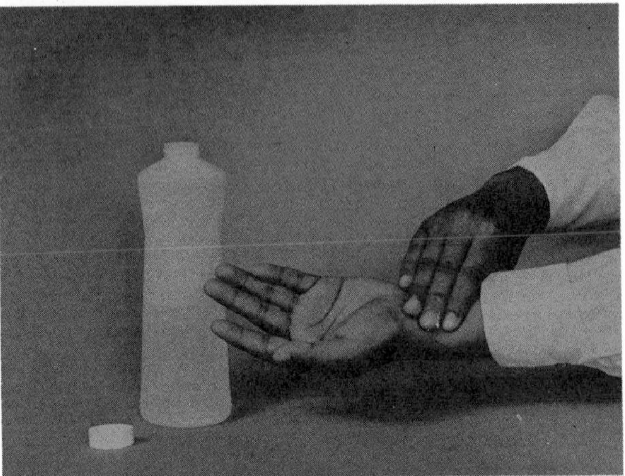

Rub a few drops of rubbing alcohol on the underside of your wrist. What happens to the alcohol you placed on your wrist? How does your wrist feel?

Do the alcohol molecules on your wrist move farther apart? How do you know that they do? What is needed to speed up molecules so that they move apart in this way?

When a liquid evaporates, it absorbs heat from whatever is around it. Suppose a liquid that needs just a little heat to evaporate it is put into pipes in a refrigerator. From what would the liquid absorb heat? What would happen to the temperature of the air and the food in the refrigerator?

The gas formed by the evaporating liquid must be moved out of the food compartment. It travels through pipes to another part of the refrigerator where a pump squeezes the molecules closer together. What must happen to make the molecules of gas stay squeezed closely together?

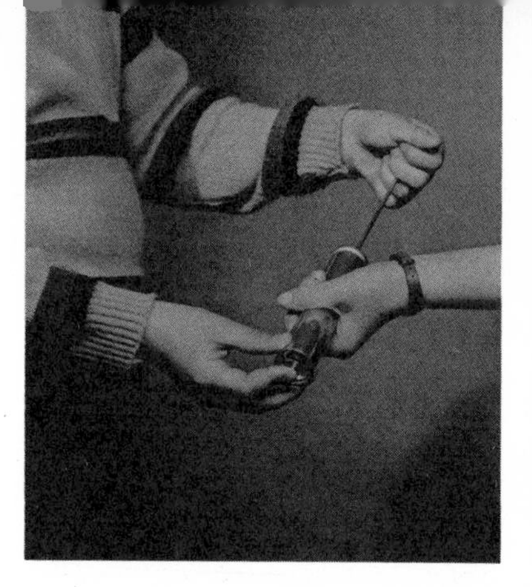

Obtain a football pump. Hold the sides of the pump at the bottom. Have another person place a finger over the opening while moving the handle up and down about five times. What do you notice?

Moving the handle up and down forces a lot of air into the pump and the molecules are squeezed together. What happens when molecules of a gas are squeezed closer together? Do you feel a change in temperature? The pump in the refrigerator squeezes and heats the gas molecules, changing the gas back to a liquid. The heat given off from the pipes of liquid at the rear of the refrigerator warms the air in the room. Would it be possible to cool a room by keeping the refrigerator door open?

Air conditioners remove heat from the air in a room in much the same way as a refrigerator removes heat from food. Why are air conditioners placed in windows with part of them outside?

What are three ways in which heat travels? What does temperature measure about the molecules of a material? When a material absorbs heat, its molecules move faster. When a material loses heat, what happens to its molecules? How does this explain expansion and contraction? Do convection and conduction depend upon motion? Does knowing what happens when molecules lose or gain heat help you explain what happens when the temperatures of materials change?

Exploring Your Learnings

Here are some ideas and vocabulary. What do these mean to you?

Words to Use

temperature (p. 115)
degrees (p. 115)
Fahrenheit (p. 116)
Celsius (p. 116)
expands (p. 123)
contracts (p. 123)
evaporates (p. 127)
boiling point (p. 128)
condensation (p. 131)
freezing (p. 133)
melting (p. 133)
conduction (p. 136)
insulators (p. 138)
convection (p. 141)
infrared rays (p. 144)
radiation (p. 144)

Ideas to Use

1. The temperature of a material is a measure of how hot or cold it is, or the speed of its molecules.
2. Temperature is usually measured with a thermometer.
3. Two common temperature scales on thermometers are the Fahrenheit and the Celsius degree scales.
4. Most materials expand as their molecules move faster.
5. Most materials contract as their molecules move slower.
6. Depending upon their temperature, water molecules may form a liquid, a solid, or a gas.
7. Solids heat by conduction and may be either insulators or conductors of heat.
8. Liquids and gases heat mainly by convection because their molecules move about freely.
9. Radiation is the movement of heat rays, or infrared rays, in every direction from something warm.
10. A material cools when heat is removed from it.

Using Your Ideas

(Do not write in this book.)

1. What is happening to molecules in pictures A, B, and C?
2. Plan an experiment to find out what happens to the freezing point of water when other substances such as sugar, or alcohol, or salt are added to it.
3. Gather different kinds of materials. Find out if they are good or poor conductors of heat. Then make a display of the different materials, labeling the two groups.
4. Put some water into a paper cup on a hot plate. Why does the water become warm enough to boil although the cup does not burn?
5. Make an air thermometer. Set up a bottle and plastic tubing as in the picture below. Put the end of the tube into a glass of water. Heat the bottle by placing your hands on the bottle until many bubbles have come out of the tube. Take your hands from the bottle. Water will rise in the tube. After the water stops moving up into the tube, mark its height. Do you notice changes in the height of the water when the thermometer is left in different parts of the room? How does this air thermometer work? How might changes in air pressure affect the accuracy of your thermometer?
6. Find out why only liquids such as alcohol and mercury are used in liquid thermometers. Is an alcohol or a mercury thermometer better for measuring high temperatures? Which is better for measuring low temperatures?

6

Weather Today and Tomorrow

In your part of the country, how much does the weather change from season to season? In some areas, people expect spring to bring warmer weather. But weather changes from day to day. You may remember a time when you thought spring was here to stay. Grass was turning green. Flowers were blooming. Then along came a snowstorm!

Some people just look outside to find out what the weather is. They may hope for good weather for the coming day or they may just guess. Why do some people watch their own weather instruments, the wind direction, and clouds in the sky?

Scientists carefully study weather to provide forecasts as close as possible to what the weather will be. You can discover some conditions that can produce different kinds of weather.

exosphere
(over 350 miles)

ionosphere
(50-350 miles)

mesosphere
(20-50 miles)

stratosphere
(7-20 miles)

troposphere (7 miles)

Temperature Change

The layer of air around the earth is called the **atmosphere** (at′ məs fir). Although the earth's atmosphere extends outward for hundreds of miles, changes in weather happen only in the air close to the surface of the earth. The layer of the atmosphere closest to the earth, called the **troposphere** (trop′ ə sfir), is about seven miles deep. When you see clouds, you are looking at clouds in the troposphere.

Weather is the result of changes in the temperature of air in the troposphere. Light rays from the sun travel through millions of miles of space before they reach the earth's atmosphere. Air is heated very little as the rays pass through it. The rays strike the surface of the earth or objects on the earth and are either absorbed or reflected back into space. Heat rays which are absorbed heat the land and water. Land and water heat the air close to the earth's surface. Do you think sunlight heats the earth's surface evenly?

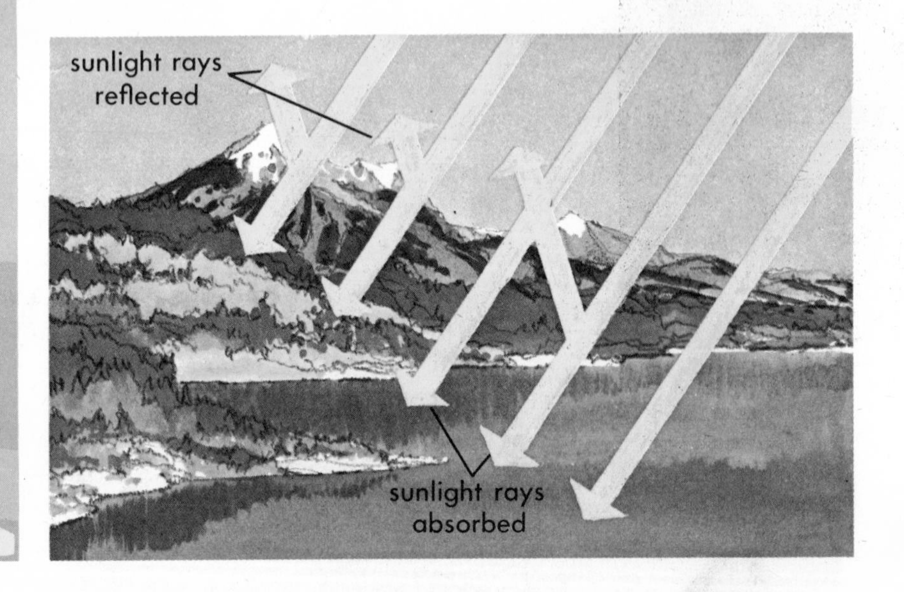

DISCOVER

Does sunlight heat the earth's surface evenly?

What You Need

flashlight
globe
ruler

1. Turn on the flashlight. Darken the room.
2. Hold the flashlight six inches from the equator on the globe as shown in the picture. Shine the light on the equator. Notice the brightness and size of the spot of light.
3. Move the flashlight straight upward so that the light strikes the globe between the Arctic Circle and the north pole. What happens to the size and brightness of the spot of light?
4. Move the flashlight straight downward so that the light strikes the globe between the Antarctic Circle and the south pole. What did you discover?

Light rays travel in straight lines. Because the earth's surface is curved, how do the light rays from the sun strike the earth in different places? Do the light rays from the sun strike the earth at more of a slant when they shine on the earth at the poles or at the equator? When light rays strike at a slant, the light is spread out over a greater area than when light rays are more direct. Do you have any ideas about the way this affects the temperature at each place?

FIND OUT

How does the slant of the sun's rays affect the temperature of the earth's surface?

EXPERIMENT

What You Need

2 shoe boxes, the same size	paintbrush
black paint	stones
white paint	2 thermometers

1. Paint the tops of the boxes black. Paint the boxes white.
2. Take the boxes outside at about ten o'clock in the morning on a sunny day. Set one box on the ground so that it receives slanted rays from the sun. Set the other box on the ground so that it is facing the sun and receives direct rays. Use stones to prop this box in the right position.
3. Read the two thermometers. Record the temperatures. Put a thermometer into each box. Cover each box.
4. Read the thermometers after ten minutes. Which box has become warmer?

Which land shown do you think receives most direct sun rays?

Are direct rays as spread out as rays which strike at an angle? Which box received direct rays? Which box became warmer? Rays which strike the equator are less spread out than those which strike the poles. Is the equator heated more than the poles? Why is air at the earth's poles colder than air at the equator?

Large amounts of cold air develop over the land and water near the poles of the earth. Such large bodies of cold air are called **cold air masses.** Do you think large bodies of warm air develop over warm land and water near the equator? Large bodies of warm air are called **warm air masses.**

Is warm air or cold air denser? When warm air and cold air meet, the warm air rises over the cold air mass. With warm air rising and cold air settling, convection currents are formed. Where would cold air masses move from the poles? Where would warm air masses move from the equator?

If the earth did not turn, these air masses would always flow directly north or south. However, because the earth turns, these air masses usually move at an angle from north to south. Because the earth's surface is uneven, these large air masses usually break up into smaller air masses.

What is a front?

Do temperatures change each time a different air mass moves into an area? By keeping temperature records, can you tell when one kind of air mass is being replaced by another? **Meteorologists** (mē′ tē ə ral′ ə jists) are scientists who study the weather. They learn about the movement of air masses.

Maps such as this one are used to show the locations of air masses

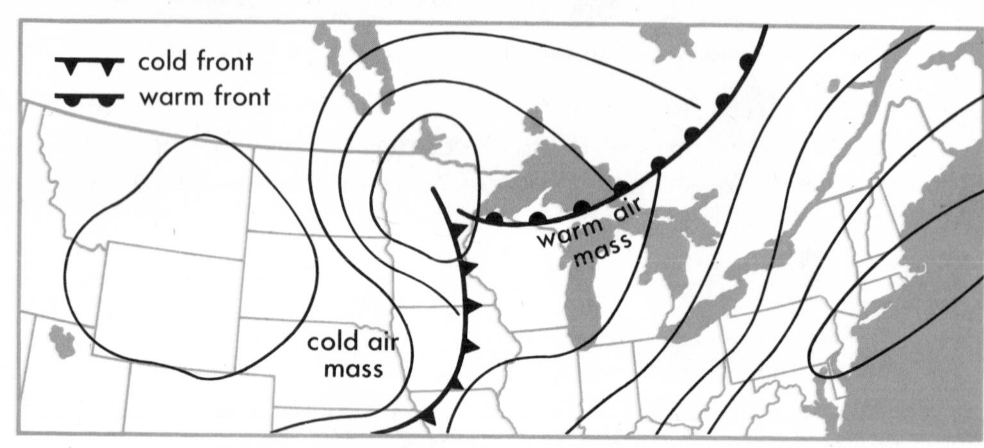

Fronts

Clouds such as these occur near a cold front.

When two air masses meet, the larger air mass moves the smaller one. Warmer air usually moves upward and colder air usually settles. The place where two air masses of different temperatures meet is called a **front.**

When cold air moves into a place where there is warm air, the place where they meet is called a **cold front.** Which kind of air would be forced upward rapidly? Large, billowy clouds may form. In the summer, these kinds of clouds may produce short, heavy rains.

When warm air moves into a place where there is colder air, the place where the warm and cold air meet is called a **warm front.** The warm front moves forward and over the colder air mass. In this case, the warmer air is cooled slowly. Flat, gray clouds may form. In summer, these clouds often produce a steady, softly falling rain that may last for days.

Can you use what you know about air masses and cold and warm fronts to explain changing weather? When a front passes over the place where you live, there is usually a change in weather. The air temperature becomes warmer or colder. How will the weather change as a cold front moves in? How will the weather change when a warm front moves in?

Humidity

Warm air which collects over the equator holds much water vapor. It is moist air. Cold air which collects over the earth's poles cannot hold as much water vapor. It is dry air. Besides knowing the temperature of an air mass, meteorologists are interested in the amount of water vapor in the air. Why might this be important for weather forecasting?

Have you ever heard someone say it is humid outside? People may describe air in this way when they are uncomfortable during warm weather. Do you know what they mean?

Air is **humid** (hū′ mid) when it contains many molecules of water vapor. Can water vapor be seen? The **humidity** (hū mid′ ə tē) is the amount of water vapor in the air.

Is there always some water vapor in the air?

FIND OUT

Where does water vapor in the air come from?

EXPERIMENT

What You Need

4 clean, empty peanut butter jars
damp soil
water
2 small potted plants
3 widemouthed gallon jars

1. Fill two peanut butter jars with damp soil. Fill the other two peanut butter jars with water.
2. Water the potted plants.
3. Place a gallon jar upside down over one peanut butter jar with soil in it. Place another gallon jar over one peanut butter jar with water in it. Place the third gallon jar over one plant. Leave one jar of soil, one jar of water, and one plant uncovered.
4. After one day, do you see anything on the inside of the gallon jars? If not, wait one more day.

Where did the drops of water that were on the inside of the gallon jars come from? How did the soil, water, and plant which were uncovered change? Did they lose water? How can you tell? Where did this water go? Where would water vapor in the air come from?

There is always some water vapor in the air. Most of the water vapor in the air comes from the oceans, lakes, and rivers of the earth. Water also evaporates from soil and plants. It passes into the air as animals breathe and perspire. Water usually evaporates from anything that is moist or wet.

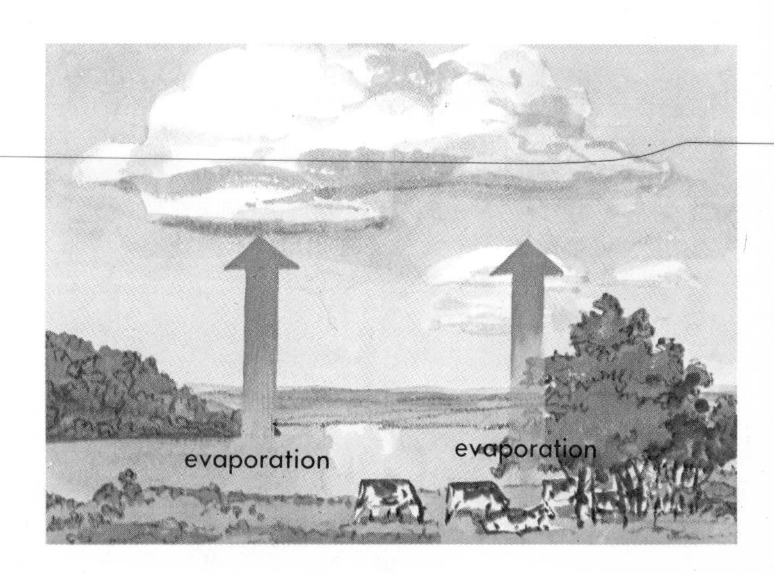

Measuring Humidity

Is the amount of water vapor in the air always the same? During some days, there is much water vapor in the air. During other days, the air is dry. A **hygrometer** (hī grom′ ə tər) can be used to measure humidity.

What part of your body may be used in a hygrometer?

DISCOVER

How is a hygrometer used to measure humidity?

What You Need

shoe box
scissors
plastic soda straw
sewing needle with a large eye
grease pencil or marker
one strand of hair, at least 6 inches long
cleaning fluid
all-purpose glue
2 paper clips

1. Cut one end out of the shoe box. Stand the box on the other end. Cut a V-shaped notch in each side of the box as shown in the picture. Make the notches large enough so that the soda straw laid across them will turn easily.
2. Push a needle through one end of the straw as far as the eye of the needle.
3. Set the straw in the notches so that the needle hangs straight down along the side of the box. Where the needle points, make a mark on the box.
4. Ask your teacher to rinse the hair in cleaning fluid. When the hair is dry, use all-purpose glue to fasten a paper clip to each end of the hair.

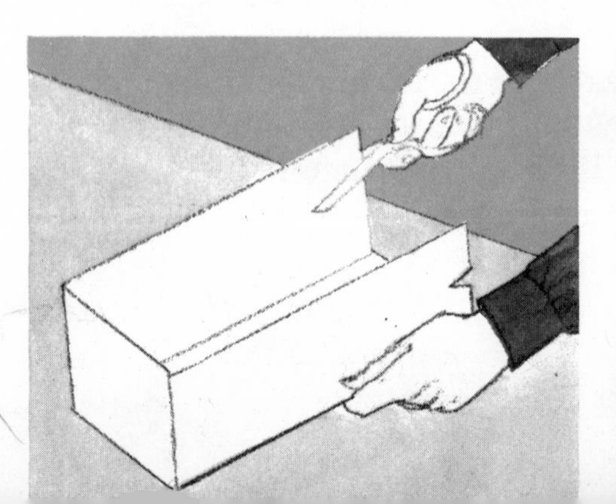

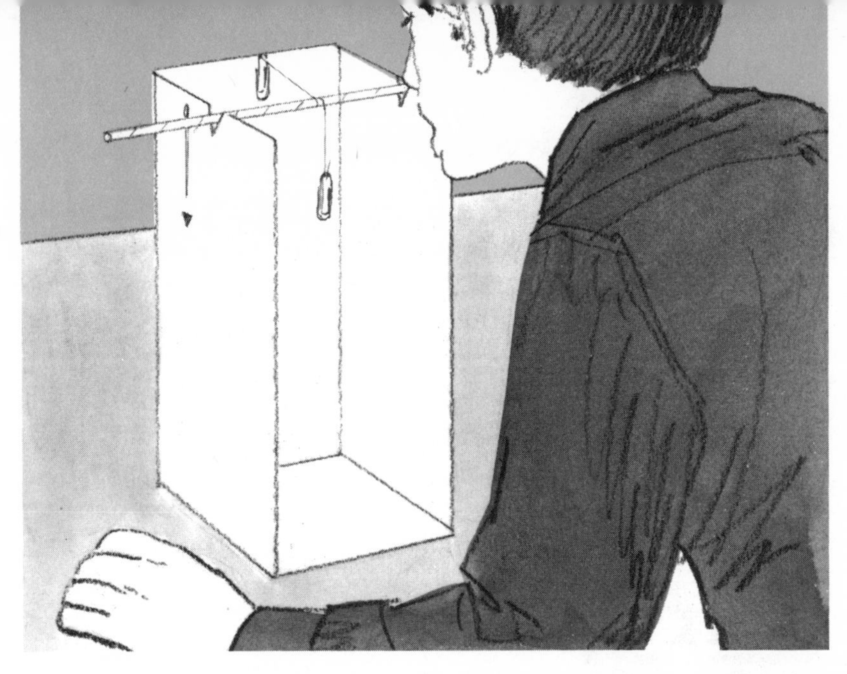

5. When the glue has dried, attach one paper clip to the box as shown. Carefully wind the hair once around the center of the straw and let it hang. The second paper clip should hang freely. The hair should not sag. The needle should point to the mark. Check these things.
6. With your mouth open, breathe slowly several times on the hair near the soda straw. Ask someone to watch the needle while you do this. What happens?

Scientists use this instrument to record both humidity and temperature on the same chart.

What did the needle do when you breathed on the hair? Why did this happen? Air from your mouth is warm and moist. Hair stretches when it is damp. The second paper clip acts as a weight pulling on the hair. When the air has a lot of moisture in it, the hair is stretched longer and the needle moves. What will happen to the length of the hair when the air around it is dry?

A hair is so sensitive to humidity that it is used in very accurate hygrometers. The hygrometer that a weatherman uses is carefully made from small metal parts, but it also contains a hair.

Kinds of Condensation

Does temperature affect the amount of water vapor that air can hold? Droplets of water which form on objects outside when the temperature falls are called **dew.** What is the process of water vapor changing to liquid water called? Dew is the result of one kind of condensation. The temperature at which a gas, or vapor, condenses to a liquid is called the **dew point.**

DISCOVER

What is the dew point in your classroom?

What You Need

shiny metal can	crushed ice
water	wooden spoon
thermometer	

1. Fill a shiny metal can half full of water. Record the temperature of the water.
2. Add the ice to the water, a few tiny pieces at a time. Stir until the ice has melted. Record the temperature.
3. Repeat step 2 until you notice tiny drops of water collecting on the can. At what temperature did water begin to collect on the can?

As air in the room touches the cold can, how is the temperature of the air affected? When air cools, can it hold as much water vapor? Why does water from the air condense on the can? When there is very little water in the air, air must be cooled a great deal to reach the dew point. When air is very moist, is much cooling needed to reach the dew point?

If the temperature at which dew forms is 32° F or below, the water vapor condenses into ice crystals instead of water droplets. Then objects such as plants and rooftops are covered with a thin coating of ice called **frost.**

Frost on a window

Clouds

When warm, moist air rises high above the earth and then reaches the dew point, what do you think forms? How is air cooled to form clouds?

DISCOVER

How are some clouds formed?

What You Need

book of matches
glass tubing, 2 inches long
rubber tubing, at least 1 foot long
one-hole stopper that fits jug opening
glass gallon jug
warm water
flashlight

1. Fit the rubber tubing over the end of the glass tubing. Insert the other end of the glass tubing into the stopper.

What is necessary for water vapor to condense?

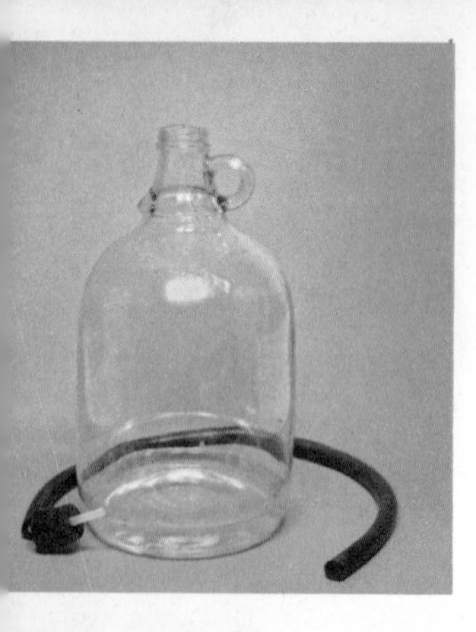

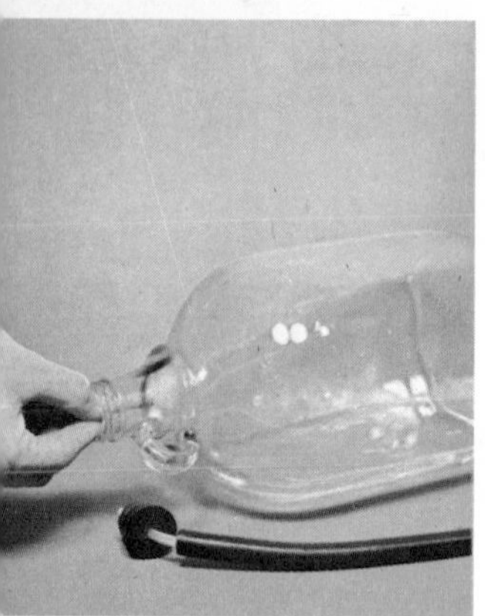

2. Add about one inch of warm water to the jug and swish it around to wet the sides of the jug. Pour out the extra water.
3. Rest the jug on its side. Ask your teacher to hold a lighted match inside the neck of the jug until the match has burned about halfway. Blow out the match. Set the jug upright.
4. Wet the stopper with water and place it tightly into the opening of the jug. Darken the room and shine a flashlight through the jug.
5. Blow air into the jug as hard as you can through the rubber tubing. Quickly remove the stopper from the jug. What do you see in the jug?

When you compressed the air in the jug, what happened to the air molecules? What happened to the molecules of water around the sides of the jug? When you removed the stopper, the molecules of air were suddenly allowed to move farther apart. The air cooled. The water vapor condensed in drops that you could see. Clouds form when warm moist air is cooled and its water vapor condenses.

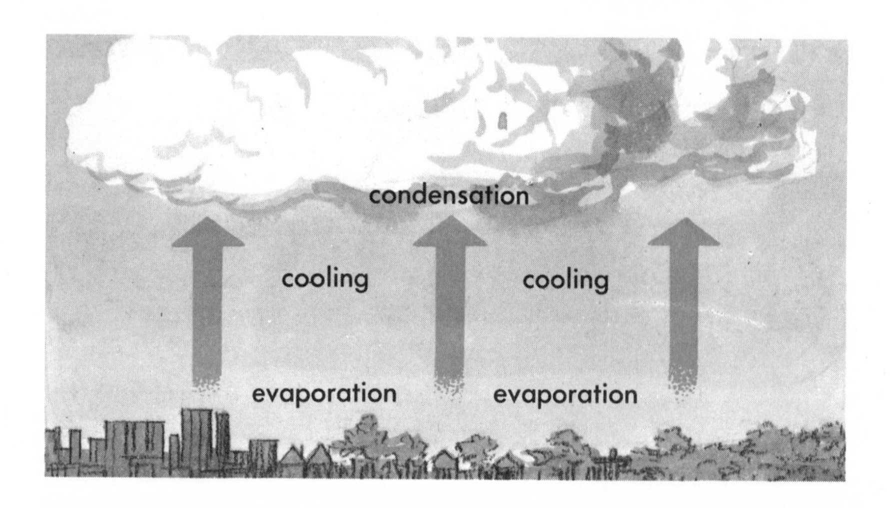

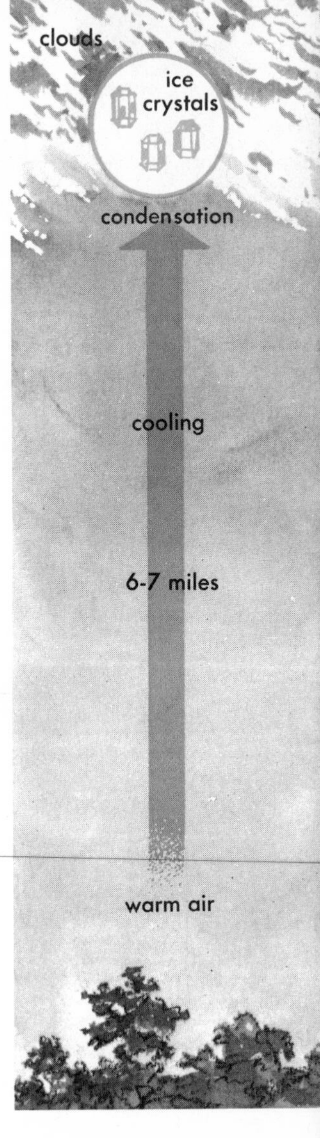

Before water vapor can condense, water molecules must have something on which to condense. On what does water vapor inside your jug condense?

Air always contains dust. Some of the dust in the air is bits of soil that have been carried by the wind. Salt from the ocean is part of the dust in the air. On what does water vapor in the air condense to form clouds?

You can do the cloud experiment by putting your mouth over the opening of the jug and blowing. Using a stopper and tubing, you can blow harder. The harder you blow, the more you compress the air. Will the cloud be thicker after the stopper is removed if the air is compressed more? Why or why not?

Air near the earth is compressed by the weight of air above it. As the air becomes warmer, what happens to the distance between its molecules? Surrounded by colder, denser air, the warm air moves away from the earth. Why does this happen? As the air moves up, it is no longer compressed as much. As air expands and cools to the dew point, clouds are formed. If air moves as high as six or seven miles before it reaches the dew point, the air may be at the freezing temperature. Then it may form clouds made of ice crystals instead of water droplets.

How are clouds named?

Cumulus clouds

Stratus clouds

Cirrus clouds

Nimbus clouds

Naming Clouds

Have you seen clouds of many different shapes in the sky? Do some clouds seem very high? Do others seem low? Meteorologists have named clouds partly according to cloud shapes and partly according to cloud height. There are three main kinds of clouds. They are **cumulus** (kūm′ ū ləs) **clouds, stratus** (strat′ əs) **clouds,** and **cirrus** (sir′ əs) **clouds.**

1. The word *cumulus* means to pile up.
2. The word *stratus* means to spread out.
3. The word *cirrus* means curly.

Name the kinds of clouds you could describe as rounded and puffy. Which would you say looked flat? Which clouds would you describe as thin and curly?

Often another word is attached to these cloud names to tell more about the height or shape of certain clouds. The picture below shows the different clouds.

Nimbus (nim′ bəs) **clouds** are storm clouds. The word *nimbo* means "rainstorm, or cloud." The word *alto* (al′ tō) means "deep or high." Clouds which have the word *alto* in their name are thick clouds.

Cloud names may sound complicated. But you can begin to figure out what they mean because the names describe the clouds. **Cirrocumulus** (sir′ ō kūm′ ū ləs) **clouds** are cirrus clouds piled up. *Cirro* (sir′ ō) is a clue that the cloud is more than five miles up. **Stratocumulus** (strat′ ō kūm′ ū ləs) **clouds** are cumulus clouds in a layer. *Strato* (strat′ ō) is a clue that the cloud is less than one mile up. **Nimbostratus** (nim′ bō strat′ əs) **clouds** are rain clouds that are spread out. They are often seen on drizzly days. **Cumulonimbus** (kūm′ ū lō nim′ bəs) **clouds** are large, tall cumulus clouds which produce thunderstorms or heavy rain.

Why does fog usually form after sunset?

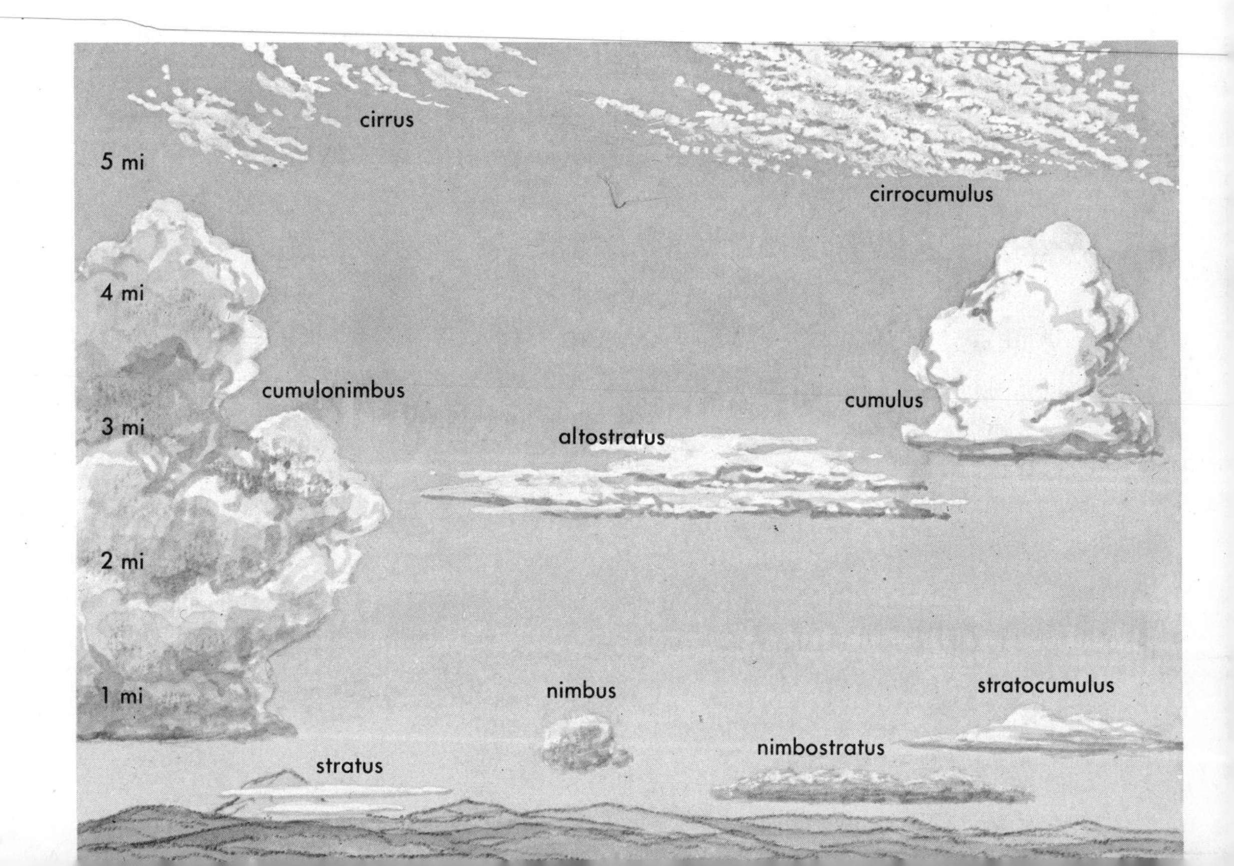

Fog

Snow

Fog is a cloud, too. Fog is formed when warm, moist air is cooled near the ground. Fog usually forms after sunset when the ground cools. Would cool air flow upward or to low places? Can you see why fog usually forms in low places? Warm air moves upward, cools, and may produce clouds. If there is enough water vapor in the warm air, the cooling may cause rain, snow, sleet, or hail. Could rain evaporate before it reaches the ground? Why might this happen?

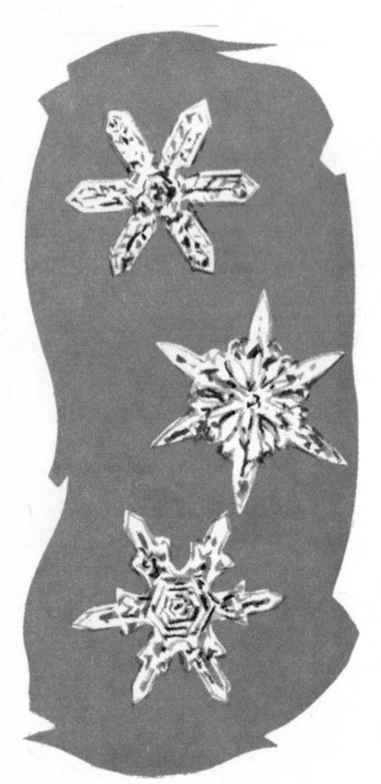

Snow, Sleet, and Hail

A snowflake begins to form when water vapor freezes. An ice crystal forms on dust in the air. The crystal of ice collects more crystals until a small snowflake is formed. When the snowflake becomes heavy enough, it falls toward the surface of the earth. What might happen if the snow falls through a layer of warm air? When raindrops fall through air which is at a temperature below freezing, what may happen? A mixture of rain and ice is called **sleet** (slēt).

Hailstones

Hailstones form in cumulonimbus clouds. Strong winds blow upward in these clouds. The top of the cloud may be at freezing temperatures, while its bottom may be warm. A raindrop in the cloud may be carried upward It freezes and forms a tiny hailstone. It falls, collects more water, and is carried upward again. As this happens many times, the hailstone grows larger and finally falls to earth. Why is a hailstone often made of many layers of ice?

The next time you see hailstones, break some open and observe the layers of ice inside. How many times was the hailstone carried upward in the cloud?

Can snow change to rain as it falls? Do you think some raindrops may change to water vapor as they fall through the air? Some rain may evaporate as it falls.

Cross section of a hailstone

Air Pressure

The weight of the air presses on the earth and produces **air pressure** (presh′ ər). Cold air masses are high density, high pressure areas. Would air in a warm air mass be as dense as air in a cold air mass? Why or why not? Would a warm air mass or a cold air mass have greater air pressure? Warm air masses are low density, low pressure areas. Within one air mass, there may be differences in pressure because of differences in temperature from place to place.

What is an aneroid barometer?

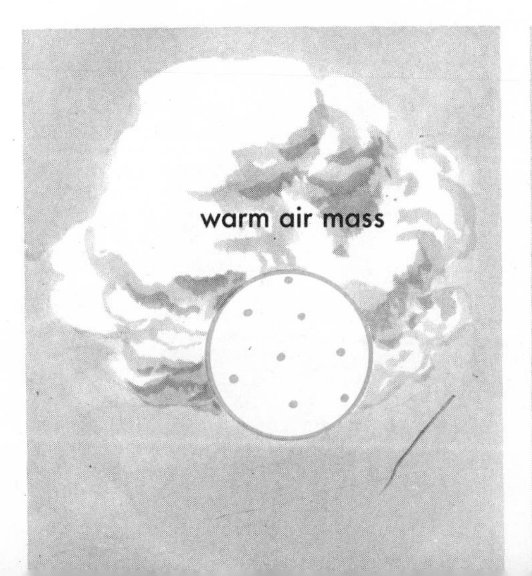

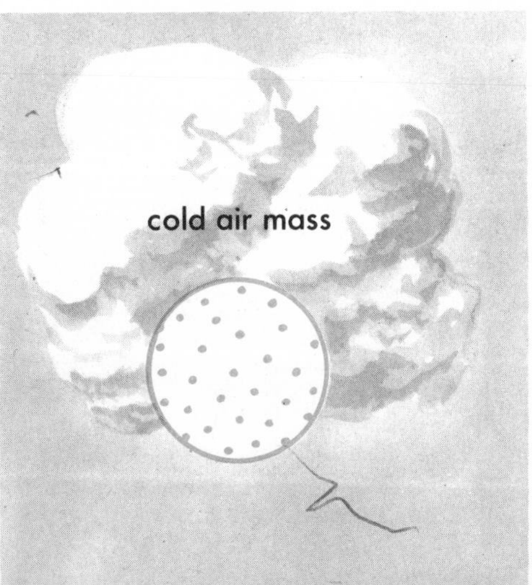

Air masses, whether warm or cool, are very large. They may be hundreds of miles across and several miles deep. Would the weight of the air in an air mass press very hard on the earth's surface? Most of the air presses at the center of the air mass. The center of a large air mass is called a "high," or high pressure area. All around this center, the air pressure is less than at the center. The outer edge of an air mass has lower air pressure. How can meteorologists tell when air pressure changes? Meteorologists use an instrument called an **aneroid barometer** (an′ ə roid′ bə rom′ ə tər) to measure air pressure.

The first barometers used to measure air pressure were mercury barometers. Mercury is a metal which is a dense liquid at room temperature. A mercury barometer is a long glass tube filled with mercury and then turned upside down in a dish of mercury. Normal air pressure holds a column of mercury 30 inches high in the tube.

It is not very convenient to have a mercury barometer in a weather bureau. Most meteorologists use an aneroid barometer which is smaller and easier to read than a mercury barometer. An aneroid barometer is built so that the pressure of air outside the barometer moves a needle along a scale. As the air pressure changes, the needle moves.

The barometer scale has numbers and lines. The numbers indicate how high the air pressure would hold mercury in the tube of a mercury barometer. The lines between the numbers indicate tenths of inches. In other words, when the pointer points to 29 the air pressure would hold mercury up in a mercury barometer to a height of 29 inches.

A. Mercury barometer
B. Aneroid barometer

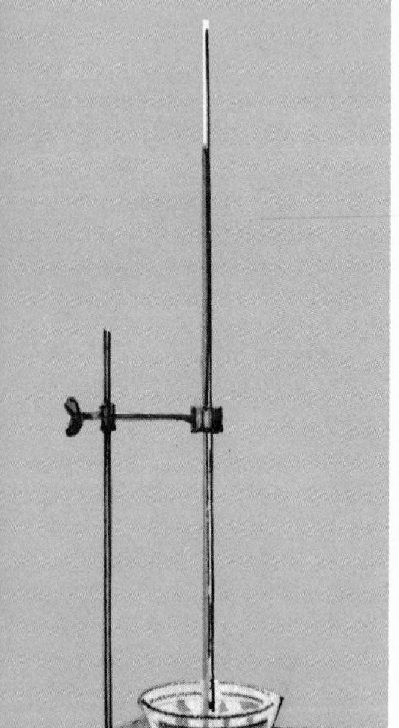

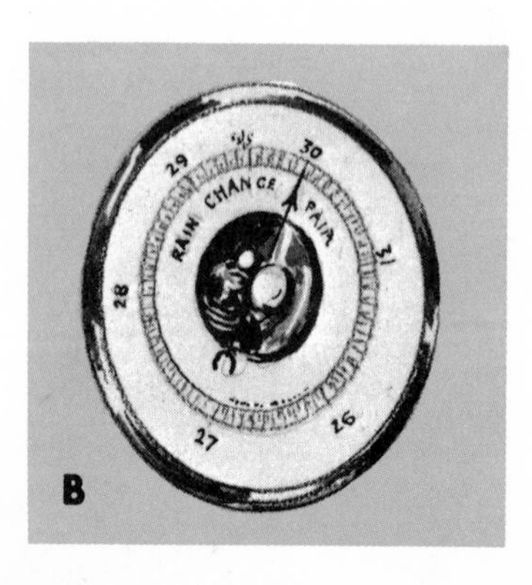

DISCOVER

How can you use an aneroid barometer to record changes in air pressure?

What You Need

aneroid barometer

1. Record the reading on an aneroid barometer. The pointer under the glass indicates the air pressure in inches of mercury.
2. Set the movable outside pointer at the same place as the pointer under the glass.
3. Tap the barometer lightly. Does the inner pointer show a higher or lower reading than before? The pressure may rise, or fall, or remain steady. Record your observation.
4. Take a barometer reading every hour for an entire day. Each time you take a reading follow steps 1 through 3.

What causes wind?

Does air pressure change as air masses move? As a high pressure area moves toward the place where you live, would the air pressure increase or decrease? After the high pressure area has passed, the pressure would decrease until the low pressure area passes. How does a barometer help in making weather forecasts? Can you feel or see other effects of a passing high or low pressure area? Do you think winds are caused by differences in air pressure? The cold, dense air of a high pressure area rushes into a low pressure area, causing winds.

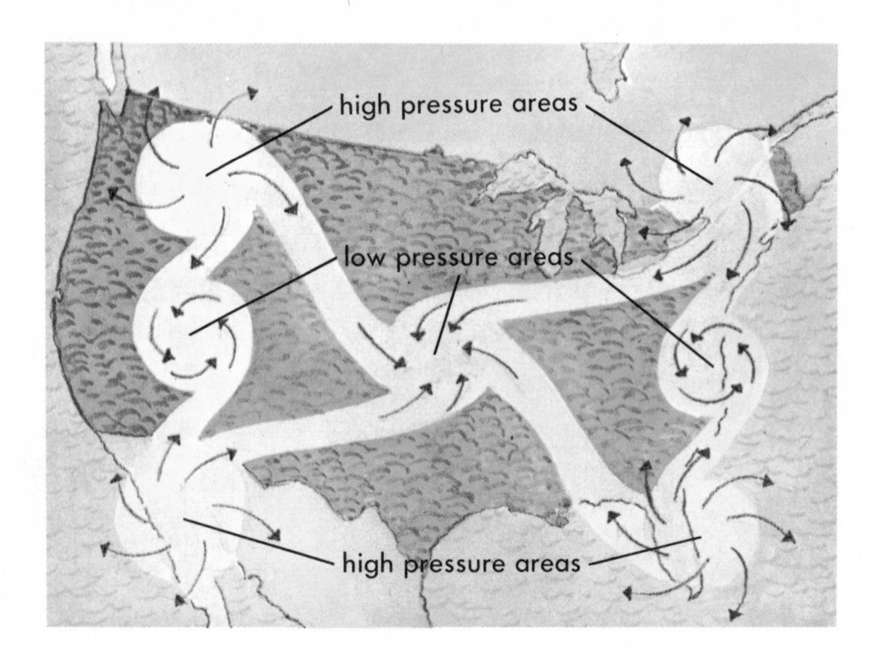

Weather Forecasts

Meteorologists use much weather information to make forecasts. By observing an aneroid barometer and the wind direction, could you make a weather forecast? Wind direction is the direction from which the wind blows. Use this chart made by the United States Weather Bureau.

Barometer Reading	Barometer Change	Wind Direction	Forecast
above 30.2	falling slowly	SW, W, or NW	warmer, fair for several days
	steady	SW, W, or NW	fair, little temperature change
between 30.1 and 30.2	steady	SW, W, or NW	fair, little temperature change
	rising rapidly	SW, W, or NW	fair, rain within two days
	falling slowly	S or SE	rain within 24 hours
	falling rapidly	S or SE	stronger winds, rain within 12 to 24 hours
	falling slowly	SE, E, or NE	rain within 12 to 18 hours
	falling rapidly	SE, E, or NE	stronger winds, rain within 12 hours
30.1 and above	falling slowly	E or NE	*Summer*—light winds, no rain for several days *Winter*—rain within 24 hours
	falling rapidly	E or NE	*Summer*—rain within 12 to 24 hours *Winter*—rain or snow with strong winds
30.0 or below	falling slowly	NE, E, or SE	rain for several days
	falling rapidly	NE, E, or SE	rain and strong winds, clearing within 36 hours, colder in winter
	rising slowly	S or SW	clearing in a few hours, fair for several days
29.8 or below	falling rapidly	S, SE, or E	severe storm shortly, clearing within 24 hours, colder in winter
	falling rapidly	N, NE, or E	severe storm and heavy rain, heavy snow and colder in winter
	rising rapidly	changing to W	clearing and colder

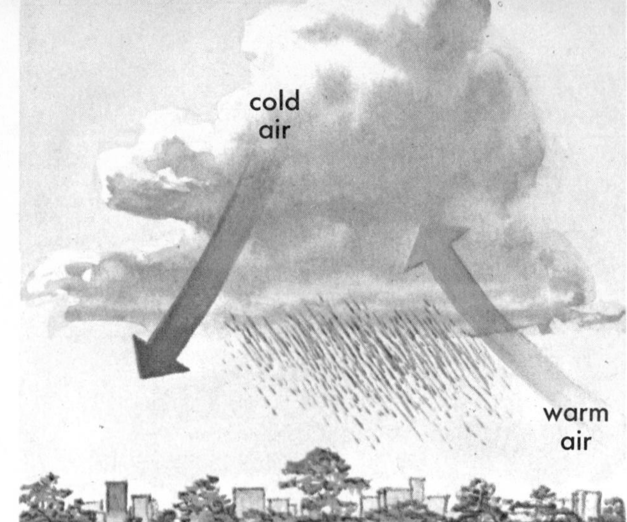

Storms

A thunderstorm can build up wherever warm, moist air is cooled quickly. As a result, a small cumulus cloud may grow to a towering cumulonimbus cloud. Its flat bottom may be only about one mile off the ground, while its top may be as high as six or seven miles off the ground.

Strong, warm winds rush up into the cloud from the direction in which the cloud is moving. Cold air rushes down out of the cloud at the other end. Within the cloud, raindrops are blown around before they fall. Scientists believe the blowing apart of drops of water helps to produce electricity which causes flashes of lightning. Often hailstones are formed in a cumulonimbus cloud.

A huge storm called a **hurricane** (hėr′ ə kān) can form over a large body of warm water. Warm, moist air is pushed upward rapidly by colder air and leaves a low pressure area. The spinning of the earth causes the winds to blow around this low pressure area. The winds may reach a speed of 200 miles per hour. With the wind, comes pouring rain. In the very center of a hurricane, there are a few miles of calm without clouds, rain, or wind. This center is called the "eye" of the hurricane.

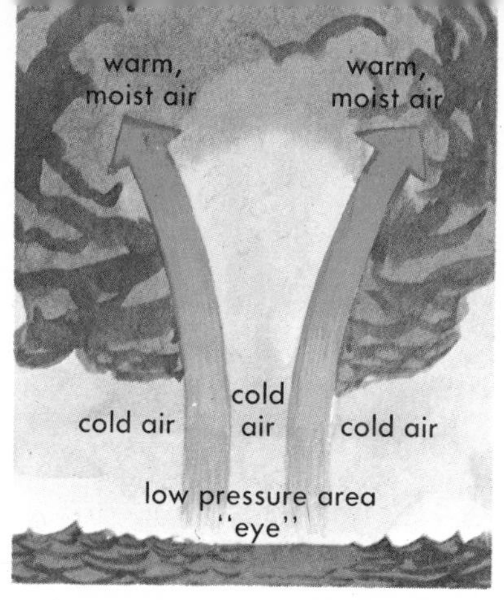

Formation of hurricane

Hurricane striking

Eye of hurricane

The conditions which form a storm called a **tornado** (tôr nā′ dō) are much like those which cause a thunderstorm. The air masses which meet and form a tornado usually have a great difference in temperature.

Warm, moist air rises rapidly in a funnel-shaped cloud. Winds may spin the cloud at speeds as high as about 500 to 700 miles per hour. Air pressure inside the funnel is very low. Sometimes this funnel touches the ground. When this low pressure area comes near buildings, the greater air pressure inside the buildings makes them explode. Dust and debris are carried up into the tornado funnel and may be dropped again some distance away.

What is a waterspout?

Formation of tornado

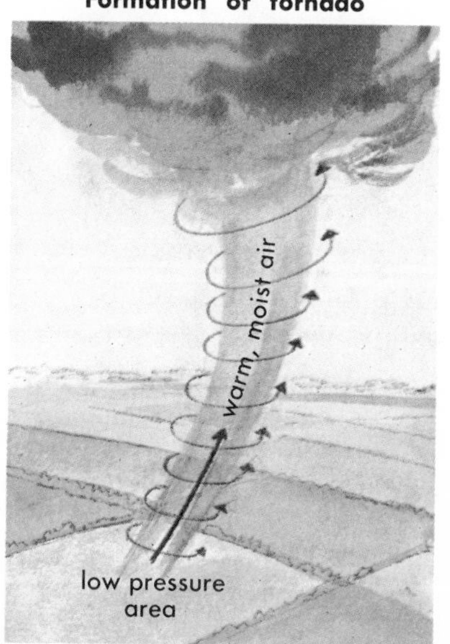

Tornado striking

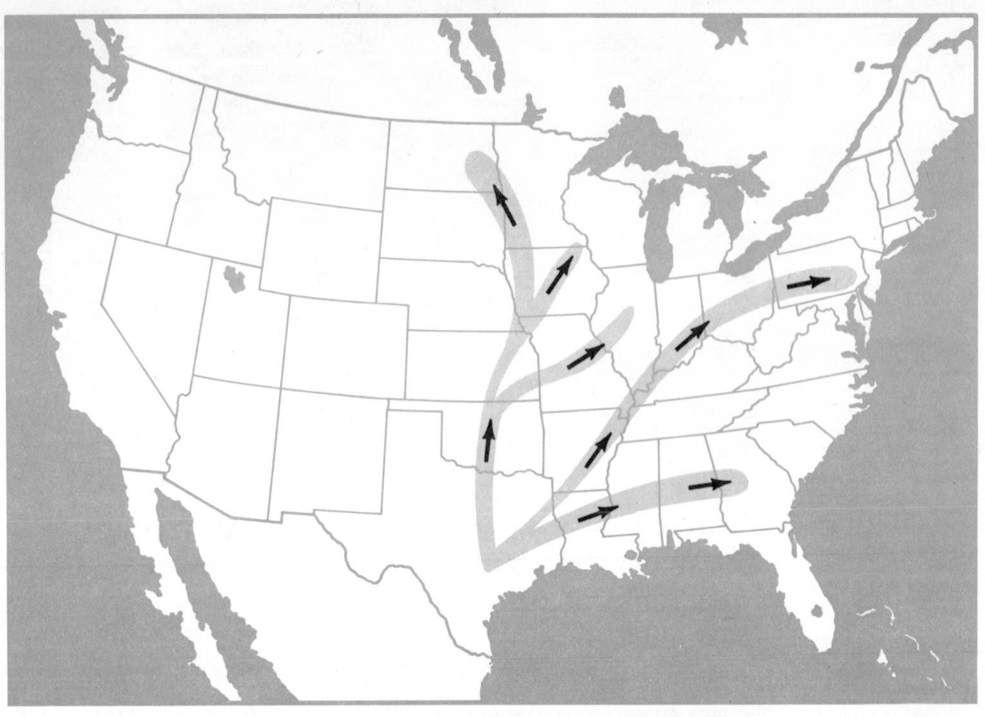

This map shows some major tornado paths.

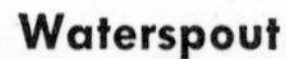

Waterspout

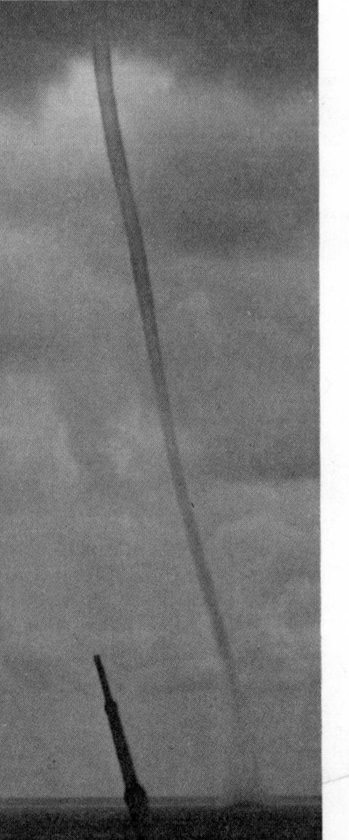

Most tornadoes which affect the United States form over hot, dry lands of the southwestern states. They usually move toward the northeast. Some tornadoes never touch the ground. Others move up and down as they travel.

Although tornadoes are dangerous and cause much damage, they are usually not as serious as hurricanes. At the most, the tornado funnel is only one mile wide. It may touch the ground for only a few minutes. A tornado usually causes less damage than a hurricane.

Sometimes a tornado forms over water. The swirling cloud gathers water. Then it is called a **waterspout.**

The study of weather is much more than reading a thermometer or a barometer. Meteorologists need much accurate information about past and present weather if they are to predict the weather of the future. And, there is still much to learn about the weather.

Exploring Your Learnings

Here are some ideas and vocabulary. What do these mean to you?

Words to Use

atmosphere (p. 152)
troposphere (p. 152)
cold air masses (p. 155)
warm air masses (p. 155)
front (p. 156)
cold front (p. 156)
meteorologist (p. 156)
warm front (p. 156)
humid (p. 157)
humidity (p. 157)
hygrometer (p. 159)
dew (p. 162)
dew point (p. 162)
frost (p. 163)
cumulus clouds (p. 166)
stratus clouds (p. 166)
cirrus clouds (p. 166)
nimbus clouds (p. 167)
cirrocumulus clouds (p. 167)
stratocumulus clouds (p. 167)
nimbostratus clouds (p. 167)
cumulonimbus clouds (p. 167)
sleet (p. 168)
hailstone (p. 169)
air pressure (p. 169)
aneroid barometer (p. 170)
hurricane (p. 174)
tornado (p. 175)
waterspout (p. 176)

Ideas to Use

1. Meteorologists are scientists who study weather changes.
2. Weather changes occur in the troposphere, the layer of the atmosphere closest to the earth's surface.
3. Because the sun does not heat the earth's surface evenly, warm and cold air masses form.
4. The place where two air masses of different temperature meet is called a front.
5. Weather changes depend upon the temperature and location of air masses.

Frost

6. Humidity is the amount of water vapor in the air.
7. Because warm air holds more water vapor than colder air, dew and frost form when the earth cools at night.
8. Clouds form when water vapor condenses on dust in the air.
9. Meteorologists have named clouds partly according to cloud shapes and partly according to cloud height.
10. Changes in air pressure, measured by an aneroid barometer, are used to forecast changes in weather.
11. Winds and storms are caused by differences in air pressure.

Using Your Ideas

(Do not write in this book.)

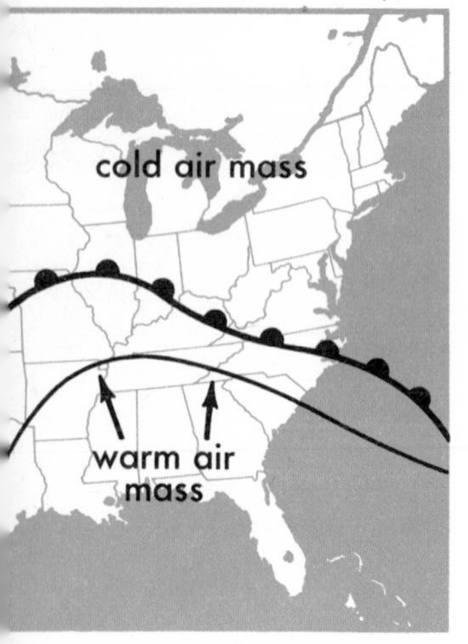

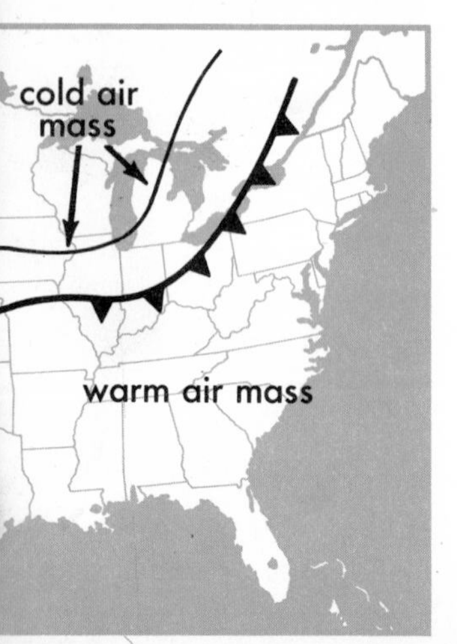

1. Compare these fronts shown at the left. Can you name them and explain how one is different from the other?
2. Find out if clouds high above the earth's surface move in the same direction as wind close to the ground. Find out what a nephoscope is and try to make one which you can use.
3. Tell how weather forecasts are important to each of the following:

farmers	airplane pilots
automobile owners	skiers
road builders	you

4. What important information can you get from a television weather forecast? Why do weather forecasters often report their predictions in percentages? *Example*: 60-80 percent chance of rain is forecast for Monday.
5. Use a camera to photograph different kinds of clouds. Prepare a collection of pictures of the kinds of cloud types which you see over a period of time.

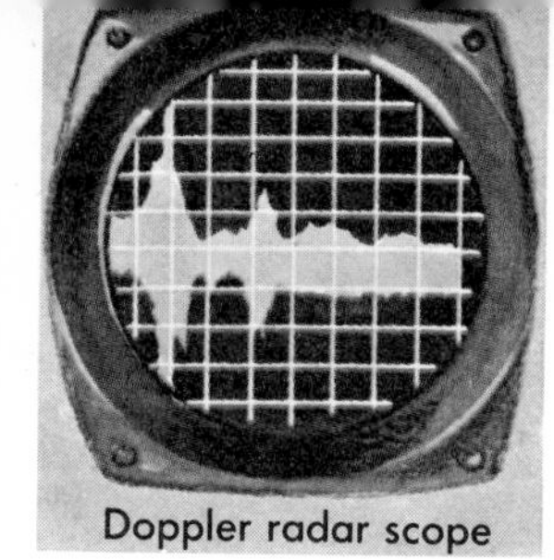
Doppler radar scope

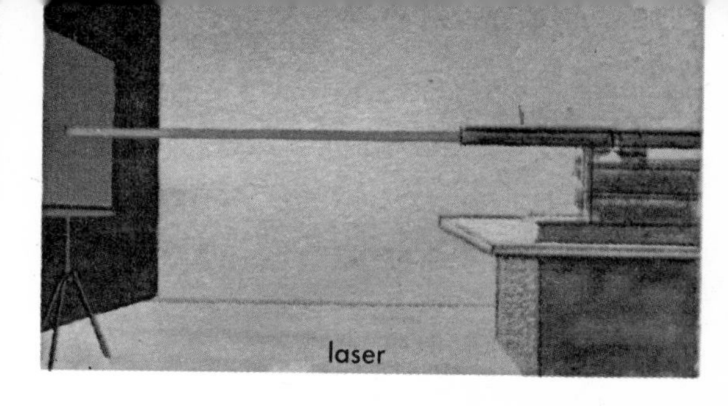
laser

6. Explain how each instrument shown in the above pictures is useful in weather forecasting.
7. Read about and report on the history of the United States Weather Bureau.
8. Collect and display weather maps from newspapers for a week or more. Use a series of weather maps to show how highs, lows, and fronts have moved from day to day.
9. Explain the difference between:
   dew and frost
   stratus and cirrus clouds
   tornado and hurricane
   high pressure and low pressure areas
10. Place a thermometer outside where it will not be in sunlight or near a building. A good way to do this is to fasten the thermometer to the north side of a tree. Read the thermometer at the same time each day for two weeks. Make a chart on which to record the temperature. Mark with a star the days on which you had rain or snow. Make a record of the temperature changes by making a graph such as the one shown in the picture.

    Look at the temperature chart and graph you made. Were there several days of rain or snow followed by a slow rise in temperature? What kind of front does this show? Label it on your graph. Was there a day with a sudden drop in temperature along with a storm? What kind of front does this show? Label it on your graph.

Dew on rose petals

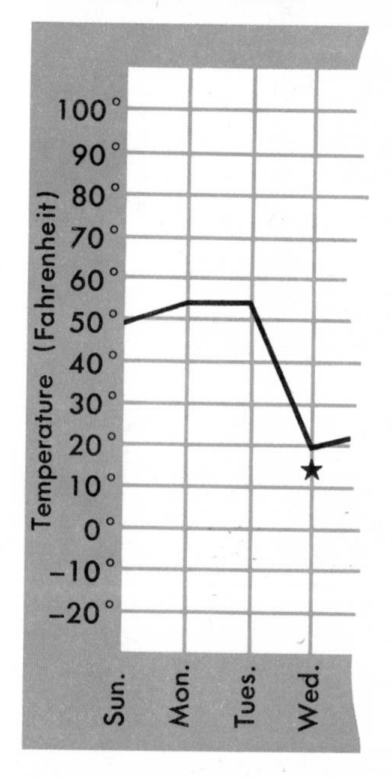

7

Exploring the Earth

At one time, this scene did not exist. In the distant past, there was probably no water on the surface of the earth. The mountains in the distance were not always as they are now. They are some of the many changes in the earth's surface that happened long ago. The surface of the earth is always being changed, slowly by wind and water, and quickly by such things as earthquakes.

Over long periods of time, scientists have gained information about the earth by exploring its surface and the ocean floor. Scientists also want to discover more about the inside of the earth. Learning about the surface and the inside of the earth can provide clues to explain the past and the future of the earth. What is happening to the earth now? What will happen to the earth in the future?

Layers of the Earth

The outer layer of the earth is called the **crust** (krust). Most of the crust is solid rock. Where the crust is above water, it is covered by a thin layer of soil. The crust under the continents is about twenty-five miles thick. Beneath mountains, it is even thicker. Under the ocean, the crust is only about three miles thick. It is covered with materials that have settled to the ocean floor.

Beneath the earth's crust is the **mantle** (man′ tl). Rock in the mantle is denser than rock in the crust.

The **core** (kôr), the innermost part of the earth, is believed to be made of heavy metals, such as iron or nickel. The core of the earth seems to be a solid or a thick liquid. The core of the earth is believed to be about 2000 miles in diameter.

Inside the Earth

Men have never been more than a few miles below the surface of the earth. But as far as men have gone into the earth, they have found solid rock. What is the earth like far below the surface?

How is information about the inside of the earth obtained?

FIND OUT

How are rocks changed deep below the earth's surface?

EXPERIMENT

What You Need

modeling clay	brick
piece of cardboard	large, irregular rock

1. Put three large balls of modeling clay on a piece of cardboard. Place a brick on one ball of clay. Place an irregular rock on a second ball of clay. Place nothing on the third ball of clay.
2. Put the cardboard in a warm place. Leave it for several hours. What happens to each ball of clay?

Did the ball of clay with nothing on it change? What happens to clay when it gets warm? Does this explain the changes you may have noticed? Deep within the earth, it is warm enough to melt hard rocks. But, something else helps change rocks inside the earth. What might this be?

Carefully lift the brick. How has this ball of clay changed? Rocks deep in the earth have heavy layers of soil and rocks pressing on them. Does this pressure help to change them?

Now carefully lift the rock and look at the clay under it. Is the shape of this clay different from the shapes of the other two? Why do you think this happened?

The outer part of the earth is mostly solid rock. In many places in the rock, there are large cracks called **fractures** (frak′ chərz). Fractures may occur in any direction in a rock. Deep below the surface, the rock is heated and squeezed so hard that it is melted. This melted rock is called **magma** (mag′ mə). Magma moves through fractures in solid rock. How can magma moving below the surface cause changes on the surface?

One instrument used to get information about the inside of the earth is the **seismograph** (sīz′ mə graf). A seismograph records vibrations deep within the earth.

Sometimes magma is forced into fractures in such a way that it causes the rock layers above it to bend and move upward. Hills and even mountains can be formed in

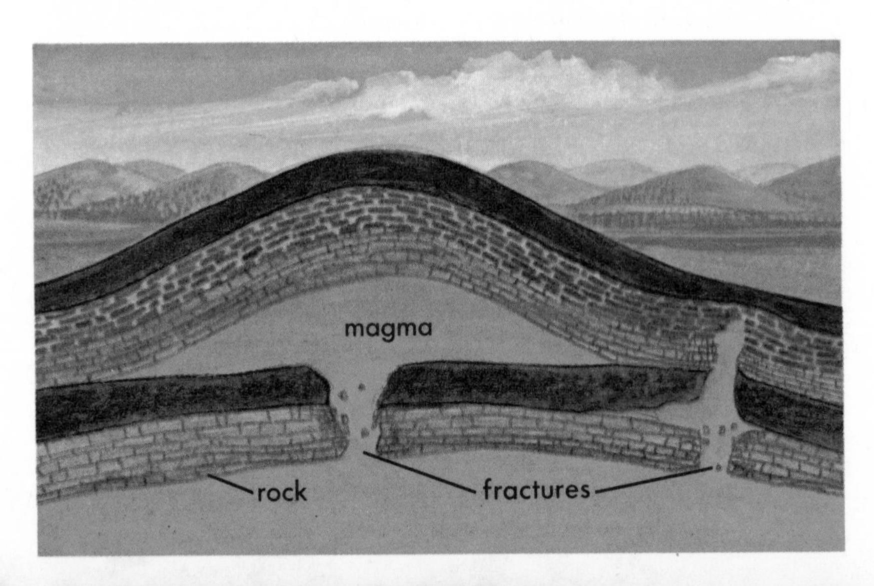

this way over long periods of time. Magma may also travel upward in a fracture and break through the surface of the earth. Magma which reaches the earth's surface is called **lava** (lä′ və). A mountain formed from lava is called a **volcano** (vol kā′ nō). Volcanic mountains may be built up very quickly.

The pressure of magma may also cause different rock layers to be pulled or pushed in different directions. What could this do to the layers of rock? When rock layers break and move, **faulting** (fôl′ ting) takes place. Faulting produces vibrations on and below the earth's surface. These vibrations can be detected by a seismograph.

One kind of seismograph

DISCOVER

How does a seismograph record the earth's vibrations?

What You Need

- yardstick
- ring stand
- wire
- tape
- pencil
- weight
- paper

What does a seismograph show about the inside of the earth?

1. Fasten a yardstick to the stand with wire and tape as shown in the picture. Use tape to fasten a sharpened pencil to the stick. Hang a weight from the yardstick.
2. Tape a piece of paper to the chalkboard. Arrange the stand so that the pencil touches the paper lightly.
3. Hit the table with your fist. Examine the sheet of paper. Jump hard on the floor. Examine the paper again. Do the pencil marks give any evidence of what has happened?

Are the marks evidence that something moved? As you hit the table or jump on the floor, you cause vibrations. The pencil made a record of the vibrations.

A seismograph works in a similar way. Part of it is fastened to a large cement post. This post rests on solid rock deep below the surface. Changes below the surface make the rock move. When the rock moves, the seismograph post moves. A seismograph gives evidence of these vibrations inside the earth. The seismograph records vibrations on a chart.

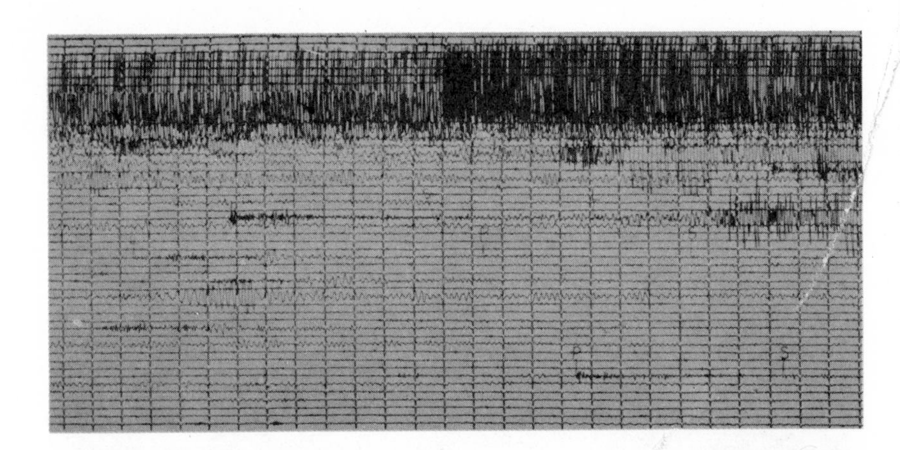

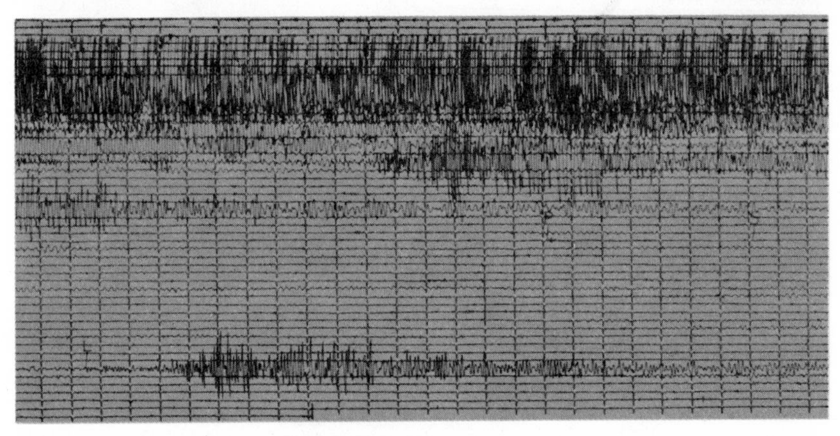

Seismograph charts

Study these seismograph charts. Can you tell which lines show slight vibrations? Can you tell which lines show strong vibrations? Faulting sometimes causes upper layers to shake, causing large cracks or upheavals on the surface. Such movements are called an **earthquake** (erth′ kwāk′).

By studying seismograph charts, scientists can tell when an earthquake began and ended. They can tell how powerful the vibrations were and how long they lasted. Because many seismographs are used at different places on the earth at the same time, an earthquake can be located as it is taking place.

How is information about the atmosphere obtained?

mi–
500 mi–
exosphere
400 mi–
300 mi–
200 mi–
ionosphere
100 mi–
50 mi–
mesophere
25 mi–
stratosphere
10 mi–
5 mi–
troposphere

The Earth's Atmosphere

By using instruments in balloons, rockets, and satellites, scientists have learned that the atmosphere has several layers that are different from each other. The chart shows the names and heights of these layers.

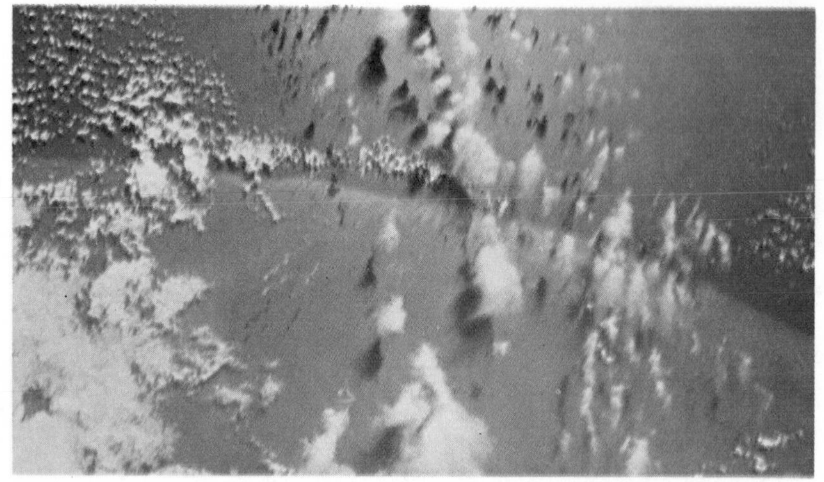

Earth's atmosphere as seen from a satellite

How many layers form the earth's atmosphere? What is the name of the layer of atmosphere in which you live?

Can you see the atmosphere? In what form are most of the materials in the atmosphere?

Air is a mixture of many gases. Look at this list of gases which make up the atmosphere. Do you recognize the names of any of them?

nitrogen	carbon dioxide	helium
oxygen	water vapor	krypton
argon	ozone	xenon
hydrogen		neon

Nitrogen, oxygen, and hydrogen are found in the air as free elements or joined to other elements as compounds. Does air contain water vapor? Is water vapor a compound? What elements are in it? Carbon dioxide is another oxygen compound in the air.

What are some other materials contained in the air? Darken the room. Shine a flashlight into the air. What do you see in the beam of light? What kinds of materials can you see in the air?

How much air do you breathe each day?

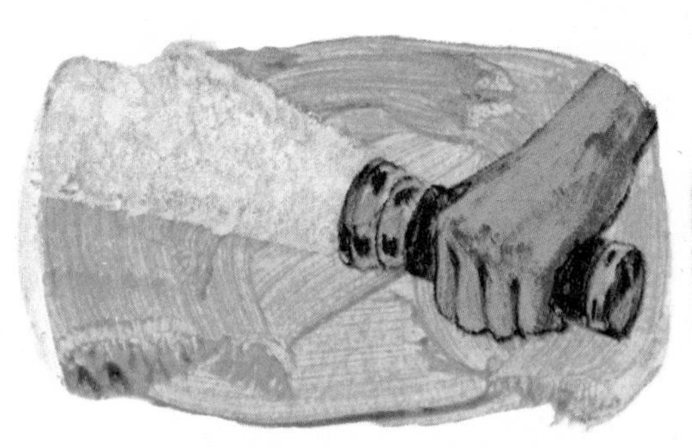

Clap two dusty chalkboard erasers together. Can bits of chalk be small enough to float in the air? Many bits of soil and rock are small enough to float in the air, too.

Ask your teacher to light a candle. With a potholder, hold a spoon in the flame. What is in the air above the flame? What collects on the spoon? How can a fire sometimes add solid materials to the air?

Air Pollution

Each day, tons of harmful chemical compounds are released into the air. Air that contains harmful wastes is called **polluted** (pə lut′ əd) **air.** These wastes are both solids and gases. Where do most of these materials come from?

Motor vehicles	86 million tons
Factories	23 million tons
Electric power plants	20 million tons
Heating systems	8 million tons
Waste disposal	5 million tons

Scientists can collect and measure the solid wastes in the air by using filters. One filter has collected solid wastes from the air. The other filter is unused. However, filters cannot collect the harmful gases in the air.

Wastes in the air are especially harmful when they collect over a city. In places where there is usually much water vapor in the air, the wastes may be trapped by the moisture in the air. Air that has wastes trapped by moisture is called **smog.** The pictures show how one city looks on a clear day and on a day when it has smog. How do you think smog affects the people who live there?

Your health depends upon the air you breathe. Each day, you breathe about 15,000 quarts of air. Scientists are very concerned about keeping this air as clean as possible. What do you think can be done about air pollution?

Wind Changes the Earth's Surface

Materials carried in the air can cause changes in the surface of the earth. **Erosion** (i rō′ zhən) occurs when materials on the surface of the earth are worn. Sand carried by strong winds may wear away parts of large rocks. This happens in much the same way that sandpaper removes part of the wood or metal surfaces across which it is moved. Wind-blown sand may wear away the lower parts of cliffs or carve rocks into unusual shapes.

What is a dust storm?

Dust storm

Sand dunes

Strong winds carrying soil are called **dust storms.** During dust storms, roads, fences, and even farm buildings have been buried. Many years ago, a great dust storm carried soil from Kansas and Oklahoma a distance of more than a thousand miles, all the way to the Atlantic Ocean. In some places, the sand collects in sand hills called **dunes** (dūnz).

DISCOVER

How are dunes formed?

What You Need

large cardboard box	small twigs
cornmeal	modeling clay
large rock	fan

1. Set the box on its side. Spread cornmeal evenly along the bottom side of the box. Use just enough cornmeal to cover the bottom side.

2. Put a large rock into the box. Cut some small leafy twigs from shrubs. Stick them into modeling clay and set them in the box.
3. Put a fan close to the box and let air from the fan blow into the box. Watch what happens to the cornmeal.

What did the cornmeal represent? What did the moving air from the fan represent? What happens to the "sand" as the "wind" strikes objects and slows down?

In what other ways does wind change the surface of the earth? As air moves across the oceans, water evaporates. Water vapor is carried up with warm air. When the water vapor cools, it condenses into tiny droplets of water. These tiny droplets of water form clouds. Clouds, pushed by the wind, move away from the ocean and travel over the land. The water droplets become larger and are too dense to float in the air. The drops fall to the earth as rain. What happens to the rain that falls on the ground?

How may soil and sand be carried many miles?

Would storms with strong winds and rain also change the surface of the earth? Tornadoes may carry soil and sand which is dropped many miles away. Rainstorms may cause floods. These floods move large masses of soil and water which uproot plants. Winds of hurricanes and other storms at sea may cause high waves that wash away parts of the coastal lands.

Tornado damage

Flood waters

Water May Cause Change

When it rains, some water usually sinks into the ground. Some water runs along hard soil or rocks. Moving water causes changes on the surface of the earth. Do you know how water erodes the surface of the earth?

FIND OUT

How can moving water erode the earth's surface?

EXPERIMENT

What You Need

shoe box	sprinkling can
scissors	clay
aluminum foil	sand
soil	gravel
book	humus
water	

1. Cut the shoe box so that it is two inches deep. Cut one end from the box.
2. Line the inside of the box and the cover with aluminum foil.
3. Put some soil into the box. With the open end downward, raise the other end of the box and place some books underneath it.
4. Place the shoe box cover under the open end of the box.
5. Sprinkle about one cup of water on the soil in the box and observe what happens to the soil.
6. Repeat the experiment with sand, gravel, humus, and powdered clay. Record your observations for each kind of material.

What evidence of erosion is along the Colorado River?

Gullies in badly eroded farmland

This river has formed the valley.

In what way can moving water erode the surface of the earth? How are different soil materials affected by moving water?

Water may move soil from places where there are few growing plants. Soil is carried downhill along with the running water. When the soil has been carried away by water, ditches called **gullies** (gul′ iz) may be formed. Can you find evidence around your school or home that soil has been eroded by water?

Fast moving rivers can carry rocks and gravel. These materials in the river help to wear down land as the river moves along. During millions of years, the Colorado River has worn away thousands of feet of rock and soil to form the Grand Canyon in Arizona.

A. The river is eroding land.
B. Many years later, the river may have eroded a wide river valley.
C. Colorado River

A

B

C

Both fast moving and slower moving water may carry away soil. Soil often contains minerals. What do you think might happen to the minerals in soil if the soil is carried away by water?

What evidence of erosion may be found in a puddle?

DISCOVER

Does water dissolve any minerals that are in soil?

What You Need

¼ cup table salt	bowl
½ cup dry soil	water
spoon	pie plate
magnifying glass	

1. Mix the table salt and the soil with a spoon. Observe the mixed salt and soil with a magnifying glass. Can you see the grains of salt?
2. Put the salt and soil mixture into a bowl. Pour some water into the bowl and mix it with the soil. Then carefully pour off the water.

3. Place the washed soil into the pie plate to dry again. Do you predict you will find any grains of salt in the soil now?
4. Use the magnifying glass to observe the dried soil. Do you find as many grains of salt in the soil as there were before? Was your prediction correct?
5. Try the same activity again. Save the water you mix with the salt and soil. Let the water evaporate. What do you predict you will find after the water evaporates?

Does this observation show that water may dissolve salt and wash it out of the soil? Will water dissolve other materials and carry them out of the soil? Try different ways of experimenting. The next time it rains, take some water from a puddle. Let the water stand for a few days so all the dirt settles to the bottom. Pour off the water into another container and let the water evaporate. What can you do to the water to speed up evaporation?

After the water has evaporated, do you find any evidence of dissolved minerals in the water? When it rains, water may move over the surface of the earth dissolving and washing away minerals which plants need to live and grow. Soil which was once good for growing plants may be left barren. What could happen to such land during a flood or a windstorm?

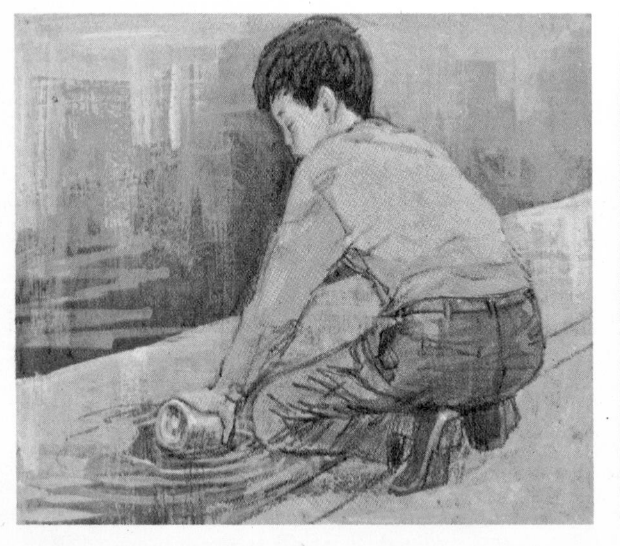

Eroded barren land

Sometimes there is a large amount of water flowing into rivers. Then rivers move swiftly, and water may flow out of the riverbeds, flooding the land. When water flows out of the riverbed, it slows down. The water leaves behind rocks and soil which it has been carrying. When the flood is over, the rivers may again flow in their usual paths. However, the soil which the flooding rivers carried is left behind on the land. Land built up in this way is called a **flood plain.** Why is such land usually rich in minerals? Why is it a place where plants grow well?

Swift moving rivers may also slow down when they flow into lakes or oceans. Then, sand, clay, rocks, and gravel carried by the rivers collect and settle to the bottom. These may form a **delta** (del′ tə).

Each year, the Mississippi River deposits more than 700 million tons of soil and rock where the river flows into the Gulf of Mexico. Locate this delta on a map. Discover where the soil might have come from.

A

B

C

D

A. River flowing in normal path
B. River beginning to flood
C. River flooding
D. River in normal path again with land left covered with new soil.

This map shows the Mississippi River delta.

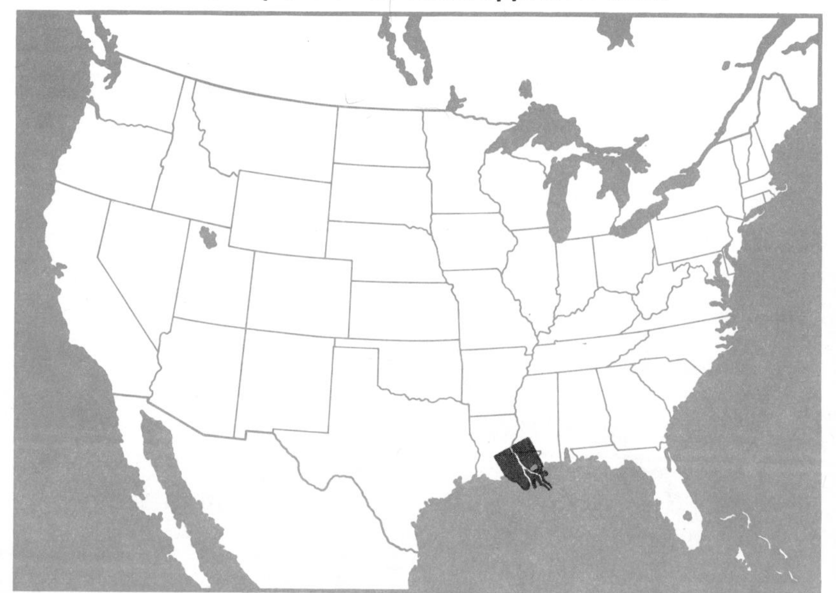

Flood plain

Surface Water

Do you know what happens to water that flows over the ground? Small streams of water may join to form a river. Rivers and streams may fill lakes or they may flow on to the ocean. Water which stays above the ground is called **surface** (ser′ fis) **water.**

FIND OUT

Why does water from rivers and lakes not sink into the ground?

EXPERIMENT

What You Need

- 2 large metal cans
- dry sand
- modeling clay or wax
- small unglazed clay flowerpot
- small glass jar
- water
- water pitcher
- aluminum foil
- spoon

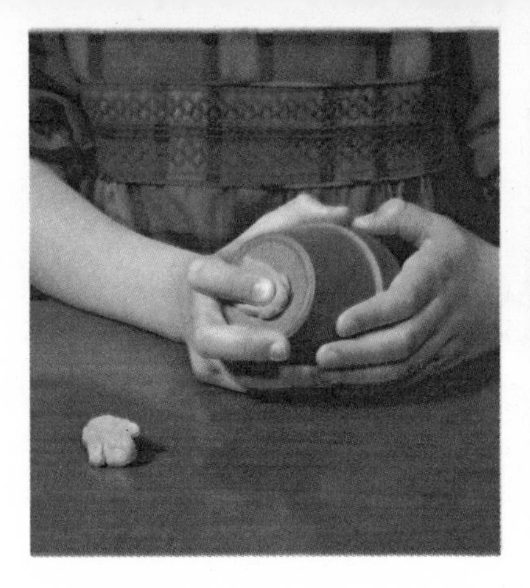

1. Fill two large metal cans halfway with dry sand. Seal the opening at the bottom of the flowerpot with modeling clay or wax.
2. Put the flowerpot into one can. Into the other can, place a small glass jar. Fill the rest of each can with dry sand around the flowerpot and jar. Do not put sand in the flowerpot or jar. Fill the flowerpot and the glass jar with water.
3. Place an aluminum foil cover over each can. Let them stand for several days.
4. After several days, use a spoon to remove some sand from around the outside of the flowerpot. Remove some sand from around the outside of the glass jar. Compare the sand from the two cans. How are they different?

Is the flowerpot made of material which is hard like a rock? Does it have tiny spaces through which water molecules can pass? Did water pass through the sides of the flowerpot? How can you tell? A material through which liquids can pass is called **porous** (pô′ rəs). Is the flowerpot porous? Soil is another example of a porous material.

Did the sand around the glass jar remain dry? Can water molecules go through glass? Glass is a **nonporous** material. Most kinds of rocks are nonporous.

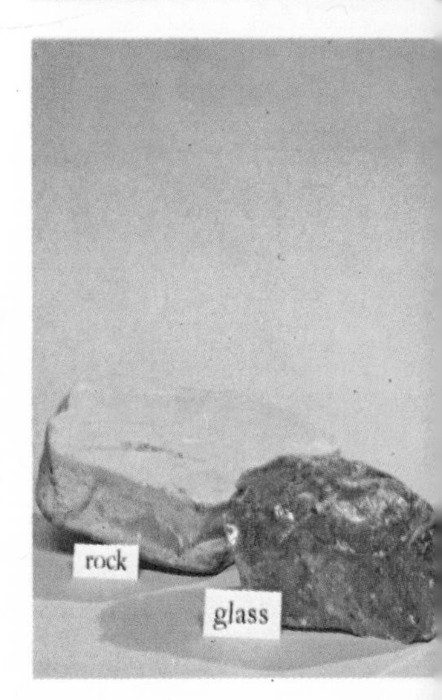

Water Below the Ground

Water sinks into soil because soil is porous. If much water falls on the surface of the ground, the water may sink to great depths. Everywhere beneath the earth's surface, there is rock. Some of this rock is porous and has spaces which water can fill. Below the porous rock layers are nonporous rocks. The water does not fill the nonporous rocks. Once water has filled the porous rock, it may "pile up" and fill spaces between bits of soil. Water which fills spaces below the surface of the ground is called **groundwater.** The height of the top surface of the groundwater is called the **water table.**

DISCOVER

What determines the height of the water table?

What You Need

large aquarium
gravel
soil
water
spoon

1. Spread the gravel to a depth of about three inches in the bottom of the aquarium. Add six inches of soil.

2. Pour water into the aquarium until the water is a little higher than the gravel.
3. Use the spoon to take soil from the middle of the aquarium and slope the soil toward the sides of the aquarium. Dig until you have a pool at the bottom. Where is the water table in the aquarium?
4. Add water to the soil around the pool. What happens to the height of the water table? What happens to the depth of the water in the pool?

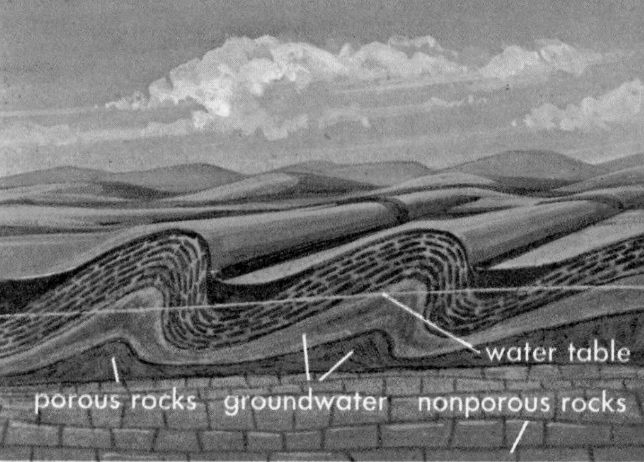

What part of the model is like nonporous rock? What part of the model is like porous rock? How high is the water table above the nonporous rock?

The nonporous rocks in the earth are not level like the bottom of the aquarium. They are higher in some places than in others, just like the land above them. Whether the land above is a swamp or a desert depends upon both the depth of the nonporous rock and the amount of rainfall. The water you see on the earth's surface as ponds, lakes, and rivers shows the height of the water table in a certain place. Did your model show how the water table forms a lake?

Can ice move?

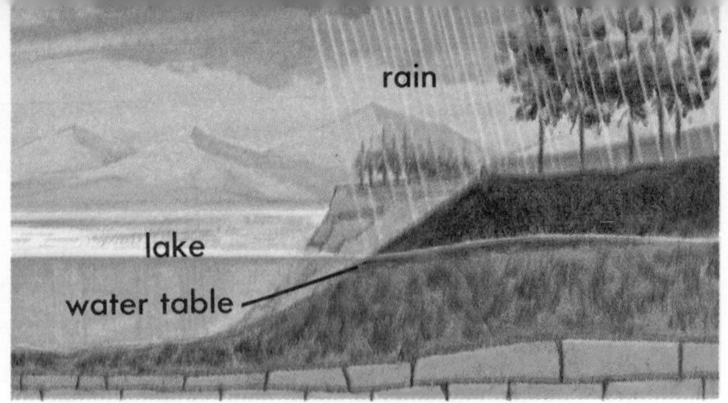

Were you able to make a lake because you uncovered the water table in the aquarium? The depth of water in a lake depends upon the water table, as well as the depth of the lake basin. How did the lake change as you sprinkled water on the ground around the lake? How does the water table depend upon the amount of rainfall?

Ice Changes the Surface

Have you ever heard of a river of ice? It is hard to imagine ice moving along like a river. However, in some places, ice moves slowly into and along mountain valleys. Huge masses of moving ice are called **glaciers** (glā′ shərz).

Glaciers may form wherever snow piles up faster than it melts. Some glaciers form high in the mountains where it is cool all year. So much snow collects in winter that all of it does not melt in summer. Year after year, the snow continues to build up. Its weight presses hard on the bottom snow so that the bottom snow is changed to ice.

Glacier

Snow in mountains in summer

As a glacier moves across hilly land, it collects rocks and gravel along its bottom and sides. Will rocks in the ice scrape and rub the earth's surface as the glacier moves along? Do you think the scraping and rubbing may wear down hills and dig valleys along the glacier's path?

Slowly, the front edge of the glacier moves to a warmer area. This edge of the glacier melts and the glacier drops rocks and soil which it carried.

Some glaciers flow into the ocean. Large pieces of ice that break off and float away are **icebergs** (īs′ bėrgz′).

Evidence shows that parts of North America, Europe, and Asia were once covered by glaciers. Scientists believe that in the past 2 million years, many huge glaciers have formed and melted away at four different times. The periods of history, when glaciers covered much more land than they do now, are often called Ice Ages. The last great glacier of the last Ice Age began to melt away about 10,000 years ago.

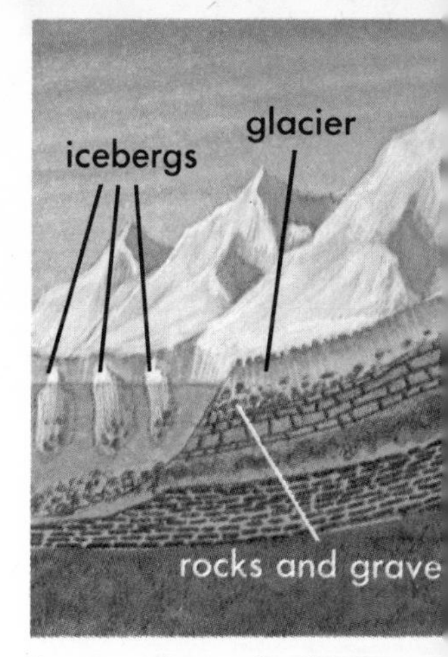

Front edge of glacier melting

Glacier

Iceberg

Map of an Ice Age

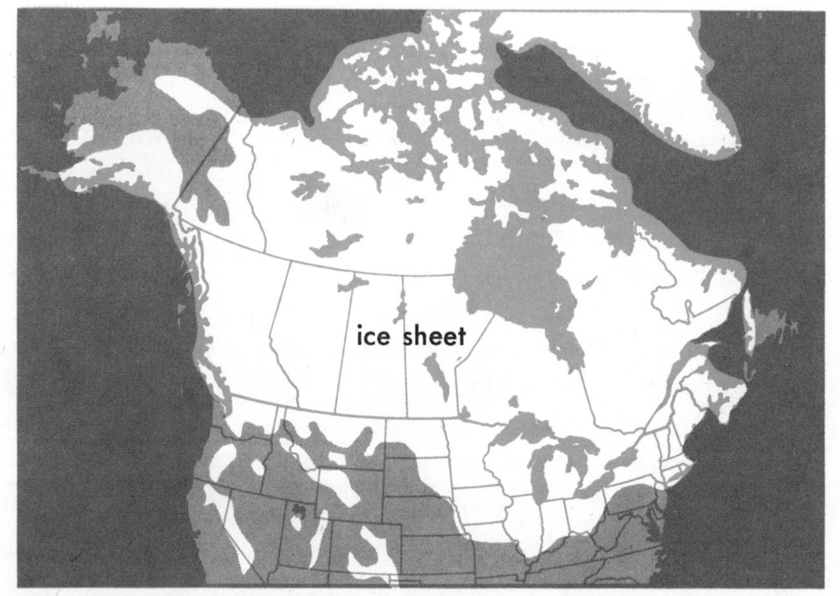

Glacier National Park

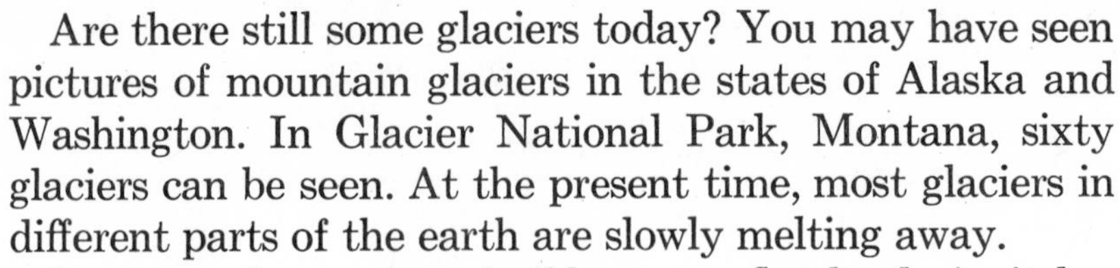

Are there still some glaciers today? You may have seen pictures of mountain glaciers in the states of Alaska and Washington. In Glacier National Park, Montana, sixty glaciers can be seen. At the present time, most glaciers in different parts of the earth are slowly melting away.

In some places, snow builds up on flat land. As it becomes very deep, the buried snow may gradually change to glacial ice. Then it begins to flow outward. Most of Greenland and all Antarctica are covered by this kind of glacier.

A glacier meets the sea

The Earth's Poles

Many scientists have camped in the Arctic, the area around the north pole. They have also lived in the Antarctic, the area around the south pole. The Arctic is entirely ocean, with no land above sea level. Most of the Arctic Ocean is covered all year by floating islands, or packs, of ice. The ice of some islands is only ten feet thick, while other ice islands are more than two hundred feet thick.

Arctic ice packs remain about the same thickness all year. The top layer of ice melts in summer and the water seeps down through cracks, spreads out, and refreezes underneath the ice.

Ice at the south pole is anchored to land, but little land can be seen. In some places, the ice is more than 15,000 feet thick. Some of the Antarctic ice is more than 100,000 years old. Samples taken from the ice show traces of coal and trees. Since it is believed coal is formed in tropical climates, what might this tell you about the history of Antarctica?

Antarctica as it is today and as it probably was 100,000 years ago

The Oceans

Does land or water cover more of the earth's surface? Use a globe to help you find out. At one time, it was thought that the floor of the ocean was nearly level and had hills and valleys similar to those on the continents. However, new scientific instruments have given evidence that the ocean floor is not as level as was thought.

Record of echo sounder

Echo sounder being used on a ship

Record of echo sounder

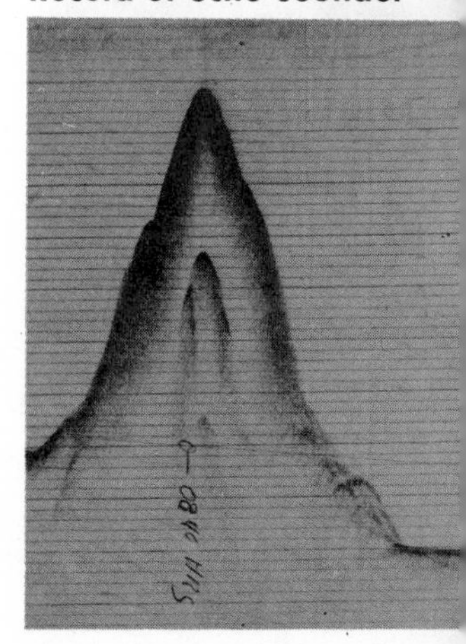

Have you ever heard sounds while you were swimming underwater? Can sound vibrations travel through water? To explore the ocean bottom, an instrument called an **echo** (ek′ ō) **sounder** is often used. Sound vibrations are sent from the bottom of a ship. These vibrations strike the ocean floor and bounce back to the echo sounder on the ship. As the echoes return, they are recorded as lines on a chart by machine. This record is a kind of picture of the ocean floor. Records of echo sounders have been studied, and it is believed that the earth's surface under the ocean is more uneven than the earth's surface on land.

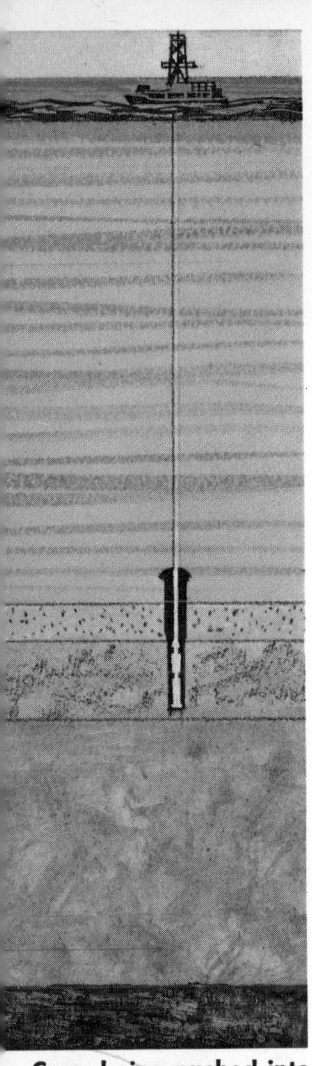

Corer being pushed into ocean floor

Top view of ocean floor

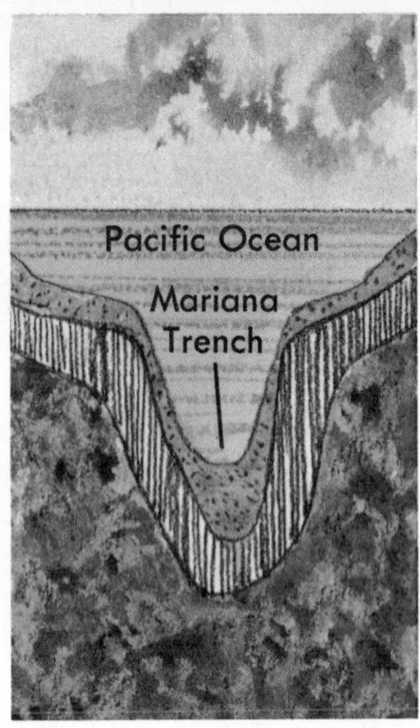

Side view of Mariana Trench

The ocean has many mountains, some more than two miles high. Both the Atlantic Ocean and the Pacific Ocean have long mountain ranges. In some places, the ocean floor has cliffs and deep canyons. The Mariana Trench in the Pacific Ocean, about seven miles deep, is the deepest place in the ocean yet discovered.

Samples of materials that have collected on the ocean floor are taken by using corers. A **corer** (kôr′ ər) is a hollow pipe which is pushed into the ocean floor by an explosive charge.

DISCOVER

How does a corer work?

What You Need

several colors of modeling clay
metal pipe or plastic tubing, 6 inches long
pencil

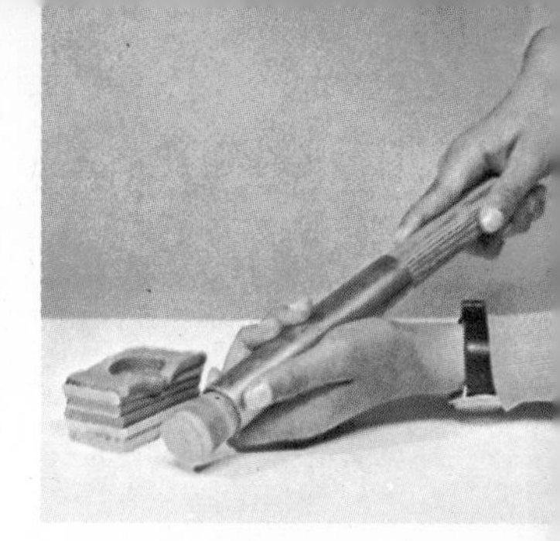

1. Arrange several thin layers of clay, each a different color, one on top of the other. Press the metal pipe or plastic tubing down into the clay.
2. Remove the tube and push the clay out of the tube with a pencil.

Taking a core sample of the ocean floor

In what way is the sample from the tube like the layers of clay? What can you find out about the layers of clay by looking at the sample?

Thousands of sample cores have been collected from the ocean floor. Some cores are over sixty feet long. What do you think can be discovered about the earth by examining the cores?

Cameras are also important instruments for gathering information about the floor of the ocean. Photographs show that in some places the ocean floor is covered with rocks. These rocks are believed to be made up of minerals such as iron, nickel, and magnesium. There are billions of tons of such valuable materials on the ocean floor. Ocean minerals of many sorts are being mined from the ocean floor.

Photographing the ocean floor

Valuable minerals on the ocean floor

Scientist taking sample of ocean water

Vessel used to explore the ocean

Ocean water is studied so that scientists can discover more about the chemicals in seawater. Thousands of samples of ocean water have been taken from different places. Some dissolved minerals are found everywhere in the oceans. But the minerals are not present in the same amounts everywhere. All ocean water is not the same. Water from different areas is constantly mixing together.

Scientists are experimenting with several kinds of undersea capsules in which people can live for long periods of time. Scientists enter and leave a capsule in diving suits to explore the ocean floor. Experiments have shown that people can live and work safely at depths of 200 feet for as long as 60 days.

Water You Use

Without water, you could live only a few days. Think about what would happen if your community could no longer provide water. Besides the use of water for drinking, what other ways is water used in your home and in your community? To provide all the water needed, your community must provide more than one hundred gallons per person each day.

Where does water you use come from? Many communities obtain water from rivers, lakes, or the ocean.

Cities located near mountains can pipe water directly from natural mountain lakes. In some places, large dams have been built to stop the flow of a river. As the water collects behind the dam, an artificial lake, or **reservoir** (rez′ ər vwär) is formed. Water flows from the reservoir to the city.

Obtaining water is not much of a problem when there is much rain and snow. Reservoirs are kept filled by surface water. However, when little rain or snow falls, reservoirs must be filled by water traveling underground. Does the supply of water depend upon the water table? If water is used from the reservoir faster than it can be replaced, what will happen to the water supply?

At one time, there was little danger in drinking from rivers and streams. Do you know why this is no longer a safe thing to do?

Rivers and streams are used to get rid of wastes. Cities and towns have sewers that empty into the water. These sewers carry wastes from homes and factories. Wastes carry germs and harmful chemicals into the water. Yet, many communities use this same water in their homes.

What is polluted water?

This town obtains water from the river.

Large dams such as this help to store water for later use.

Rivers and lakes become polluted by people and factories.

Water being filtered

At one time, there were few cities and factories. The small amount of waste that flowed into rivers and lakes was not very harmful. Few poisonous wastes entered the water.

Now there are many more cities and factories adding wastes to the water. Many lakes and rivers have so much waste in the water, it is not even safe for swimming. Water that is dangerous to health is called polluted water.

Most of the water that reaches your home must be purified in a number of ways. Chemicals are added to water to make some materials in the water settle to the bottom of large tanks. Then a little chlorine is added to the water to kill some germs that remain. The water is then sprayed into the air so that fresh air and sunlight can remove odors. Finally, the water is filtered through sand and gravel.

Since water is often used faster than it can be supplied, each person should do what he can to save water. This does not mean that you must be thirsty or skip a needed bath. However, every drop counts, even those from a leaky faucet. You may be surprised how much water can be wasted this way in a very short time. What can you do to help save water?

The amount of water on the earth does not change very much. But keeping water in the right places and keeping it clean enough are problems. Millions of gallons of water are lost from reservoirs every day by evaporation. Can you think of a way this problem might be solved?

FIND OUT

How might the loss of water by evaporation be prevented?

EXPERIMENT

What You Need

2 drinking glasses	cooking oil
water	teaspoon
tape	

1. Fill the two glasses with the same amount of water. Mark the glasses with tape at the top level of the water.
2. Add a teaspoon of cooking oil to one glass.
3. Let both glasses stand in a warm place for days. What difference do you notice? What caused the difference?

Scientists think that certain chemicals might stop evaporation. Like the oil in your experiment, the chemicals form a cover over the surface of the water in a reservoir. They prevent molecules of water from escaping into the air. Scientists are testing this way of preventing evaporation.

Many dams have been built to slow down the movement of surface water and to collect it in reservoirs. Then the water can be used before it flows into the ocean.

Is ocean water safe for drinking?

Many cities are now purifying sewage and garbage before it is released into lakes and streams. Factory owners are removing harmful chemicals from the water they use before returning it to lakes, rivers, and streams.

Water for the Future

What can be done to use the present water supply more wisely? More and more water will be needed as the population increases. The use of ocean water might provide enough water. However, ocean water cannot be used for drinking unless the salt is removed from it.

Ocean water can be desalted in a number of ways. The water can be frozen and the top layer of ice, which does not contain much salt, can be scraped off and used. Electricity can be used to separate the chemicals in salt and remove them from water. However, these ways are quite complicated and expensive.

The easiest way to remove salt from water is to evaporate the water, but this process is also expensive. Much fuel is needed to evaporate large amounts of ocean water. As a result, scientists are experimenting with ways to use the sun's heat to evaporate seawater. In the future, the use of atomic fuels may provide inexpensive water from the ocean. The search for ways to make use of ocean water is one of science's most important problems today.

How can man make use of ocean water?

Ocean water can be evaporated to remove salt from the water.

The Changing Earth

The earth is always changing. Wind and water shape the surface by erosion. Soil and minerals are constantly carried by wind, streams, rain, and floods. Waves beat away at shorelines and rivers build deltas. Dust storms may suddenly change acres of land, and normal winds may carry enough sand to carve the side of a mountain.

Beneath the earth's crust, pressure and heat combine to change rocks within the mantle and core. As deep rocks shift and change, the surface is changed, too.

Shifted rocks beneath the earth's surface cause the surface to change, too.

Exploring Your Learnings

Here are some ideas and vocabulary. What do these mean to you?

Words to Use

crust (p. 182)	dunes (p. 192)
mantle (p. 182)	gullies (p. 196)
core (p. 182)	flood plain (p. 199)
fractures (p. 184)	delta (p. 199)
magma (p. 184)	surface water (p. 200)
seismograph (p. 184)	porous (p. 201)
lava (p. 185)	nonporous (p. 201)
volcano (p. 185)	groundwater (p. 202)
faulting (p. 185)	water table (p. 202)
earthquake (p. 187)	glaciers (p. 204)
polluted (p. 190)	icebergs (p. 205)
smog (p. 191)	echo sounder (p. 207)
erosion (p. 191)	corer (p. 208)
dust storms (p. 192)	reservoir (p. 211)

Ideas to Use

1. Studying the earth above and below its surface helps scientists to explain the history of the earth.

Scientist using instrument to study the inside of the earth

Water treatment plant

2. The earth has an outer crust, a middle layer called the mantle, and an inner core.
3. Earthquakes may be caused by faulting, which is a breaking and moving of rock layers.
4. Polluted air and smog contain harmful chemical compounds which are released into the air as waste solids and gases.
5. Moving water, wind, and ice change the surface of the earth by erosion.
6. Rivers and other surface waters carry soil and minerals which are deposited and form flood plains or deltas.
7. Because soil is porous, water sinks through it to become groundwater.
8. Glaciers may form wherever snow collects faster than it melts.
9. The Arctic and the Antarctic are covered with snow and ice all year long.
10. Scientific instruments are used to study the ocean floor and movements below the earth's surface.
11. Because cities and factories are polluting rivers and lakes with wastes, water in reservoirs must be treated before it can be used.
12. Beneath the earth's crust, pressure and heat change rocks and cause shifts which change the earth's surface.

Using Your Ideas

(Do not write in this book.)

1. Make a model which shows the three layers of the earth.
2. Collect pictures and clippings from magazines and newspapers which show or tell how the earth is changing. Use them in a scrapbook or on a bulletin board.
3. To make a model glacier, pour freshly mixed plaster of paris and water into a soil-covered valley made of modeling clay and soil. How does the glacier move and carry materials?
4. Plan an experiment to show how the size of materials carried by running water depends upon the speed of the water.
5. Read about and report on the nuclear-powered submarine Nautilus. Why is its trip to the north pole so famous?
6. Find out what a bathyscaphe is. What kind of information has been obtained with the use of a bathyscaphe?
7. Find out how air in some kinds of air conditioners and furnaces is filtered to remove solid materials.

USS Nautilus

Bathyscaphe

8. Read about and report on famous volcanoes such as Paracutin, Vesuvius, Krakatoa, and Mauna Loa.
9. Find out how moving groundwater can form caves. Find out what stalactites and stalagmites are.
10. Learn what a geyser is. With your teacher's help, find out a way to make a model of a geyser.
11. Find out how chlorine kills germs in water. Germs are made of material similar to egg white. Place some egg white in water. Add a few drops of washing bleach which contains chlorine. *Be careful* not to get any in your eyes, on your skin, or on your clothing. Observe what happens.
12. Make a still which produces fresh water from salt water with the sun's heat. Add a cup of salt water to the pan. Face the slanted glass toward the sun.

13. Read to find out what causes a spring and an Artesian well. Report on what you find out.

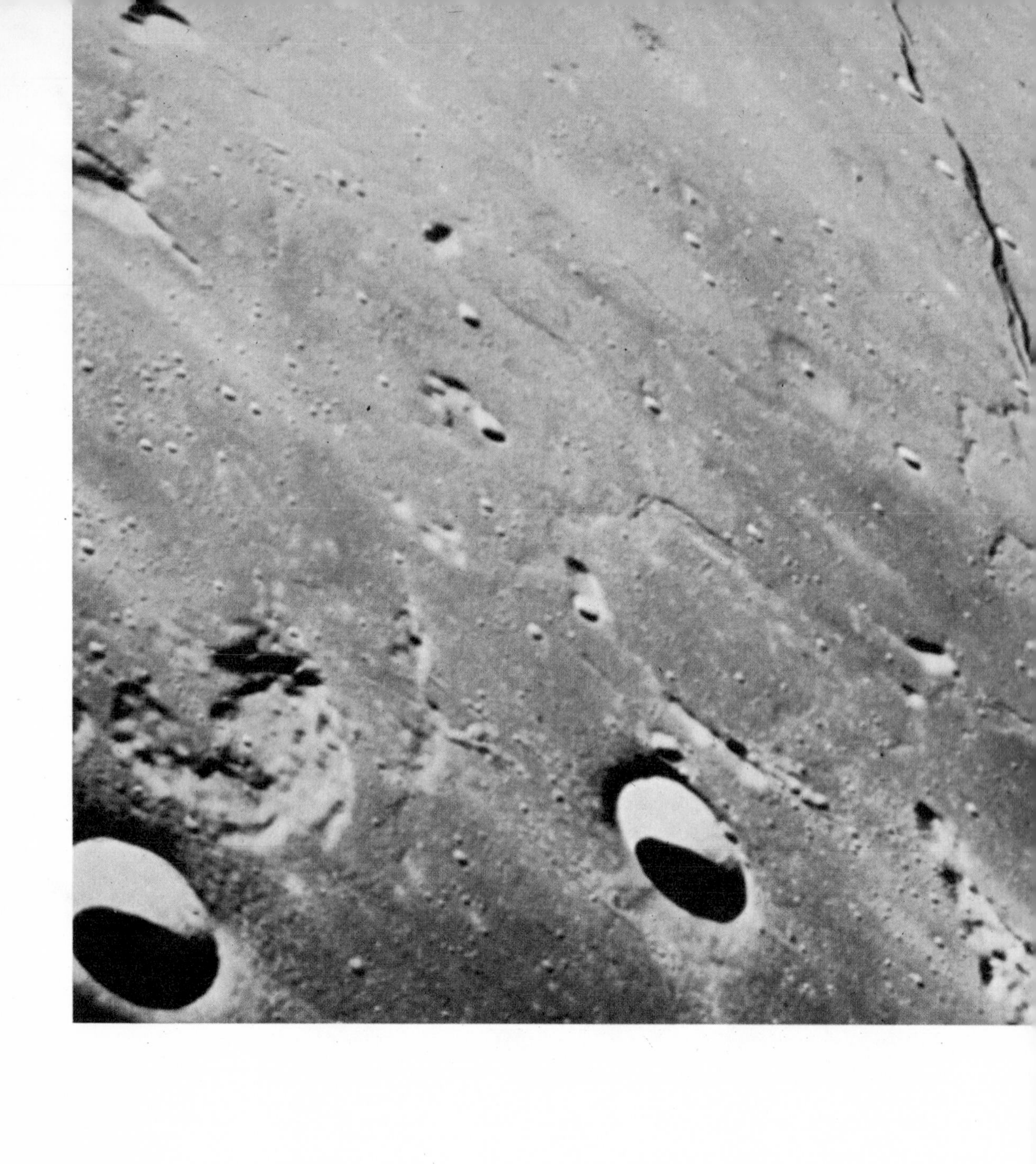

8

The Sun and the Moon

Of all the heavenly bodies, the sun and the moon have always interested man the most. In this photograph, you see part of the moon, the heavenly body closest to the earth. No other heavenly body can be seen so clearly from the earth. How do you think this picture was obtained?

The moon travels along with the earth as the earth journeys through space. And that journey which never ends is around and around the sun. Do you know that you would never see the moon at all if the sun did not light its surface?

All the stars in the sky are suns. Because our sun is the closest star, it can be studied more carefully than the others. Scientists have discovered what the sun is made of. How do you think it continues to give off light and heat day after day, year after year?

Studying the Sky

Long ago, people had ideas about the sun, the moon, and the earth. Some people believed that the earth was flat and feared that a ship could sail off the earth's edge. Ancient Egyptians thought that the earth was covered by a bowl-shaped sky. Chinese people once believed that the moon was eaten by dragons every month! These are some of the ways people explained the things they saw.

For hundreds of years, people have been studying and learning about the moon, the sun, the stars, and other heavenly bodies. The study of heavenly bodies is called **astronomy** (əs tron′ ə mē). Scientists who study astronomy are called **astronomers** (əs tron′ ə mərz).

Astronomer looking through a telescope

The Sun

On a clear night, you can see hundreds of stars. Do some seem to twinkle? Do some appear to have colors? Most stars are trillions of miles away. Have you ever wished you could get a closer look at a star to find out more about it?

There is one star near the earth that is easily studied. This star is the sun. Would knowing about the sun help you understand the more distant stars?

What do you already know about the sun? What is it made of? Why does it give off heat and light? A great deal has been learned about the sun with the use of special instruments.

The sun was photographed several times a day for eighteen months. Many photographs were taken by a camera telescope carried high above the surface of the earth by a huge balloon. Other instruments, carried by balloons and rockets, have been used to collect information about the sun.

Balloons such as this one carry cameras to photograph the sun.

Surface of the sun

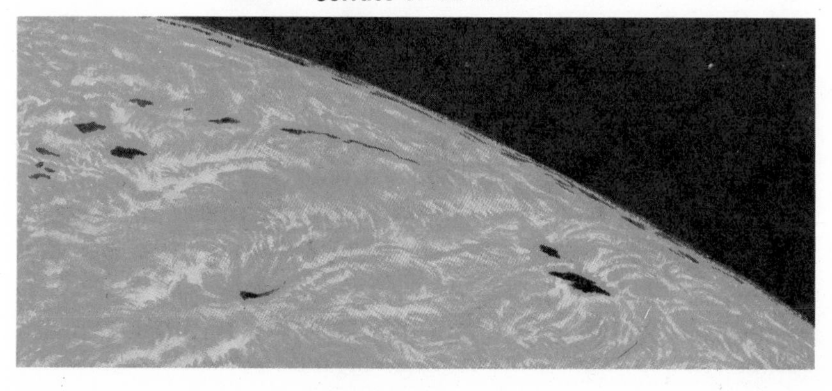

What are sunspots?

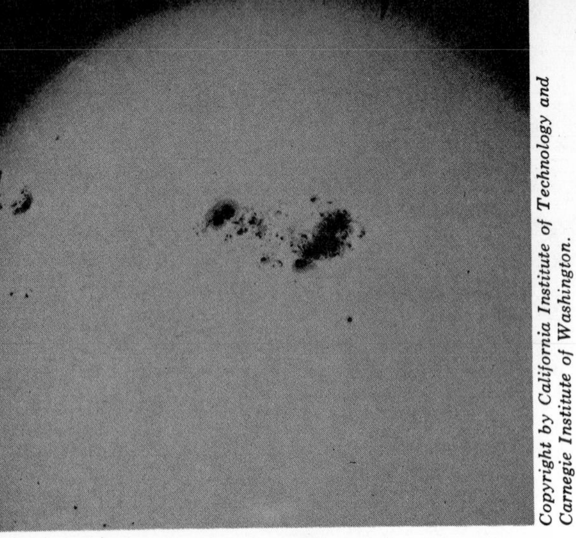

Sun as seen through a telescope

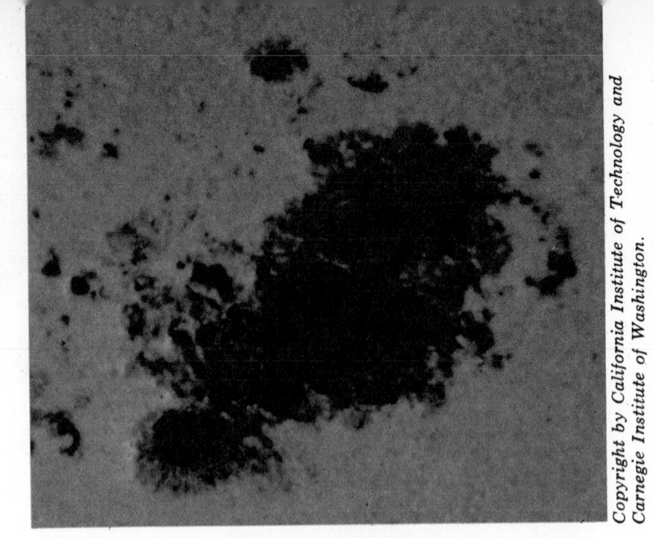

Closeup of sunspots

The picture shows the sun as it looks when photographed through a telescope. Do you observe light and dark areas? The light areas are many times wider than the earth's diameter. The light areas are hotter than the rest of the surface of the sun. These areas rise to the surface of the sun from the sun's hot center.

Dark spots, or **sunspots,** on the sun were observed and reported by Chinese astronomers as early as the year 300 A.D. For a time, the spots were believed to be planets between the earth and the sun. Later, it was observed that these spots were on the sun itself. The dark spots are areas which are cooler than the rest of the sun's surface.

Although sunspots are cooler than the rest of the sun's surface, they are still very hot. A sunspot is an area of electrically charged gases. The charged gases send out billions of charged particles into space. Can you think of a way in which sunspots might affect the earth?

A large number of sunspots seem to appear on the sun quite regularly about once every eleven years. At such times, radio messages and signals on the earth may be difficult to receive. How might this affect airplanes and ships which depend upon radio signals for direction?

Sunspots may last for hours, weeks, or even months. Because astronomers observe that the sunspots seem to move across the sun's surface from one side to the other, the astronomers believe that the sun turns, or **rotates** (rō′ tāts). How do you think they were able to find out that the sun takes twenty-five days for one rotation? How long does it take for the earth to make one rotation? Which rotates faster, the sun or the earth?

Astronomers believe that the sun is made mostly of hydrogen gas and helium gas. Inside the sun, hydrogen atoms are being changed to helium atoms. This kind of change is called a **nuclear reaction** (nü′ klē ər rē ak′ shən). Nuclear reactions on the sun change many million tons of hydrogen to helium every second.

Much heat and light are given off during nuclear reactions. The surface temperature of the sun is about 10,000° F, hot enough to melt rocks! Inside the sun, where the heat and pressure are greatest, the temperature is believed to be 30,000,000° F. Besides hydrogen and helium, the sun is believed to be made of the same elements found in the crust of the earth. In the sun, all the elements are so hot that they are gases.

What elements are in the sun?

These sun gases extend about 132,000 miles above the sun's surface.

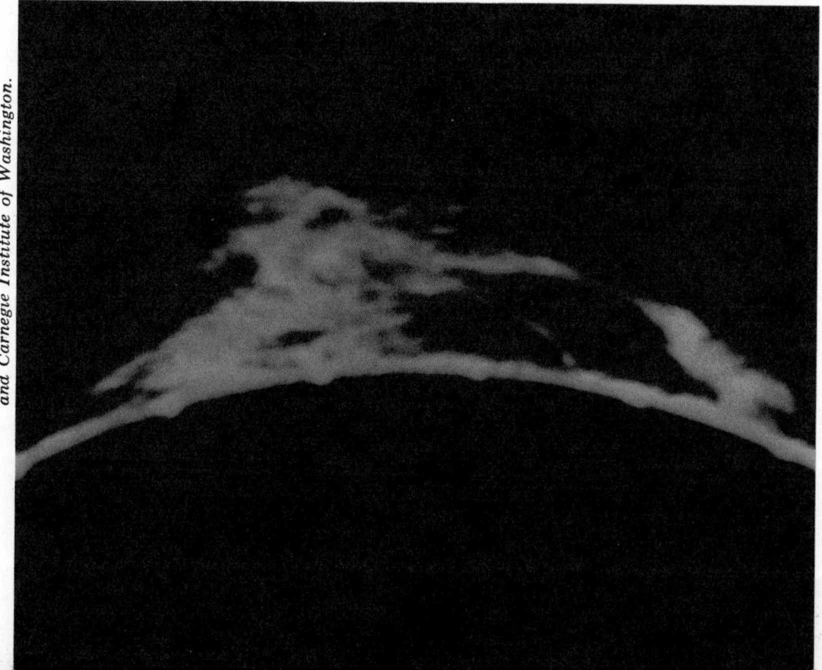

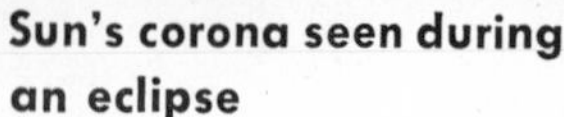

Sun's corona seen during an eclipse

Sun's red layer of gases

Just above the surface of the sun is a layer of glowing gases called the **corona** (kə rō′ nə). The corona of the sun extends millions of miles out into space. What keeps the gases of the corona from flying into space? The corona is attracted to the sun like the atmosphere of earth is attracted to earth, by gravitation. Below the corona is a red layer of gases usually seen during an eclipse. This layer is hydrogen and calcium. The central mass of the sun is made up mostly of hydrogen, helium, calcium, sodium, magnesium, and iron.

The sun is a medium-sized star, but it is very large when it is compared to the earth. Compare the size of the sun to the size of the earth. The earth has a diameter of 8,000 miles, and the sun has a diameter of 865,000 miles. About how many times greater in diameter is the sun?

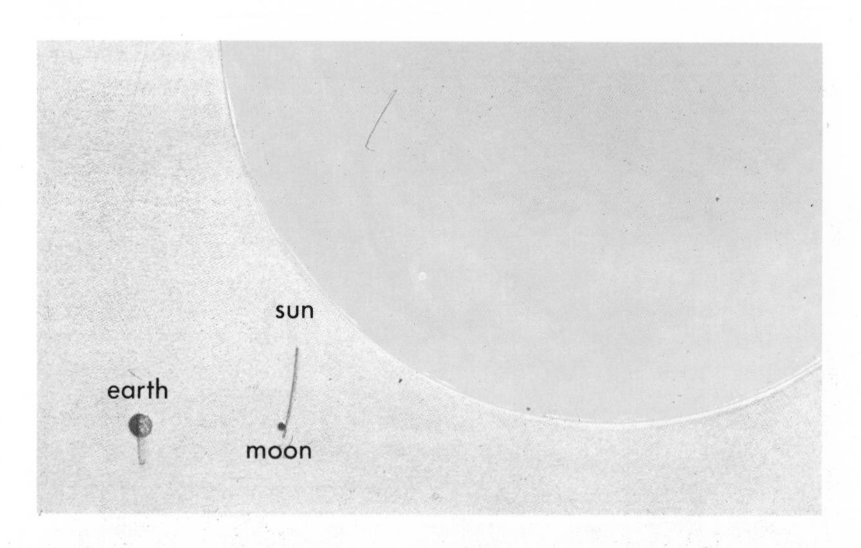

The Moon

Of the heavenly bodies, which one is closest to the earth? People on earth have spent much time and effort studying the moon. The earth's moon is only about one-fourth the diameter of the earth. What is the moon's diameter in miles?

Many **moon probes** (prōbz) have been carried out to gather information about the moon. Some instruments were launched into space by rockets to photograph the moon's surface. Others landed on the moon's surface.

In July, 1969, astronauts Armstrong, Aldrin, and Collins made a 240,000 mile journey to the moon in the spacecraft Apollo 11. Armstrong and Aldrin landed on the moon and were the first humans to walk on the moon's surface. This was man's 33rd manned spaceflight in history.

Can all the moon's surface be seen from earth?

Path of Apollo 11

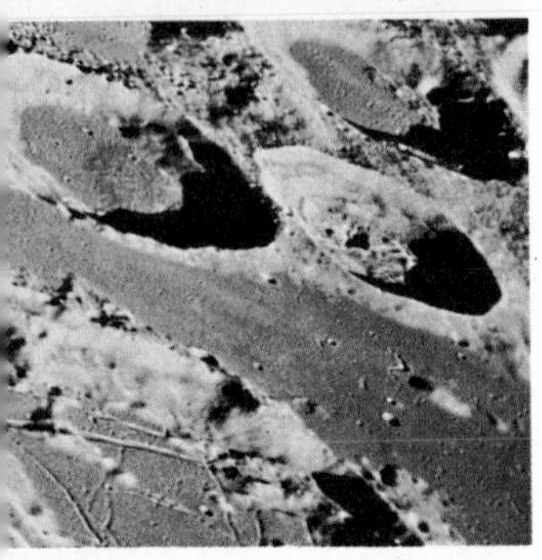

Surface of moon

The astronauts tested their ability to move about in the one-sixth gravity field of the moon. They collected rock and soil samples which will help man to learn more about how the moon and the earth began.

Armstrong reported, "The surface appears to be very, very fine grained. It's almost like powder." The astronauts left a seismograph on the moon to measure moonquakes and other vibrations, and they left a small mirror to reflect laser beams sent from California back to earth.

The moon rotates and it also moves around the earth, or **revolves** (ri volvz′). If the moon both rotates and revolves, why can people on earth see only one side of the moon?

An earth-moon model might help you to understand why you can see only one side of the moon from the earth. Make a large circle on the floor with a piece of chalk. Stand in the center of the circle. You will be an observer on the earth. Have a person represent the moon and revolve around you, following the chalk line. Have him always keep his face toward you.

Does your "moon" rotate as it revolves? How many times does your "moon" rotate as it revolves once? See if you can draw a step-by-step diagram of how your model works. Does your model help you explain why you never see the other side of the moon from the earth?

The hidden side of the moon is shown in gray. The dark side is shown in blue.

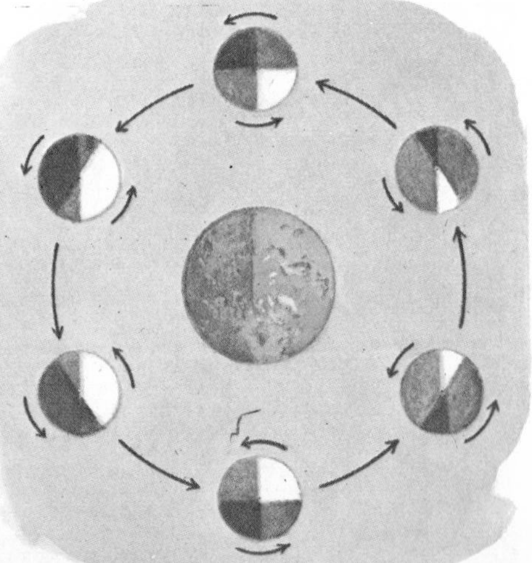

You cannot see one side of the moon from the earth because the moon rotates as it moves in a path around the earth. The moon rotates once completely about every twenty-seven days. It takes just about the same amount of time for the moon to make one trip around the earth.

Phases of the Moon

DISCOVER

Why do you sometimes see only part of the moon?

What You Need

basketball	chalk
white tape	flashlight

1. Using white tape, mark a basketball with an "X".
2. Make a large circle on the floor with chalk. Mark the circle with positions 1, 2, 3, and 4 and A, B, and C as shown in the picture.

What causes phases of the moon?

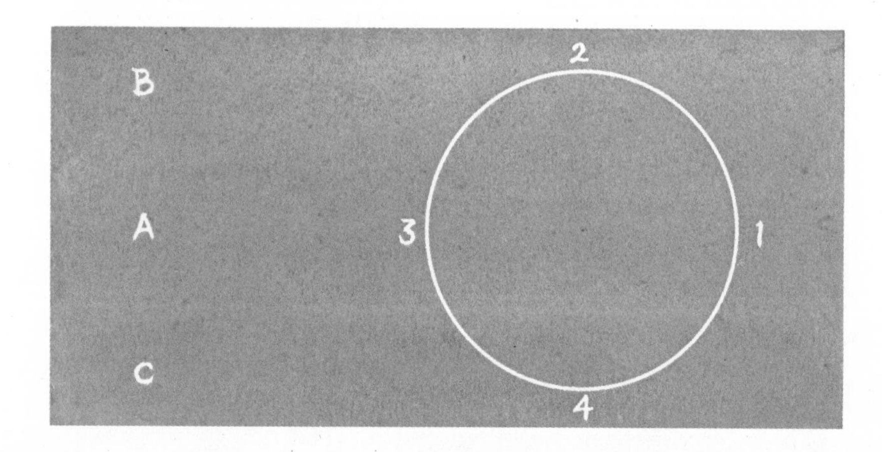

3. Seat five people on the floor with their backs to the center of the circle.
4. Have another person hold the ball at arm's length from his body. He should hold the ball at its top and bottom with the "X" facing away from his body *at all times.* He should stand facing the center of the circle at position 1.
5. Have other people hold the flashlight at positions A, B, and C. They must make certain the flashlight is aimed at the ball at all times.
6. Darken the room and have the person at A turn on his flashlight. Have the person with the ball sidestep around the circle very slowly.
7. The flashlight should be moved by passing it from one person to another person as follows:

Ball	*Flashlight*
1 to 2	A to B
2 to 3	B to A
3 to 4	A to C
4 to 1	C to A

What do the people in the center of the circle represent? What does the basketball represent? What does the flashlight represent? Could a person in the circle see the "X" at all times? Was the "X" always lighted? How much of the ball was always lighted?

The "X" side of the ball was toward the center at all times. At one time, the "X" side was lighted completely, at another time, the "X" side was completely dark. Most of the time, only part of the "X" side was lighted.

Why does the moon seem to change shape? As the moon moves around the earth, how much of it is lighted by the sun? Do you always see all the lighted portion? Changes in the way the moon appears are called **phases** (fāz′ əz) **of the moon.**

These pictures show how the moon looks at different times. Look at a calendar to find out when to look for each phase during the month. You may want to use the ball and flashlight again to see if you can recognize each phase.

What is the terminator line?

When astronauts in spacecraft circle the moon, they cross the area where the sunlit part of the moon meets the dark part of the moon. This area on the moon where light meets dark is called the **terminator** (ter′ mə nā′ tər) **line.**

Do you think the moon is much like the earth? The moon appears to be a bare, rocky place with sandy soil and many craters. There seem to be no plants, animals, or water.

From the moon, the sky appears dark at all times, even on the "day" side of the moon. There is no air or dust in the space around the moon to reflect sunlight toward its surface. From the moon, many more stars can be seen than from the earth. Why?

Astronauts on the moon can see sunlight reflected from the earth. This earthshine is eight times brighter than moonlight shining on the earth.

Earth as seen from the moon

Because there is little or no air on the moon, the moon has no air pressure. Temperatures on the moon's surface rise to about 240° F or higher, on the side facing the sun. On the side away from the sun, the temperature drops to about 280° F below zero. Explain why temperatures change greatly on the moon from day to night.

Gravity in Space

Why do objects have weight on the earth? What force pulls things toward the center of the earth? Weight is a measure of the force of gravity on something. Does the force of the earth's gravity affect things far beyond the earth?

All matter has gravitation. Would the moon, a star, a book, a pencil, and a grain of sand all have gravitation? The strength of gravitation depends upon the mass of material. The moon is much smaller than the earth. Do you think the gravitational pull of the moon is as strong as the gravitational pull of the earth? Would you weigh more on the moon or on the earth?

Shadows in Space

What two things are necessary to make a shadow? Do you think the earth, the moon, the other planets, and their moons can cast shadows? Bodies in space may cast shadows.

What happens when the moon blocks some of the sun's light? Sometimes the earth moves through the shadow of the moon. Other times, the moon moves through the shadow of the earth. When either of these things happens, an **eclipse** (i klips′) takes place.

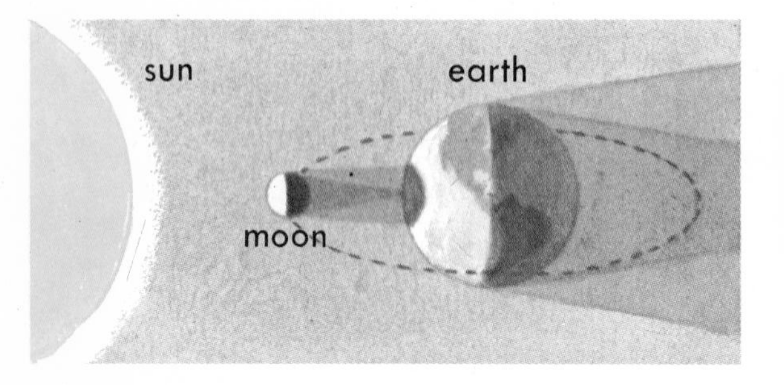

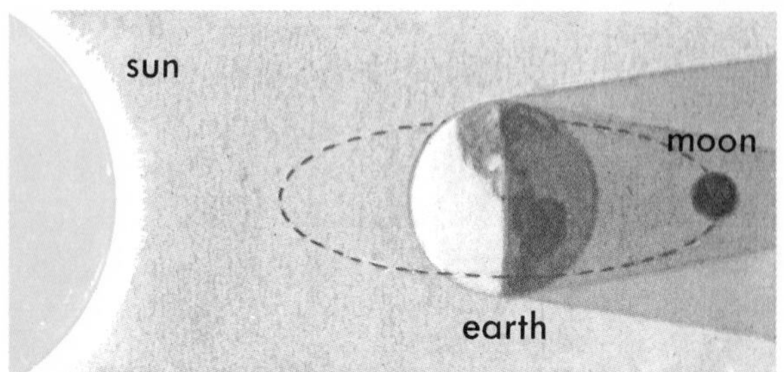

DISCOVER

What happens when the moon blocks some of, or all of the sun's light?

What You Need

volleyball	string
tennis ball	filmstrip projector or flashlight

1. Set the volleyball on a table. Imagine that the volleyball is the earth.
2. Fasten a string to the tennis ball. Imagine that the tennis ball is the moon.
3. From one side of the room, shine a filmstrip projector or bright flashlight on the volleyball. Darken the room. Where should you hold the "moon" by the string so that its shadow strikes the earth? This model represents an eclipse of the sun or a **solar** (sō′ lər) **eclipse.**

What is the shape of the "moon's" shadow on the "earth"? What change can you make in your model to make this shadow larger? What change can you make in your model to make the shadow smaller?

Persons in the shadow of the moon may see a total eclipse, during which all the sun appears to be darkened. Or, persons in the shadow may see a partial eclipse, during which only a part of the sun is darkened. Use the models to demonstrate each type of eclipse. Make drawings to show how the sun might appear to persons on the earth.

Does a solar eclipse occur each month?

Solar eclipse

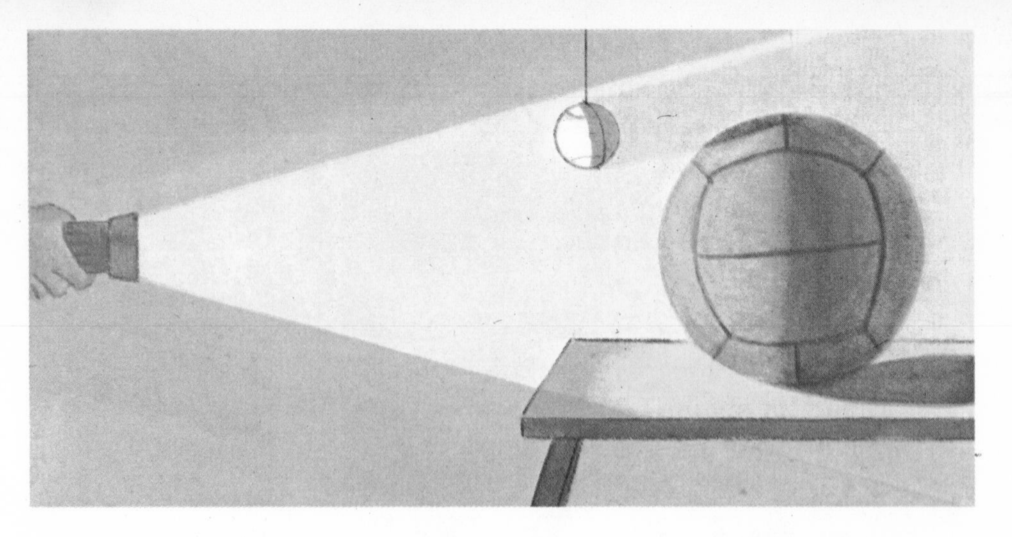

In what phase is the moon at the time of a solar eclipse? Use your models to show that a solar eclipse can take place only at the time of the new moon. A new moon occurs once each month.

Use the models to show a reason why there may not always be an eclipse of the sun at the time of the new moon.

DISCOVER

What happens when the earth blocks some of the sun's light from the moon?

What You Need

volleyball	string
tennis ball	filmstrip projector or flashlight

1. Use the same models to represent the earth and moon. Turn on the light source. Darken the room.
2. Hold the "moon" so that it is in the shadow of the "earth." This model represents an eclipse of the moon or a **lunar** (lü′ nər) **eclipse.**

When the moon is completely in the shadow of the earth, a total eclipse of the moon occurs. How would the moon look seen from earth? Can you hold your model of the moon so that it represents the position of the moon during a partial eclipse of the moon? Make a drawing to show how the moon might appear seen from the earth. Why does a partial eclipse of the moon show that the earth's surface is curved?

Lunar eclipse

In what phase is the moon at the time of a lunar eclipse? Use your models to show that an eclipse of the moon can take place only at the time of the full moon. A full moon occurs once each month. Use the models to show why there is not always an eclipse of the moon each time there is a full moon.

Day and Night

Do you have to travel into space to be in the earth's shadow? As the earth rotates, do you move into and out of the earth's shadow? Why is it dark every night?

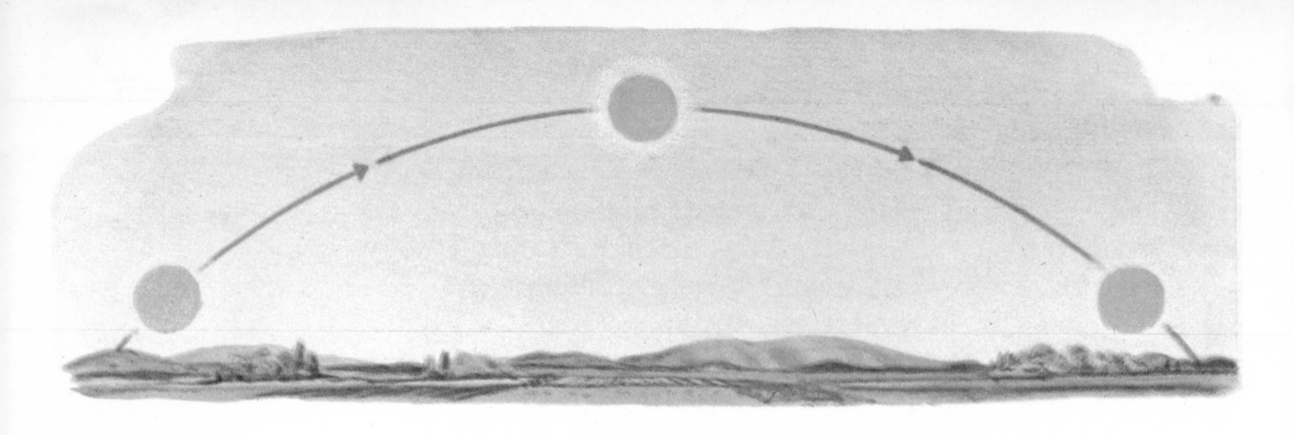

The sun appears to move across the sky from east to west.

How much of the earth is lighted by the sun at one time? As the earth turns, the sun seems to rise, move across the sky, and then set. While the sun is above the horizon, is it day or night? While the sun is below the horizon, is it day or night? The earth turns from west to east. Why does the sun appear to rise in the east and set in the west?

DISCOVER

What is one way to record the sun's daily path?

What You Need

shoe box	pin
black paint	small rock
paintbrush	sponge
scissors	ammonia
aluminum foil	gallon jar and lid
tape	pan, 9″ × 13″
ammonia print paper	tongs

1. Paint the cover and inside of a shoe box black.
2. In the center of the cover, cut a hole about two inches square. Fasten aluminum foil over this opening with tape.

3. Curve a piece of ammonia print paper with its reverse side toward the inside of the shoe box (chemical side up). Fasten it in place with tape.
4. Use tape to fasten the cover onto the box. With a pin, punch a small hole in the aluminum foil.

5. Early on a sunny day, take the box outside. Set it where it will be in sunlight all day. Face the cover of the box toward the south. Tip the box by placing a rock under it as shown in the picture.
6. After sunset, remove the ammonia print paper.
7. Soak the sponge in ammonia and put it into the gallon jar. Handle the sponge with tongs. Do not breathe the ammonia vapor.
8. Then put the ammonia print paper into the jar so that the paper does not touch the sponge. Place the lid on the jar. The ammonia fumes will develop your print.

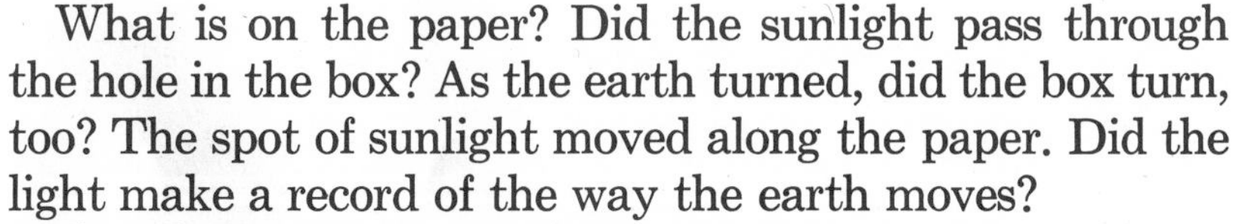

What is on the paper? Did the sunlight pass through the hole in the box? As the earth turned, did the box turn, too? The spot of sunlight moved along the paper. Did the light make a record of the way the earth moves?

As you observe the sun from day to day, you may notice another change. Is the sun always the same height above the horizon at the same time each day?

Does the length of a shadow change from season to season?

FIND OUT

How does the sun's position in the sky change from day to day?

EXPERIMENT

What You Need

paper	cork
tape	toothpick
all-purpose glue	pencil

1. Place a table by a window that faces south. Tape a piece of paper to the tabletop.
2. Glue a cork to the center of the paper. Stick a toothpick into the center of the cork.
3. The toothpick will make a shadow on the paper on sunny days. Use a pencil to mark the end of the shadow on the paper. Make a mark at exactly the same time every day for one or two weeks. Does the length of the shadow change?

Upon what does the length of the shadow depend? When the sun is high above the horizon, the shadow is shorter than when the sun is low. Whether the shadow became longer or shorter each day depends upon the time of year that you made your record. From December 21 until June 21, the shadow should become shorter each day. From June 21 to December 21, the shadow should become longer.

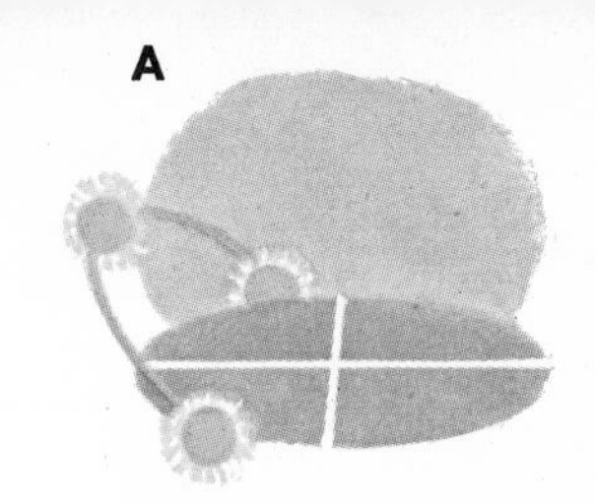

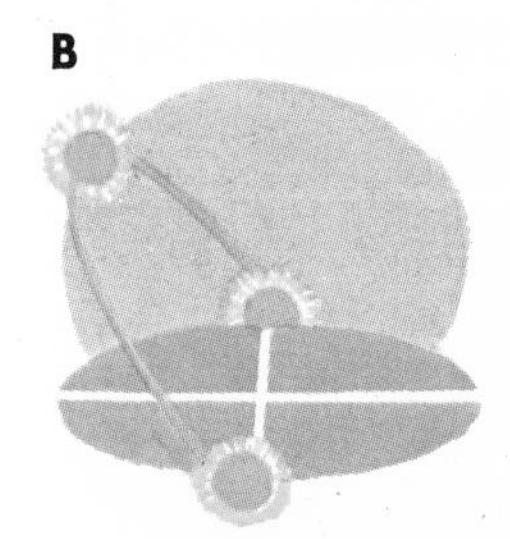

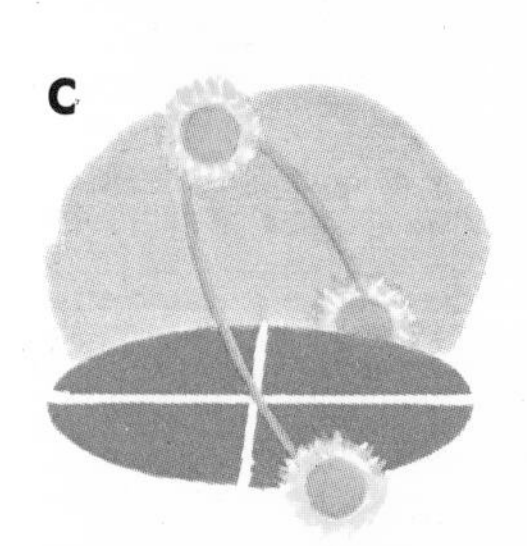

A. December in North America

B. March in North America

C. June in North America

A Model of Earth

Examine a model of the earth called a **globe** (glōb). Why do you use a ball to represent the earth in your experiments? A globe is a kind of map of the earth that is much like the earth itself. By studying the globe, there are many things about the earth which you can understand better.

Find the north pole on the globe. Find the south pole on the globe. These are the **geographic** (jē′ ə graf′ ik) **poles.** The **magnetic** (mag net′ ik) **poles** of the earth are close to these points. Try to locate them on the globe. Look on the globe for a line halfway between the north pole and the south pole, which is labeled **equator** (i kwā′ tər). The equator marks the globe into northern and southern parts. The **axis** (ak′ sis) of the earth is an imaginary line running through the earth between the geographic poles.

What are latitude and longitude lines?

Do you know what a sphere is? Is the earth sphere-shaped? The Greek word *hemi* means half. What do you think a hemisphere is? On the globe, find the place where you live on the earth. Do you live in the northern hemisphere or the southern hemisphere?

Is the equator the only line marked around the globe? Lines marked around the globe parallel to the equator are counted in degrees. These lines are called **latitude** (lat′ ə tüd) **lines.** The equator is at 0° latitude. At 66½° north and 66½° south are two latitude lines with special names. Can you find them? What are these latitudes called?

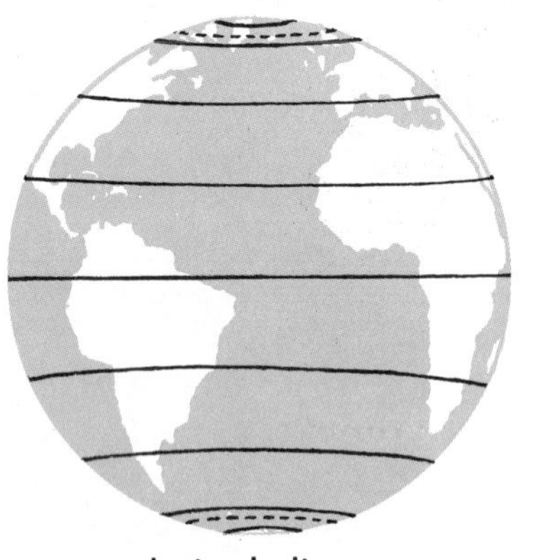

latitude lines

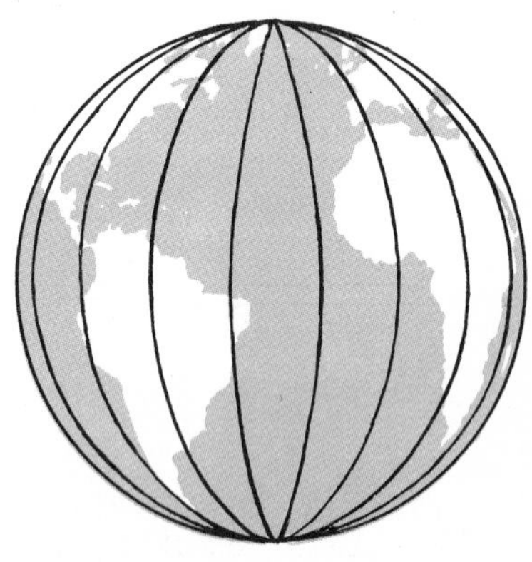

longitude lines

The lines marked on the globe from north pole to south pole are called **longitude** (lon′ jə tüd) **lines.** Longitudes are also counted in degrees. Find the place where you live on the globe. At about what degree latitude and what degree longitude do you live?

Changing Shadows

Knowing about a globe will help you in your experiments to discover more about the earth.

FIND OUT

Why are shadows longer during some parts of the year?

EXPERIMENT

What You Need

- chalk
- compass
- label marked "north"
- light bulb, 100-watt
- light socket
- extension cord
- globe

1. With chalk, draw a large circle on the floor to represent the earth's path around the sun. Mark the center of the circle.
2. Locate the north wall or corner of the room with a compass. Label this wall "north."
3. Mark the circle as follows: north side, "December"; west side, "March"; south side, "June"; and east side, "September."

What two movements of the earth cause shadows to change?

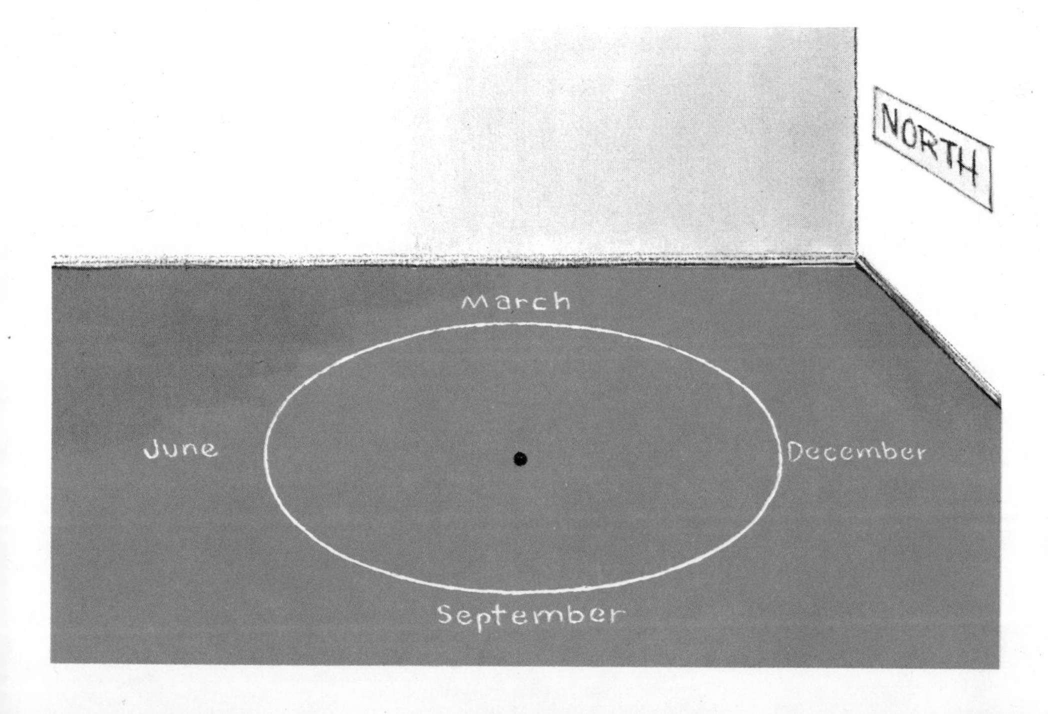

4. Darken the room. Place the lighted bulb at the center of the circle to represent the sun.
5. Set a globe on the floor at the "June" side, with the earth's north pole pointing toward the north wall. Is the axis straight up and down or slightly slanted? This represents summer in the northern hemisphere. Is the earth's north pole slanted toward the sun or away from the sun?
6. Move the globe to the place marked "December" while keeping the north pole of the globe pointed toward the north wall. Is the earth's north pole slanted toward the sun?

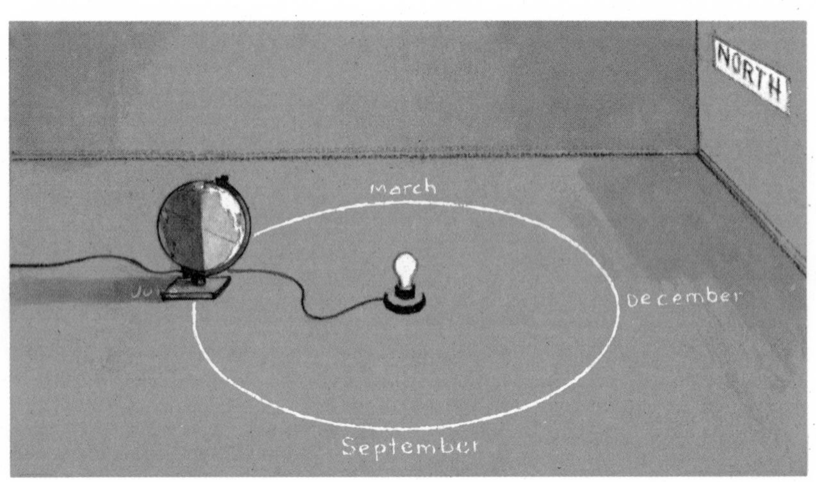

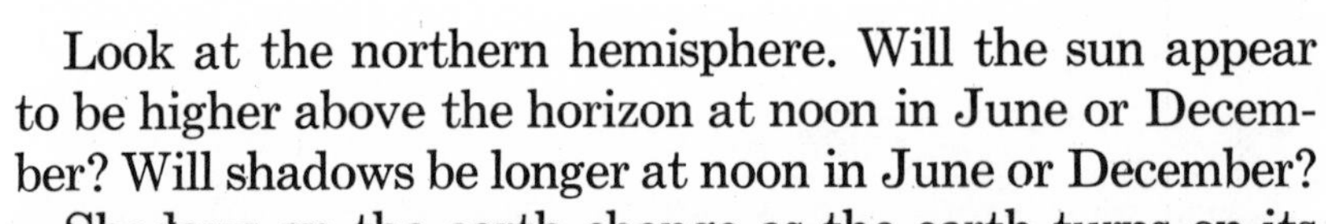

Look at the northern hemisphere. Will the sun appear to be higher above the horizon at noon in June or December? Will shadows be longer at noon in June or December?

Shadows on the earth change as the earth turns on its slanted axis and moves in its orbit around the sun. In June, is the northern hemisphere slanted toward the sun? In December, is the northern hemisphere slanted away from the sun or toward the sun?

At what time does the sun rise and set in summer where you live?

At what time does the sun rise and set in winter where you live?

Long Days and Short Days

Are there more hours of daylight in summer or in winter in the northern hemisphere? In summer, the sun rises early and sets late. In winter, the sun rises late and sets early. What makes the difference in the length of the days and nights?

FIND OUT

Why does the length of day and night change with the seasons?

EXPERIMENT

What You Need

- globe
- masking tape
- light bulb, 100-watt
- light socket
- extension cord
- chalk circle you used in the last experiment

1. On a globe, stick a small piece of masking tape at each line of longitude where it crosses the arctic circle, the equator, the line of latitude where you live, and the antarctic circle.
2. Set the globe at "December" on the chalk circle. The north pole of the globe should point toward the north wall.

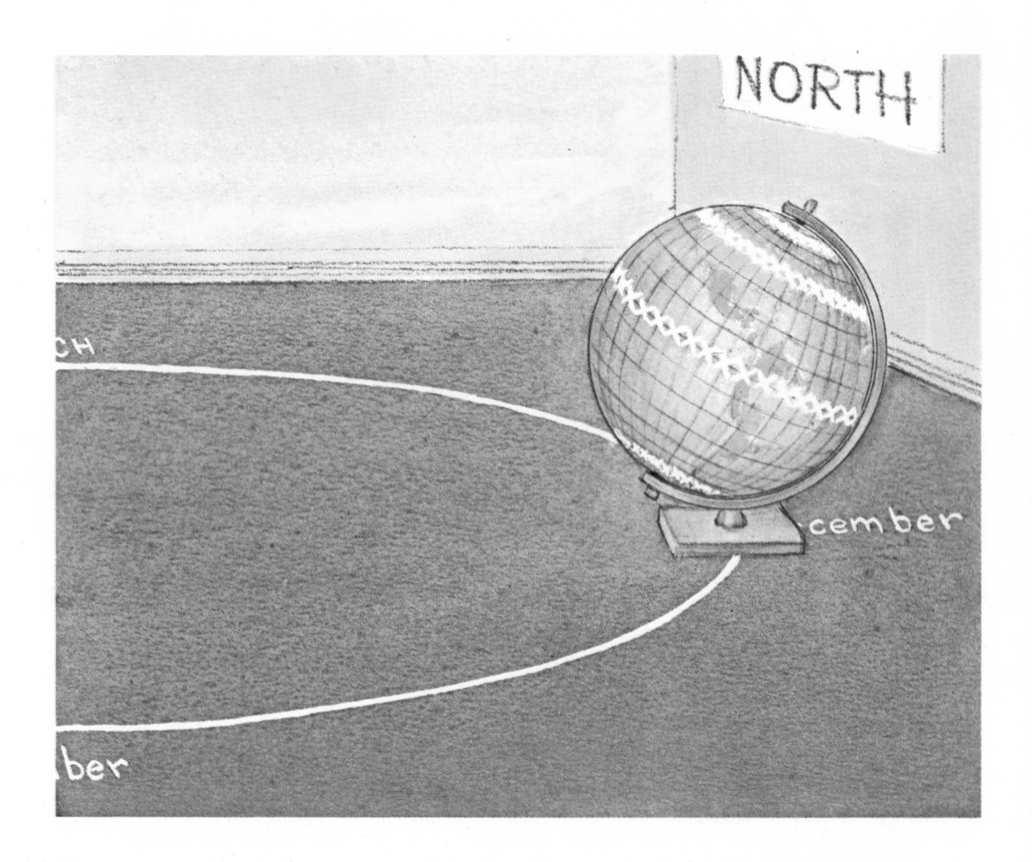

3. Darken the room. Set the lighted bulb on the floor at the center of the circle. How much of the earth is lighted? How many of the pieces of masking tape are lighted at the arctic circle, at your latitude, at the equator, and at the antarctic circle? Record the results.

4. Move the globe to "March"; then to "June"; then to "September." At each position, the north pole of the globe should be pointed toward the north wall. Count the number of pieces of masking tape lighted at each position and record the results.

Each piece of masking tape lighted at each latitude represents one hour of daylight. During what month is the shortest day of the year where you live? During what month is the longest day of the year where you live?

During what months are the days and nights the same length everywhere on the earth? Where on the earth are days and nights the same length all year long? Where on earth is it possible to have twenty-four hours of daylight? When does this happen? Where on the earth is it possible to have twenty-four hours of darkness? When does this happen?

Exploring Your Learnings

Here are some ideas and vocabulary. What do these mean to you?

Words to Use

astronomy (p. 222)
astronomers (p. 222)
sunspots (p. 224)
rotates (p. 225)
nuclear reaction (p. 225)
corona (p. 226)
moon probes (p. 227)
revolves (p. 228)
phases of the moon (p. 231)
terminator line (p. 232)
eclipse (p. 234)
solar eclipse (p. 235)
lunar eclipse (p. 236)
globe (p. 241)
geographic poles (p. 241)
magnetic poles (p. 241)
equator (p. 241)
axis (p. 241)
latitude lines (p. 242)
longitude lines (p. 242)

This ring nebula far out in space contains many suns and planets and moons.

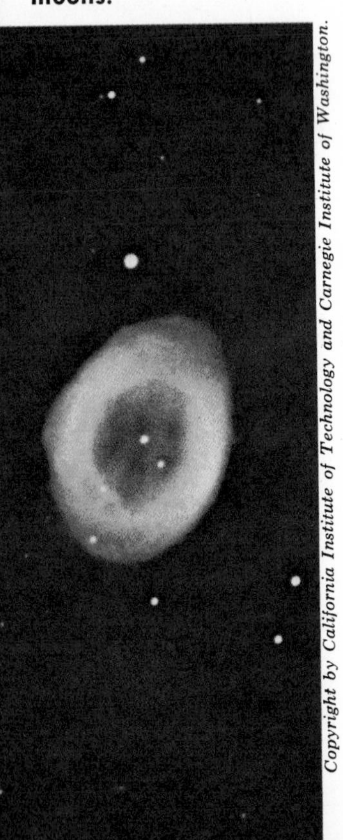

Ideas to Use

1. The study of heavenly bodies is called astronomy.
2. The sun is made mostly of hydrogen gas and helium gas.
3. Nuclear reactions inside the sun give off much heat and light.
4. The sun is neither the largest star nor the smallest star in the universe.
5. You cannot see one side of the moon from the earth because the moon rotates as it revolves around the earth.
6. There is very little air around the moon.
7. Eclipses, night, and the phases of the moon are all caused by shadows in space.

8. A globe is a kind of map of the earth that has a shape much like the earth's.
9. Shadows on the earth change as the earth revolves around the sun.
10. Because the axis of the earth is slanted, the length of days and nights changes as the earth travels in its orbit.

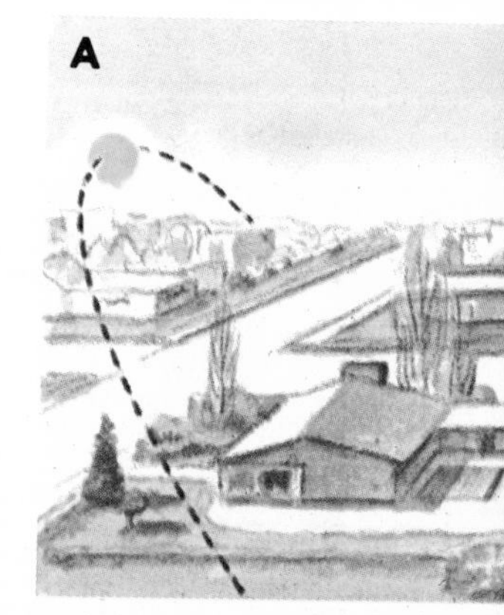

Using Your Ideas

(Do not write in this book.)

1. Identify the pictures. Tell which shows an eclipse of the sun, summer in North America, winter in North America, and an eclipse of the moon.

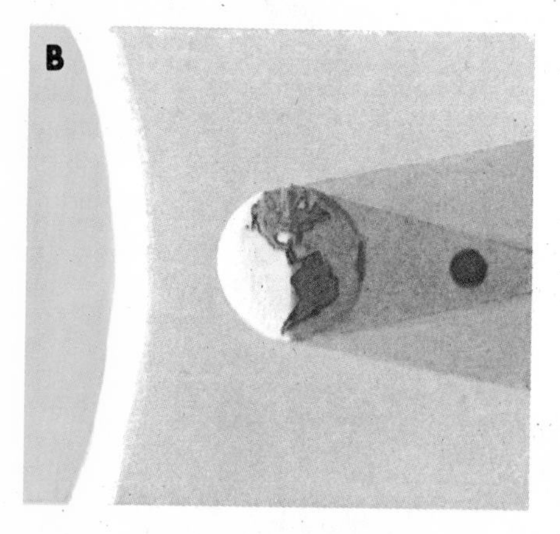

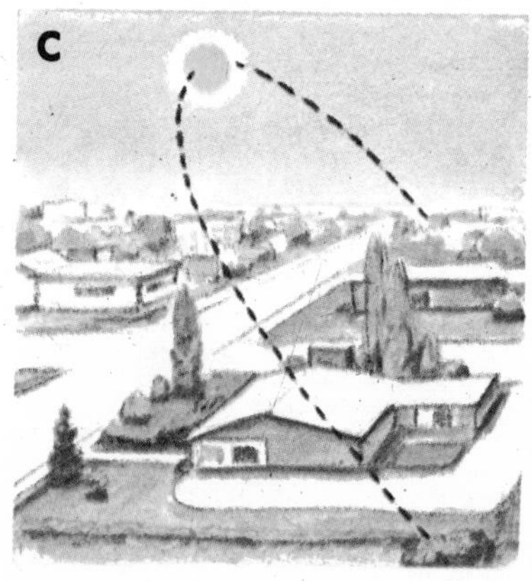

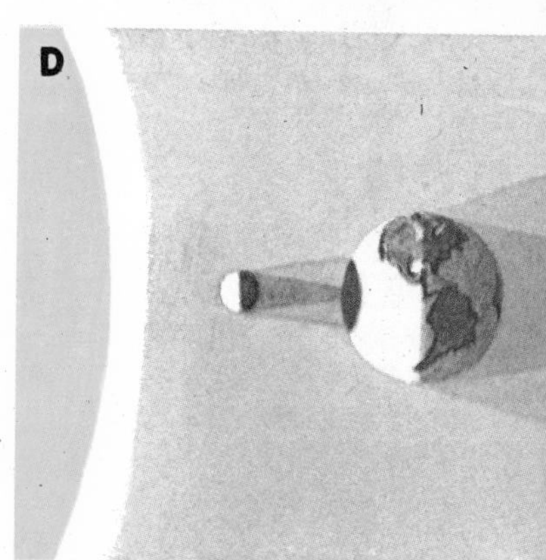

2. The pull of gravity is six times greater on the earth than it is on the moon. Find out how high and how far you could jump on the moon.
3. Read to find out how far away other planets are from the sun. Report on one of the planets.
4. Find out the meanings of these words: asteroid, aurora, dwarf star, equinox, lunar module.

Into Space With Satellites

After a rocket helps to launch a satellite into space, where does the rocket go? On its trip back to earth, it is guided by a reentry system, mounted on the front of it. In this picture, inside the clear globe, is a model of a reentry system.

Once a satellite is in space, what forces cause it to orbit the earth? Man-made satellites sometimes fall back toward earth after a certain length of time. Do you know why? You can discover how satellites provide many different kinds of information to further man's understanding of both the earth and space.

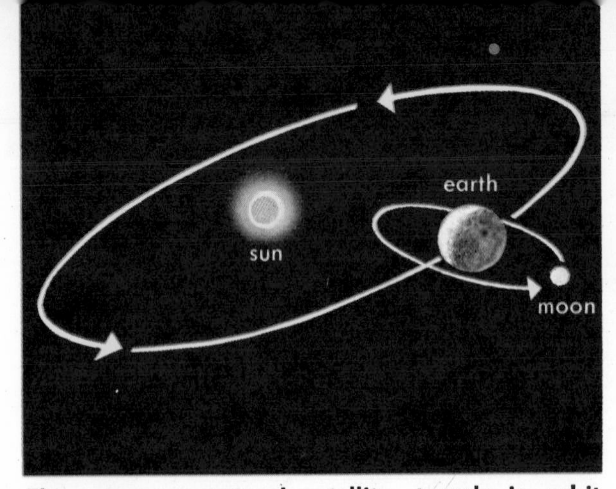

The moon, a natural satellite, travels in orbit around the earth.

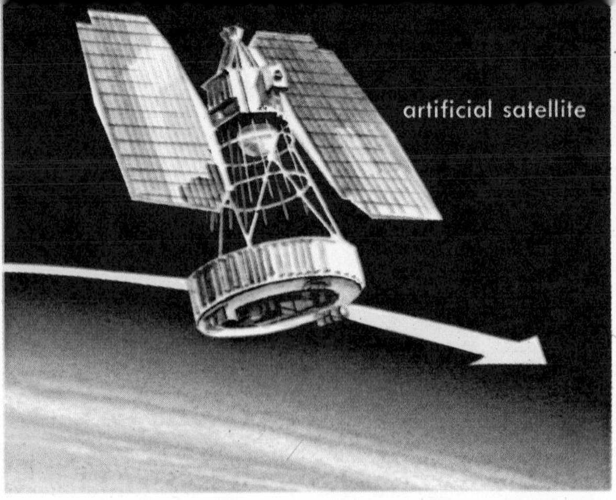

An artificial satellite travels in orbit around the earth.

Satellites—Old and New

A **satellite** (sat′ l īt) is any object in space that travels in an orbit around a larger body. Is the moon a satellite of the earth? Is the earth a satellite of the sun? **Artificial** (är′ tə fish′ əl) **satellites** are satellites made and sent into space by man. What do you think **natural** (nach′ ər əl) **satellites** are? Are the earth and the moon natural satellites?

Many kinds of man-made satellites have been **launched** (lônchd), or sent into space. One of the first satellites launched weighed only about three pounds. Most satellites weigh several hundred pounds and carry instruments which gather and record information about space.

Launching Satellites

Before a satellite can begin its journey, it must be given a thrust. A **thrust** is a push opposite to the force of gravity. The thrust must be strong enough to lift the satellite from the earth. Satellites are launched into space by huge rockets. Have you ever wondered what makes rockets move?

Put on a pair of roller skates. Stand on a smooth floor with your feet together. Ask someone to hand you a basketball. Holding the ball in front of you with both hands, throw it away from you as hard as you can. What happens? In which direction does the ball move? In which direction do you move? Can you explain what happened?

Scientists use an idea they call **action-reaction** to explain what happened. Whenever two objects act on one another, the force of the first object on the second object is equal to the force of the second object on the first object. The two forces that the objects have on each other are in opposite directions. It makes no difference which of the two forces is the action force, or which is the reaction force because both forces act at the same time. Can you think of other examples of action and reaction forces? These pictures may help. For each picture, the arrow shows the direction of one of the forces. What is the other force in each picture?

DISCOVER

How do action and reaction forces work in a rocket?

What You Need

balloon

1. Blow air into the balloon and pinch the neck. What is pushing out the sides of the balloon?
2. Let go of the balloon. What do you observe?

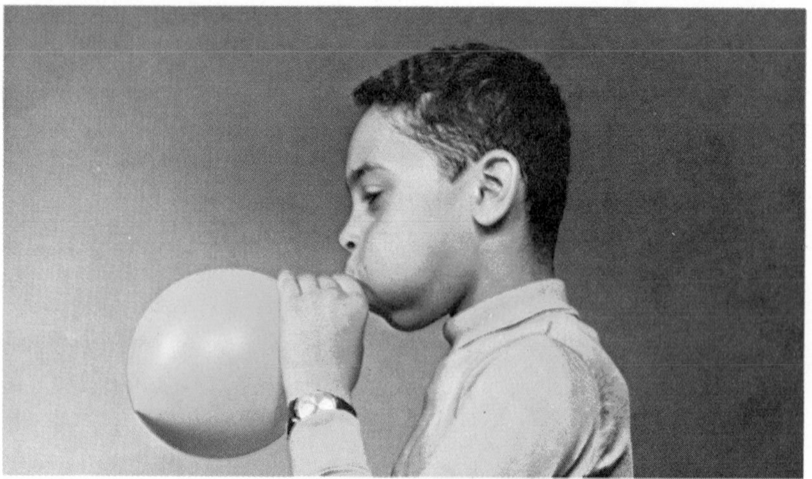

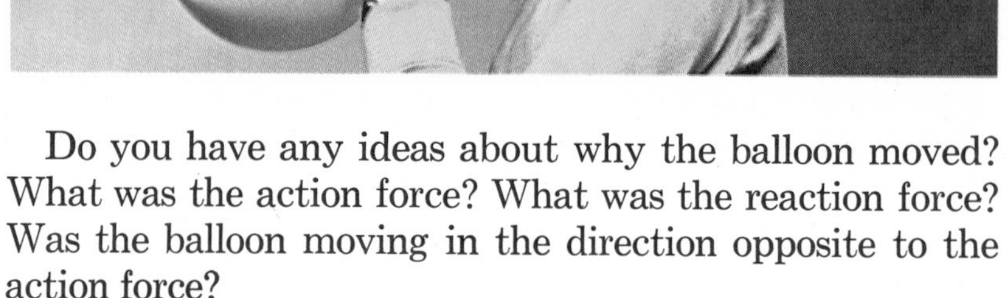

Do you have any ideas about why the balloon moved? What was the action force? What was the reaction force? Was the balloon moving in the direction opposite to the action force?

A rocket has an engine in which fuels are burned. The burning forms gases which move out of the rocket through an opening at the back of the engine. As the gases move in one direction, the rocket moves in the opposite direction. What provides the thrust to a rocket? Why is a rocket engine called a reaction engine?

Rocket Power

Both jet and rocket engines provide thrust by action-reaction forces. There is one important difference between a jet engine and a rocket engine. Do you know how they are different?

Jet airplane

Rocket

To burn, fuels need oxygen. A jet airplane operates in air. Where do you think the jet engine gets the oxygen it uses? Rocket engines can work in space where there is little or no air. Where would a rocket in space get a supply of oxygen to burn its fuel?

Rockets carry fuel and oxygen in separate tanks. The oxygen gas is compressed and cooled to form a liquid. As the rocket engine starts, some fuel and oxygen mix in the engine. The fuel burns. Gases push against the inside of the engine and leave through the opening at the back with great force. What is the action force in a rocket engine? What is the reaction force?

How fast must a rocket travel to launch a satellite?

Cross section of rocket

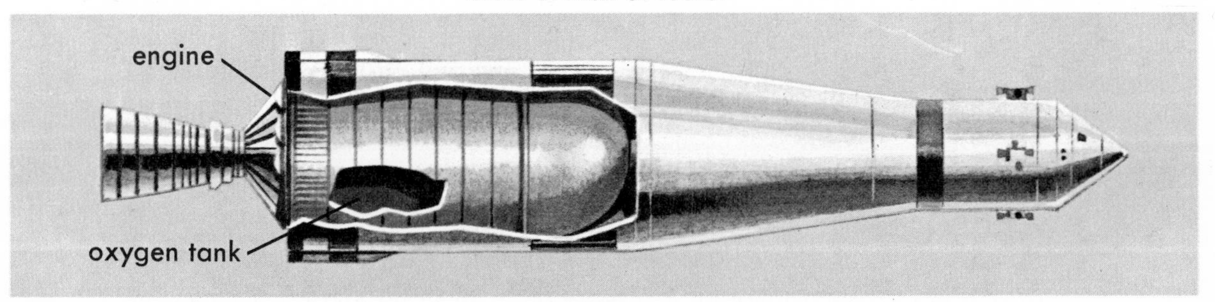

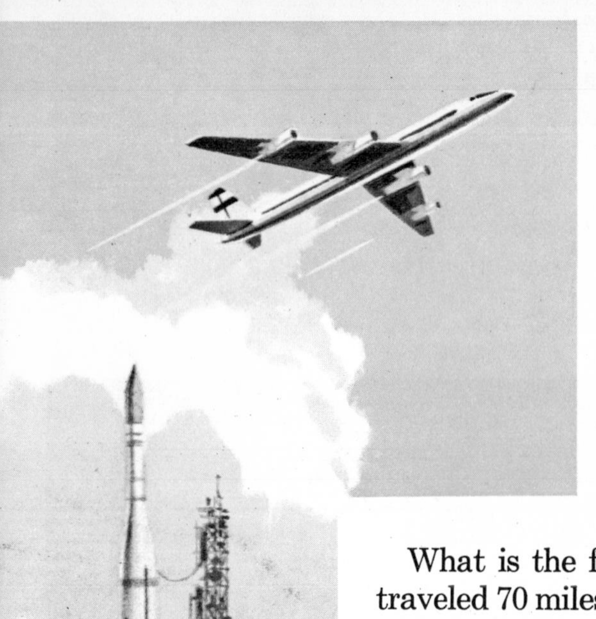

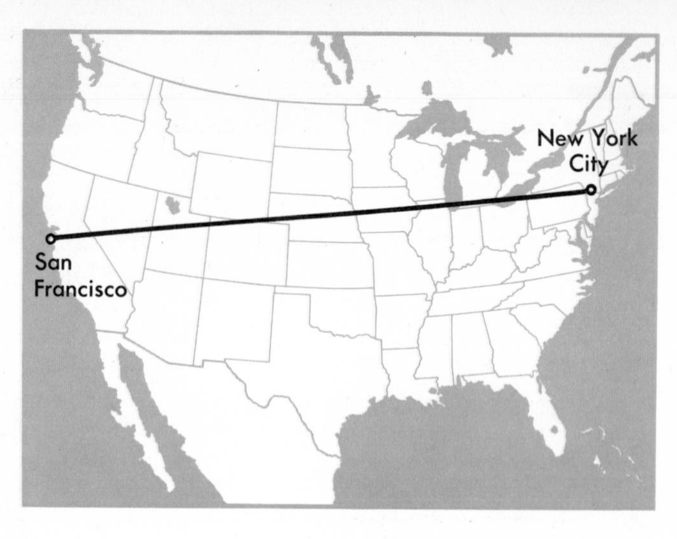

What is the fastest you have ever traveled? Have you traveled 70 miles per hour in a car? Perhaps you have gone as fast as 600 miles per hour in a jet airplane. The speed of a jet is like walking compared to the speed at which a rocket must travel to launch a satellite. It must travel about 17,500 miles per hour, or 300 miles per minute. At a speed of 17,500 miles per hour, you could travel from New York City to San Francisco in about ten minutes!

FIND OUT

Why can the thrust of balloons be different?

EXPERIMENT

What You Need

- 2 thick soda straws
- small wooden spool
- all-purpose cement
- shoe box
- scissors
- modeling clay
- tape
- file card, 3″ × 5″
- grease pencil or marker
- tape measure
- balloons of different sizes

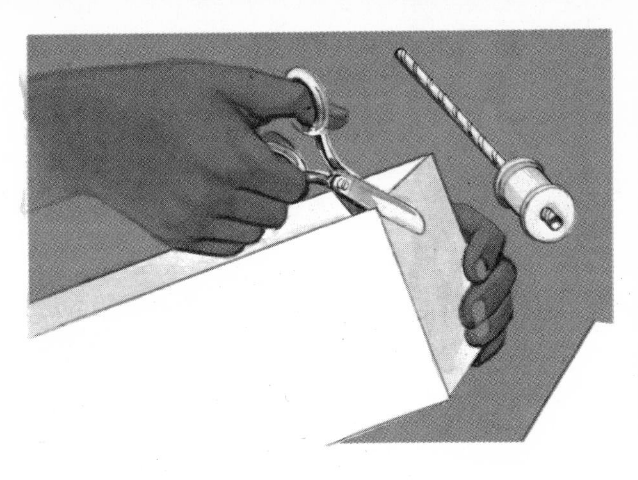

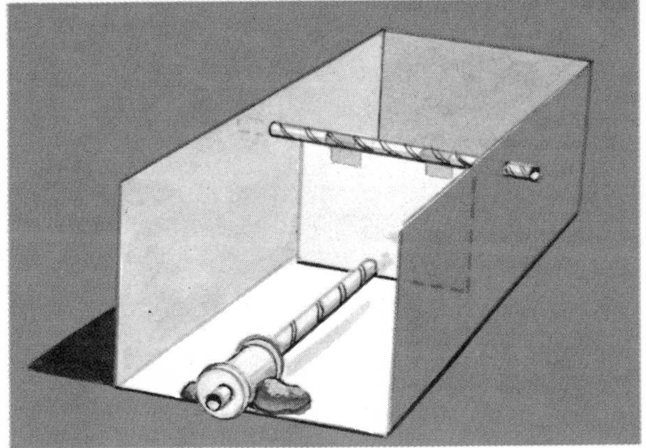

1. Make a test stand to hold your balloons. Put a thick soda straw into a small spool. Seal it with all-purpose cement.
2. Cut one closed end out of a shoe box, as shown. Put the spool into the open end of the shoe box by setting it on a piece of modeling clay.
3. Make an indicator to measure the thrust. Six inches from the closed end of the box, make a hole in each side through which a straw can be placed. Put the other straw through the holes. Tape the middle of the straw across the top of the file card.
4. Make a scale on the inside of the box, as shown in the picture.
5. Blow up a balloon. Twist the neck to prevent the air from escaping. Measure the distance around the balloon, using a tape measure. Record this measurement.

What does the thrust of a rocket depend upon?

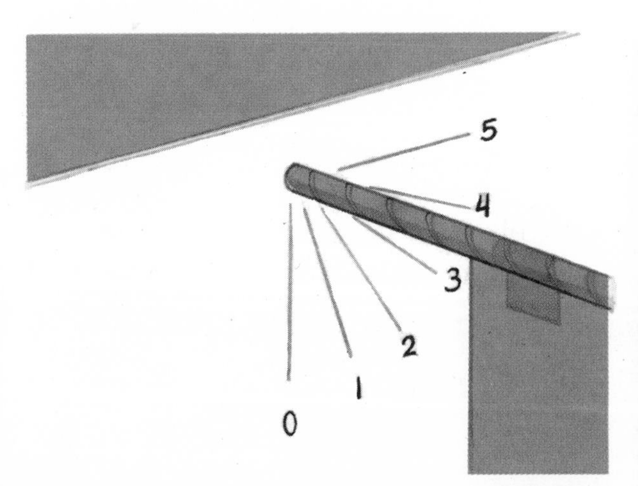

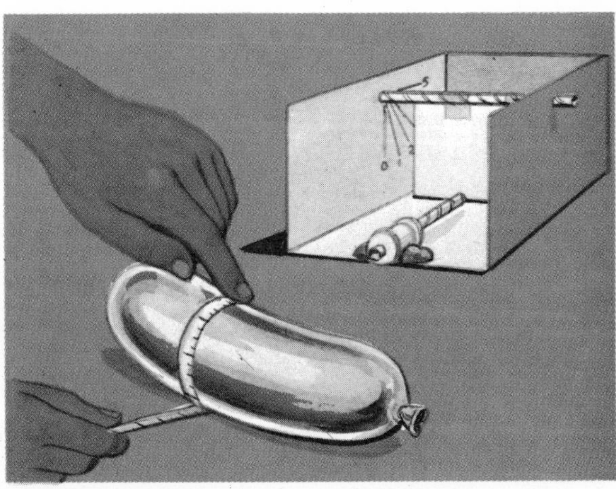

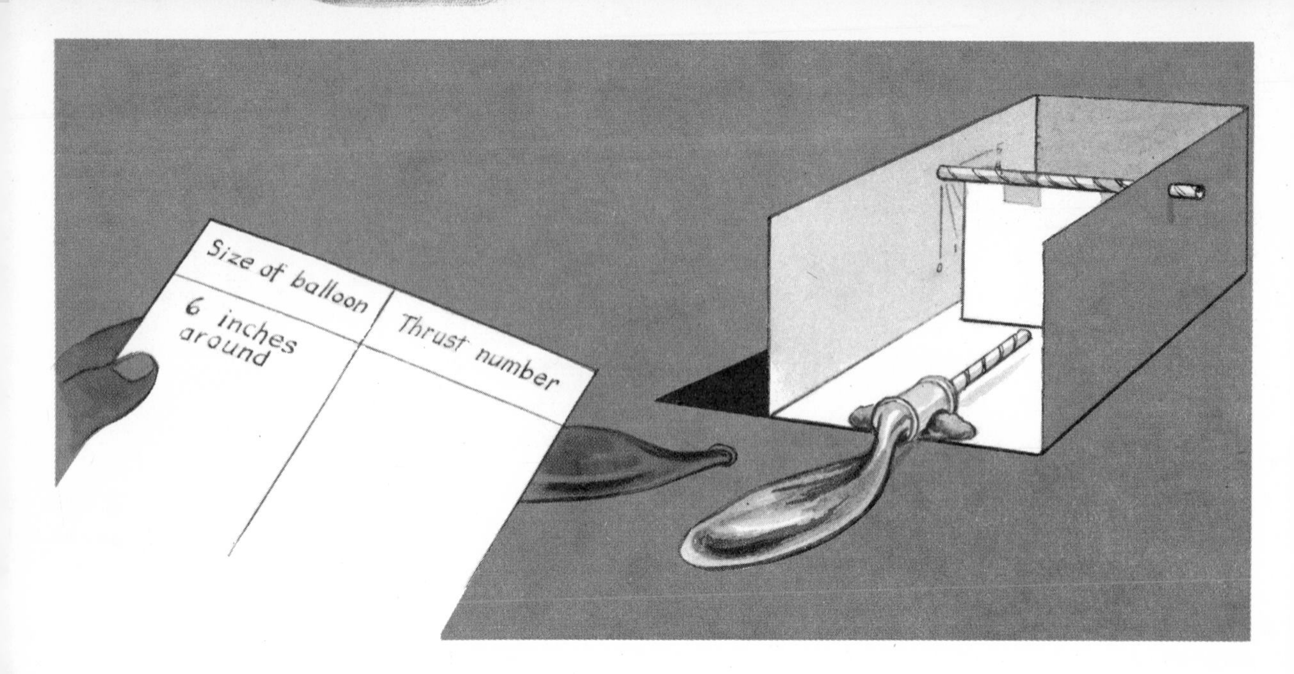

6. Place the opening of the balloon over the spool in the test stand. Let air escape from the balloon. Measure the thrust by watching to see how far the card moves along the scale. Record the thrust of the balloon.
7. Repeat steps 5 and 6 with different balloons. Blow up each to full size and measure it. Try some balloons of the same size blown up to the same size. Record the results.

Which have more thrust, the large balloons or the small balloons? Why? Why don't all balloons of the same size have the same thrust?

The thrust of a rocket engine depends upon the kind of fuel used, how fast the fuel burns, and the shape of the rocket's end. The greater the thrust, the more weight the rocket can carry and the faster it can travel.

Thrust is measured in pounds. Some of the first satellites were launched into space by a rocket with only 27,000 pounds thrust. Compare this to information about the latest rockets.

Satellite Rockets

Several rockets are joined together to launch satellites. Each rocket is a **stage** (stāj), or part, of the total rocket. Each stage has an engine and tanks for fuel and oxygen. One rocket engine fires, providing thrust. After this first stage has burned all its fuel, it separates from the other stages and is left behind. After the separation of one stage, another rocket fires and separates. Each rocket fires at a different time.

Each time a stage separates from the rocket, the rocket is smaller and weighs less. Why can the fuel of the remaining stages move the rocket faster?

What pulls everything on the earth?

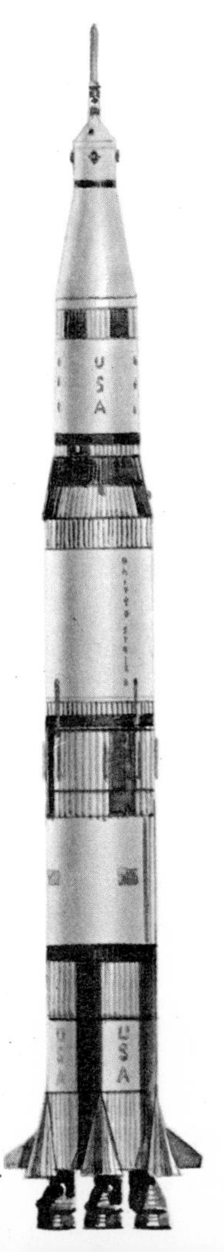

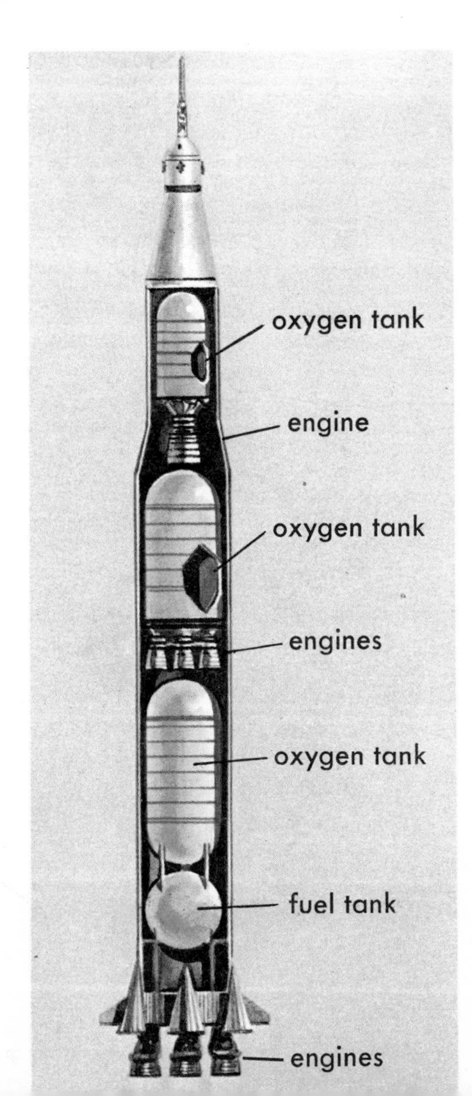

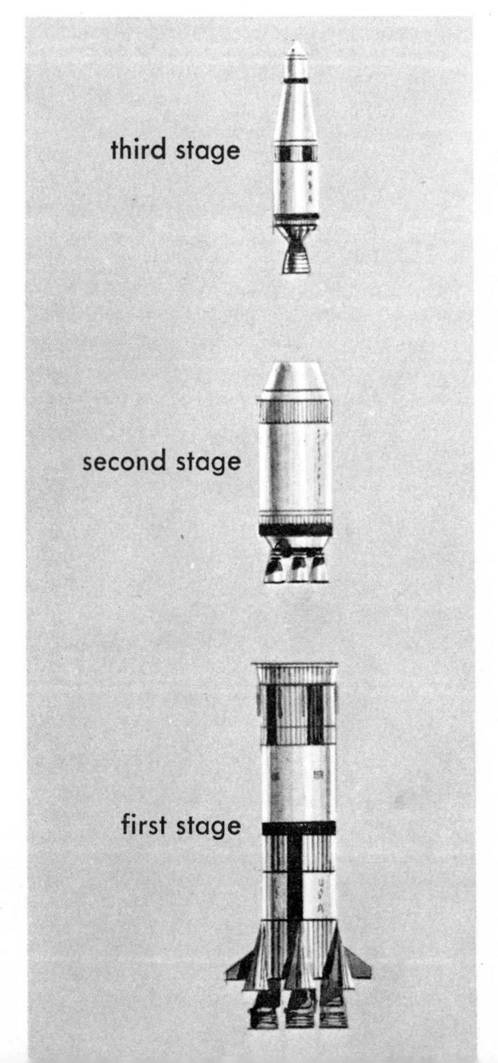

The satellite separates from the last stage. The **nose cone,** or front end, may also separate from the satellite. The nose cone and last-stage rocket may orbit with the satellite. How does the satellite stay in orbit?

Gravity pulls on everything on the earth. The heavier something is, the more strongly it is pulled toward the earth's surface. However, when an object on the end of a string is spun in a circle, what happens to the object? What can cause a force which will pull against gravity? What happens to the object when it stops moving?

Gravity pulls on a satellite, but as long as the satellite moves rapidly, it stays in orbit. If it begins to slow down, it may start to fall toward the earth. Explain the forces that keep a satellite in orbit.

Satellites in Orbit

Satellites do not usually orbit the earth in a circle. How is the shape of the orbit different from a circle?

Use a drawing compass to draw a circle on a piece of heavy cardboard. The circle should be four inches across. Use a ruler to draw a line through the center of the circle, from one side of the circle to the other. Put a thumbtack into the cardboard at each end of the line. Cut a piece of string one foot long and tie its ends together. Place the loop around the thumbtacks. Put a pencil inside the loop as shown in the picture. Move it around the circle as far away as the string will allow. Keep the string tight. How is the shape you just drew different from a circle? This shape is called an **ellipse** (i lips′).

If a satellite travels in an orbit that is a circle with the earth at the center, will it always be the same distance from the earth? Will the satellite always be the same distance from the earth if it has an orbit that is an ellipse?

Scientists can figure out in advance what the high and low points of the orbit of a satellite will be. They select the orbit of a satellite according to the kind of information they wish to obtain.

Tracking Satellites

Once a satellite is in orbit, it is important that scientists know where it is at all times. Using instruments to follow a satellite in orbit is known as **satellite tracking** (trak′ ing).

What can scientists learn by tracking a satellite?

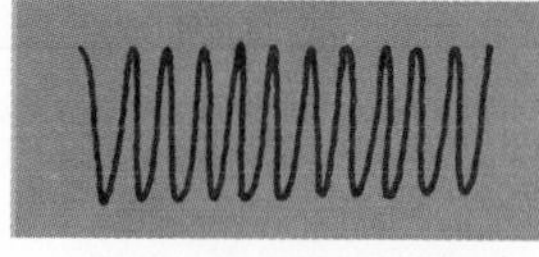

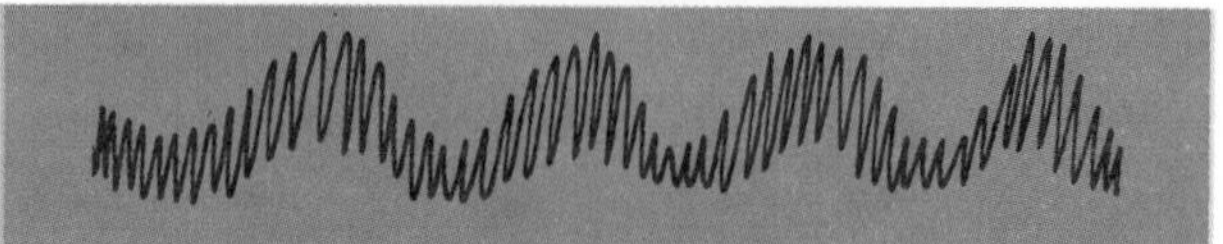

A. This radio telescope picks up signals from satellites.

B. Records of some satellites' signals

One way to track a satellite is by means of radio signals. Each satellite has at least one radio. Signals from the satellite's radio are picked up by large antennas on the earth at receiving stations. Such receiving stations are located all over the world, on land and on special ships at sea. Each time a satellite makes a trip around the earth, its signals can be picked up by one or more of these stations. By tracking a satellite, scientists can figure out its speed and direction as well as its distance from the earth.

Satellites have also been tracked by large camera-telescopes. Camera-telescopes photograph the satellites as they pass. Even when there are clouds, photographs may be taken. A kind of film is used which takes a photograph of the heat rays which a satellite reflects.

A type of camera which photographs satellites passing overhead

Photograph of satellite entering earth's atmosphere

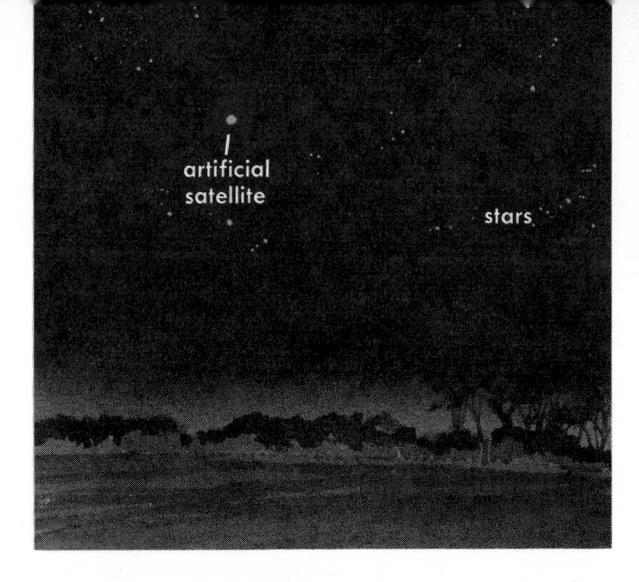

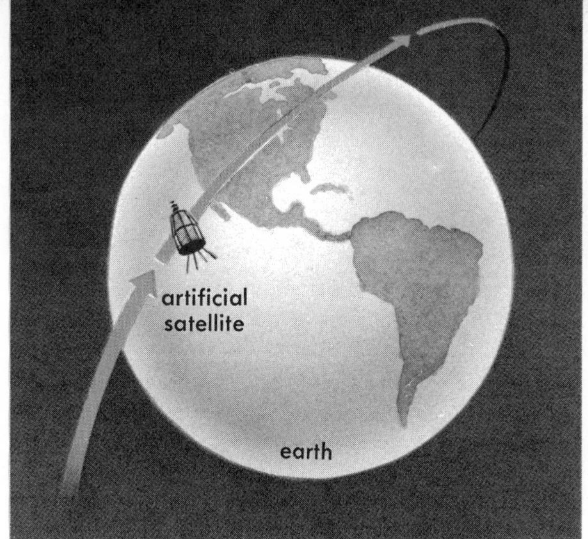

Would you like to try watching for a satellite? Watch the newspapers for announcements and you may be able to see one of the largest kinds of satellites without a telescope or binoculars. Usually the newspaper will tell you when to watch and the direction in which to look.

A satellite moves around the earth in a west to east direction. Will it always travel across the sky in the same direction? What do you know about the way the earth rotates? A satellite will sometimes be seen traveling from northwest to southeast. At other times, it may be viewed traveling from the southwest to the northeast. Can you explain why?

DISCOVER

Why does a satellite's orbit seem to change direction?

What You Need

large hoop
tape
globe

As a satellite moves, what is always turning beneath it?

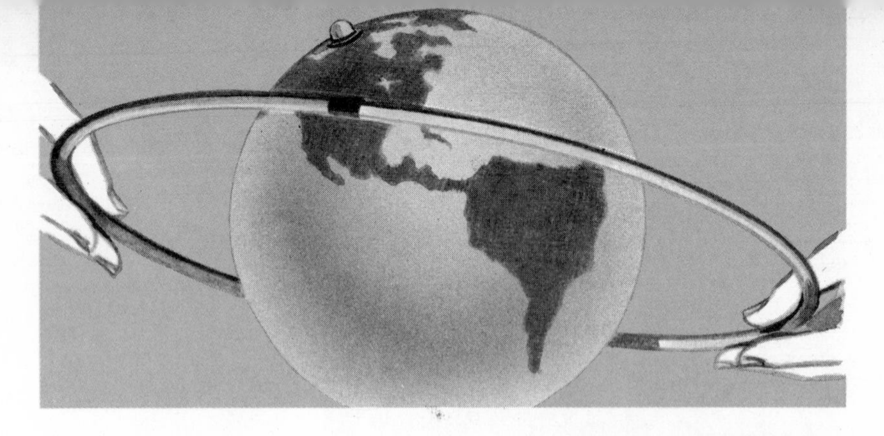

1. Place a piece of tape around one place on the hoop to represent the satellite. The hoop shows the orbit of the satellite.
2. Hold the hoop at an angle around the globe. Turn the globe so that you are facing North America.
3. Move the hoop so the path of the satellite crosses the United States from the state of Washington to Florida. This orbit is northwest to southeast.
4. Keep the hoop at the same angle. Move to the other side of the globe. Turn the globe so that you are again facing North America. Observe the satellite orbit again.

If you were watching from earth, in which direction would the satellite in this experiment first be seen? In which direction would it be moving?

Although the satellite travels in the same direction all the time, the earth turns beneath it. For this reason a satellite may appear to travel across the United States from northwest to southeast. At other times, it may appear to travel from the southwest to northeast.

Seeing Satellites

Can an artificial satellite reflect light from the sun? Can the satellite always be seen?

DISCOVER

If a satellite passes over the place where you live during the day or late at night, can it be seen easily?

What You Need

aluminum foil	flashlight or projector
white thread	globe
all-purpose glue	

1. Make a small ball of aluminum foil to represent a satellite. Fasten it to a white thread with glue.
2. Shine the light from a strong flashlight or a projector on the globe. Darken the room.
3. Stand facing the dark side of the globe. Have someone hold the thread so that the "satellite" hangs between the light and the globe. Why would the satellite be hard to see during the day?
4. Now stand where you can see the globe half lighted and half darkened. Have someone hold the satellite so that it is in the shadow of the globe. Why would it be hard to see the satellite at night?
5. Stay where you are. Have someone hold the satellite so that it is directly opposite you. Can the satellite be seen easily now? Why?

When can you see a satellite most easily?

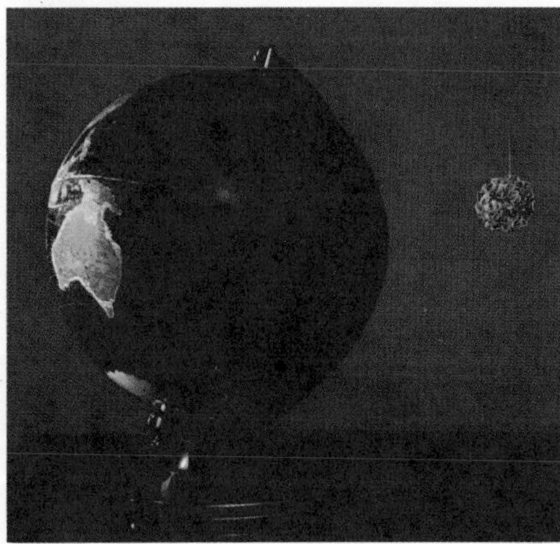

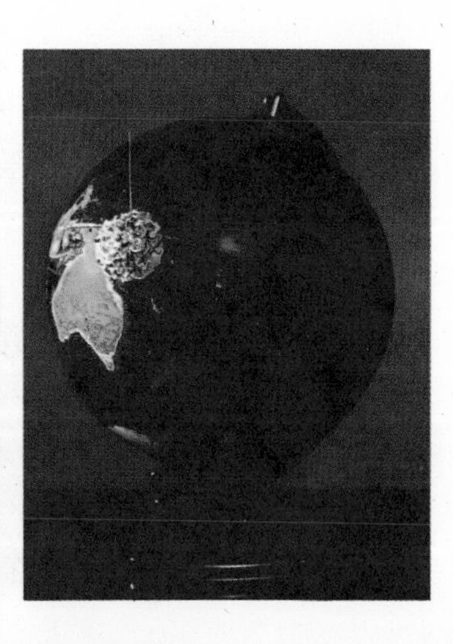

Is a man-made satellite much like the moon? When can a satellite be seen? Is it lighted by the sun? In a daylight sky, the lighted part of the moon can sometimes be seen because the moon is quite large. It reflects enough light to be seen even in daylight. Why can a satellite not be easily seen in the daylight sky? How does the light it reflects compare to the brightness of the sunlight?

You can usually see the moon at night because it does not often pass into the earth's shadow. A satellite is closer to the earth than the moon is and is smaller than the moon. A satellite is in the earth's shadow for part of every trip around the earth. Why might you not be able to see it at times?

A satellite is seen most easily shortly after sunset or just before sunrise. At these times, the satellite is usually well lighted by the sun and may be seen in a dimly lighted sky.

Satellites—Up and Down

Some satellites stay in orbit only a few weeks, while others stay in orbit for months or years. Have you wondered why some satellites stay up longer than others?

A. Scientists think the moon has been a satellite of the earth for millions of years.

B. Artificial satellites vary in how long they stay in orbit.

A

B

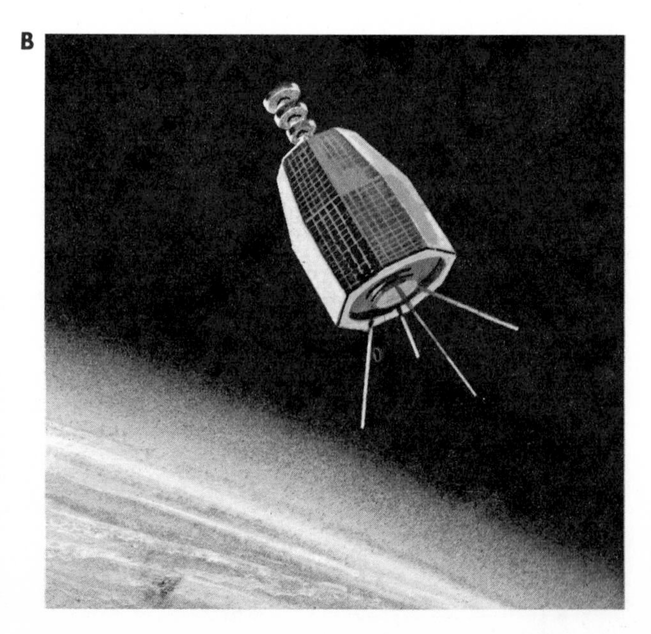

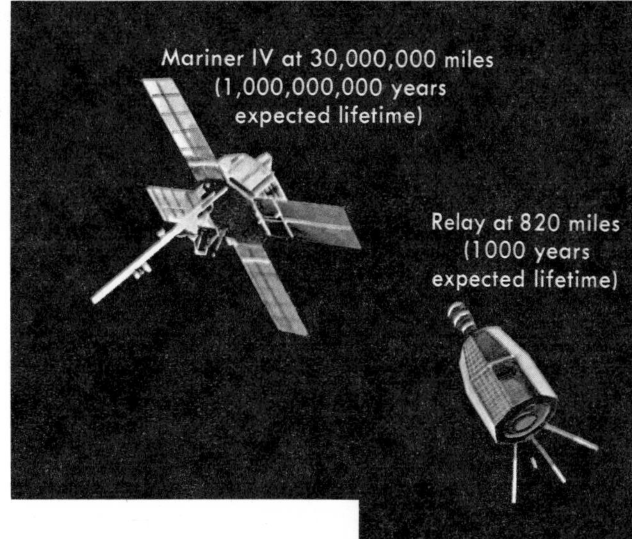

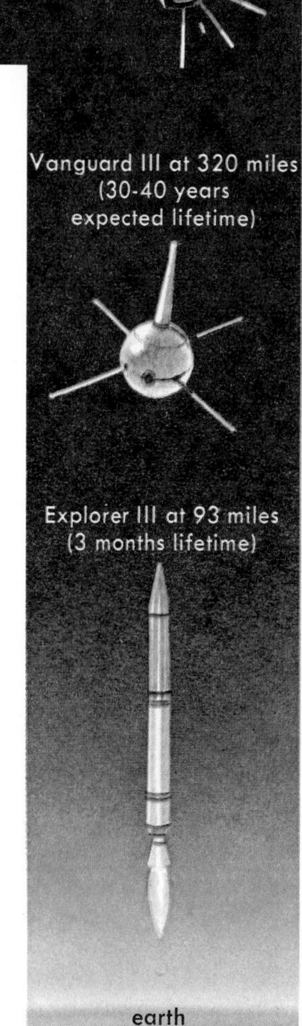

Get two pieces of paper exactly the same size. Crumple one piece into a ball. Drop both pieces of paper at the same time. Which falls faster? Can you explain why one piece falls faster than the other?

Do both pieces of paper have the same mass? Do both fall through air? Would air push upward more on one piece than on the other? Why do you think so? The force holding back something which passes through or over a material is called **resistance** (ri zis′ təns).

The air around the earth extends outward for hundreds of miles. Do you think there are more air molecules closer to the earth than farther out? Why? Would air near the earth have more resistance than air farther out?

How long a satellite stays in orbit depends partly upon how closely it travels to the earth in its orbit and how heavy it is. Would a satellite which passes through more air be slowed down more? The more it slows down, the sooner a satellite is pulled to earth by gravity. Why might a satellite that comes within three hundred miles of the earth last only a few months? A satellite that passes the earth farther out may last for years. What happens to satellites which have been pulled out of orbit by the earth's gravity?

Satellite during reentry into the earth's atmosphere

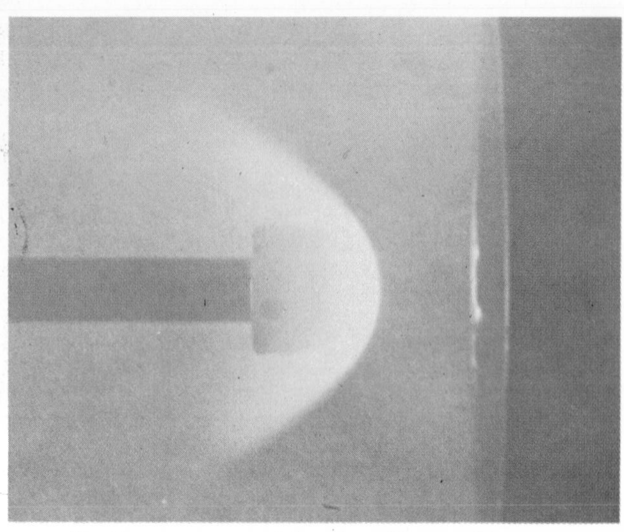

Testing a material for the effects of heat

Satellites fall, but do they reach the earth? As a satellite falls through the air around the earth, air molecules bump into it. The bumping of air molecules against the satellite at this speed causes much heat. The satellite heats to high temperatures. What happens to something which is heated to very high temperatures in the presence of oxygen? What do you think happens to a satellite which falls toward earth?

Satellite Instruments

Before the first man-made satellites were launched from earth, scientists knew very little about the space beyond earth. There were many questions. For example, are there many molecules of gases or pieces of matter in space? Do you have many questions, too? By sending instruments into space in satellites, scientists are learning more. And they are discovering new questions to be answered by further exploration.

This picture shows some of the instruments which have been helpful in learning about space. Information which the instruments gather is recorded by a special tape recorder. When a satellite passes over radio tracking stations on the earth, the information stored on tape is sent to earth as radio signals.

Instruments used in a satellite must be small and lightweight. One satellite carried a radio the size of a book of matches. Can you explain why the instruments are usually specially made? Scientists and engineers have been hard at work making satellite instruments smaller and smaller.

What is a solar cell?

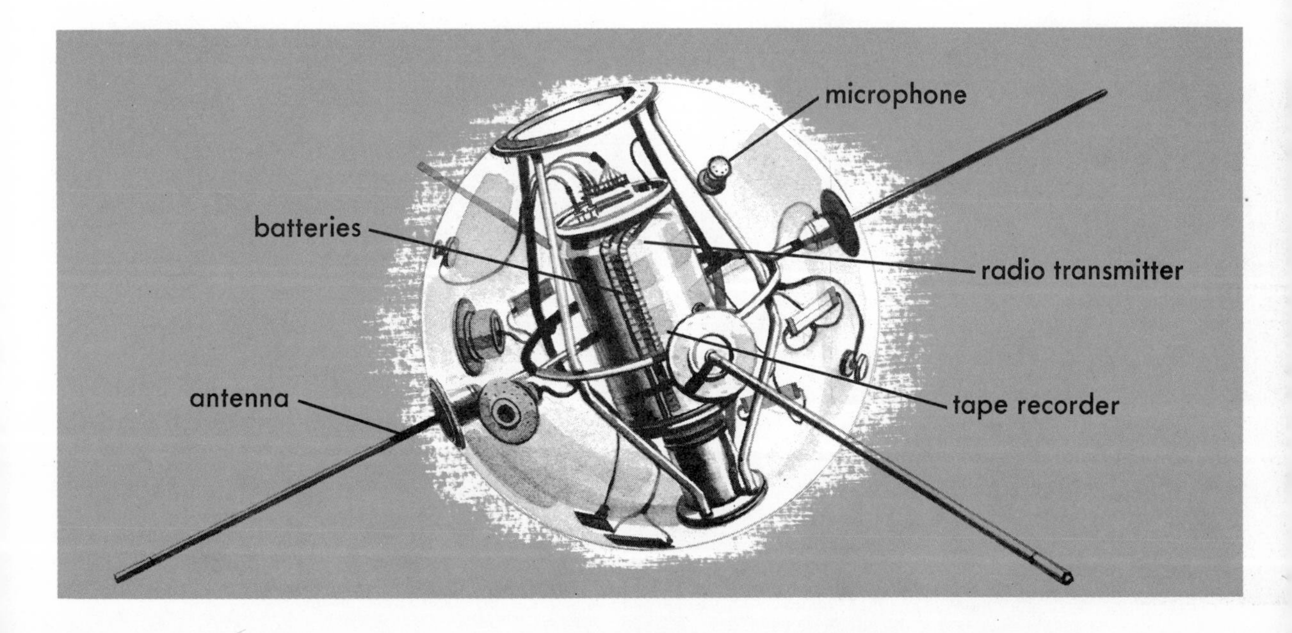

Thousands of solar cells are in this section of a spacecraft.

No matter how small the instruments of a satellite may be, they need to be operated by some source of power. What might produce electric power for satellites?

Have you ever heard of a **solar** (sō′ lər) **cell?** A solar cell looks like a thin piece of metal. When light shines on a solar cell, electricity is produced. Why would solar cells be valuable for use in satellites? Solar cells produce electricity as long as they are in sunlight. But each solar cell gives off only a small amount of electricity. Many must be used in each satellite to produce the electricity needed.

Man-made satellites may be grouped by the kinds of jobs they do. **Weather satellites** have instruments which send weather information back to earth. Some weather information is recorded by equipment in or on these satellites. Camera equipment photographs the earth's weather.

Satellites which send radio signals have been launched as **navigation** (nav′ ə gā′ shən) **satellites.** Planes and ships receiving these satellite signals use them to find their position. Even in stormy weather, navigation satellites help planes and ships to stay on course.

A. Communication satellite

B. Weather satellite

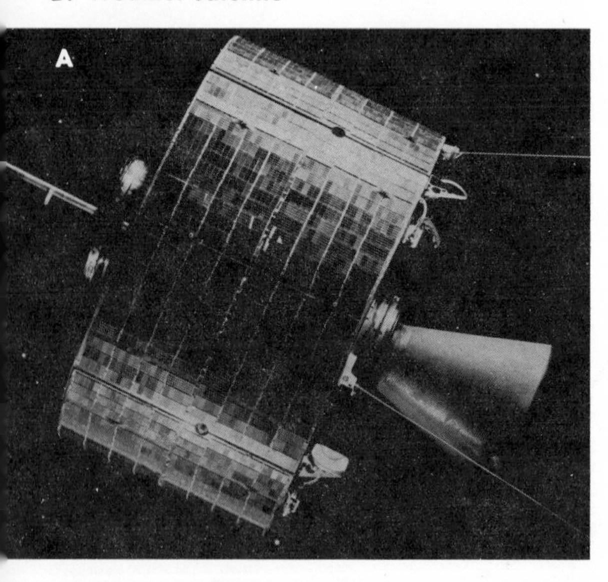

A. Experimental satellite

B. Communication satellite

A whole series of satellites which have special equipment for detecting and recording information have been launched. These are **experimental satellites.** These satellites have measured radiation from the sun, measured some effects of earth's magnetism, and tested the way space travel affects living things.

Communication (kə mū′ nə kā′ shən) **satellites** are launched to help in sending messages from one place on earth to another. Radio, television, and telephone messages have been sent using communication satellites. If you have ever seen live television programs that came from across the oceans, they were probably sent by satellite.

Satellites are also used for military purposes. Some of these are communication or navigation satellites built for use by the armed forces. Others are launched with equipment for making tests. These are all satellites which orbit within the earth's atmosphere.

What jobs do some other man-made satellites do?

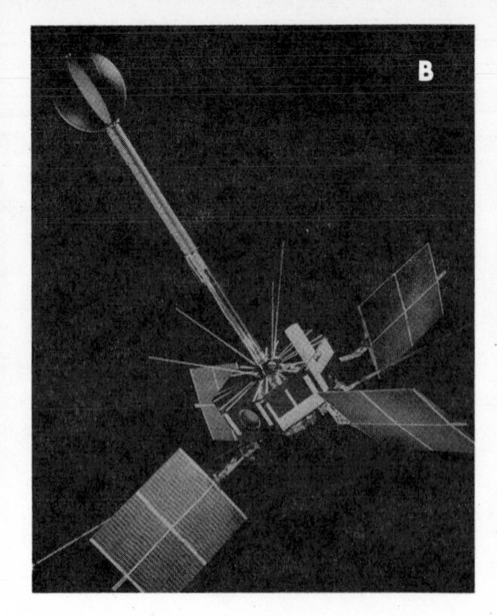

A. Moon probe

B. Planetary probe

C. Interplanetary probe

Another group of spacecraft have been sent far into space. Moon probes have been sent to and around the moon. **Planetary** (plan′ ə ter′ ē) **probes** have passed close to certain planets and have collected information about them. Some spacecraft are **interplanetary** (in′ tər plan′ ə ter′ ē) **probes.** These gather information about space between heavenly bodies.

Make a chart like the one below and use it to record some information on earth satellites and space probes.

Spacecraft	Date Launched	Importance
Explorer I	Jan., 1958	first U.S. satellite
Vanguard I	March, 1958	discovered irregular shape of earth
Project Score	Dec., 1958	broadcast voices from space
Vanguard II	Feb., 1959	first weather satellite
Pioneer V	March, 1960	gathered information about deep space
Mariner II	Aug., 1962	gathered information about Venus
Ranger VII	July, 1964	took photographs of moon
Luna 10	March, 1966	first satellite to orbit moon
Surveyor 3	April, 1967	dug up soil on moon
Zond 5	Sept., 1968	orbited moon, made soft landing on earth
Mariner IX	May, 1971	took photographs of Mars

Exploring Your Learnings

Here are some ideas and vocabulary. What do these mean to you?

Words to Use

satellite (p. 252)
artificial satellites (p. 252)
natural satellites (p. 252)
launched (p. 252)
thrust (p. 252)
action-reaction (p. 253)
stage (p. 259)
nose cone (p. 260)
ellipse (p. 261)
satellite tracking (p. 261)
resistance (p. 267)
solar cell (p. 270)
weather satellites (p. 270)
navigation satellites (p. 270)
experimental satellites (p. 271)
communication satellites (p. 271)
planetary probes (p. 272)
interplanetary probes (p. 272)

Ideas to Use

1. A satellite is any object in space that travels in an orbit around a larger body.
2. Whenever two objects act on one another, the force of the first object on the second object is equal to the force of the second object on the first object.
3. Both jet and rocket engines provide thrust by action-reaction forces.
4. The thrust of a rocket engine depends upon the kind of fuel used, how fast the fuel burns, and the shape of the opening through which the gases escape.

Gemini 6 was a satellite that orbited the earth.

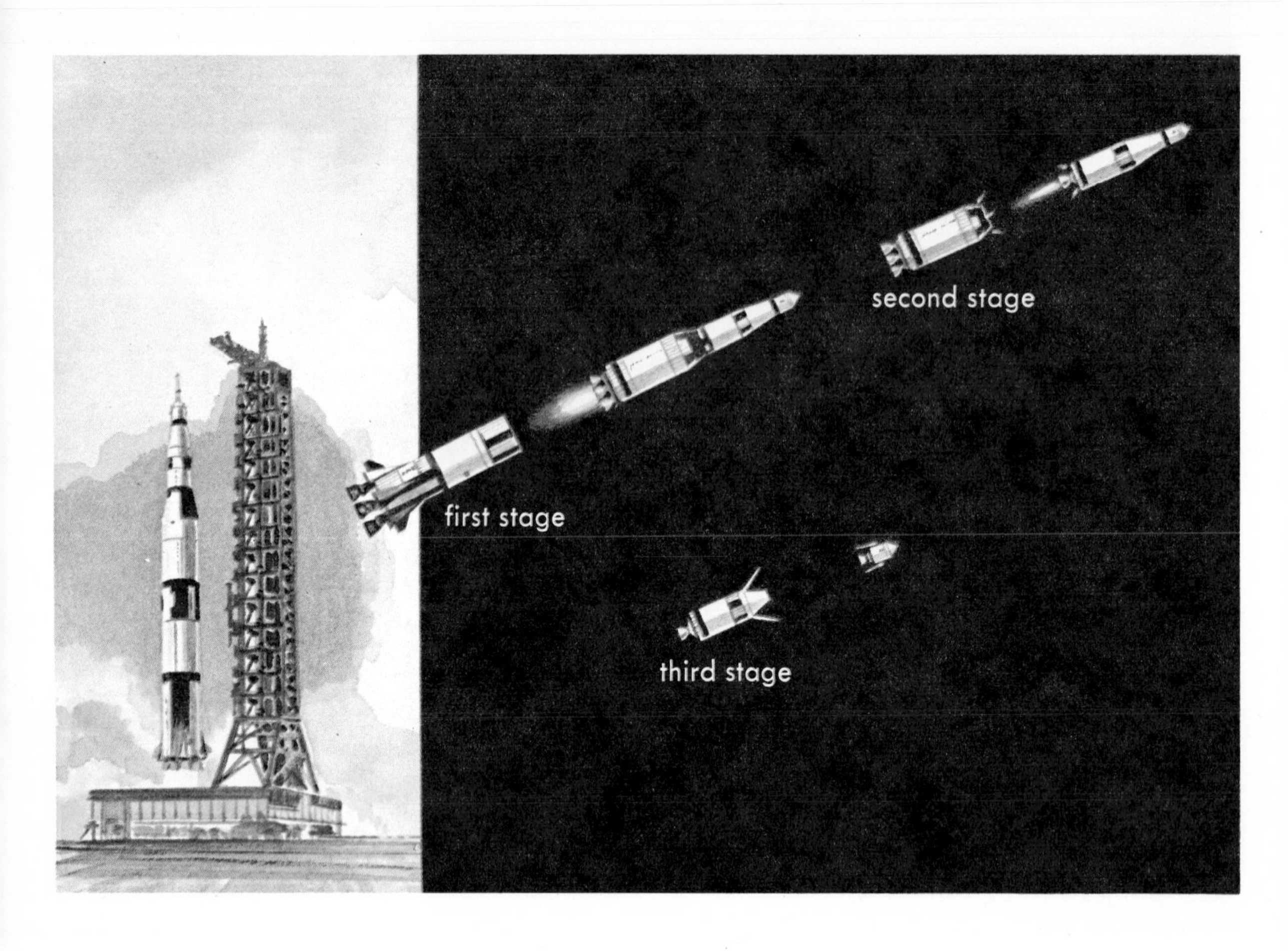

5. After a rocket stage has burned all its fuel and oxygen, it usually separates from the other stages.
6. A satellite is kept in orbit by the force of gravity and by the forward force of the satellite.
7. By tracking a satellite, scientists can figure out its speed and direction as well as its distance from the earth.
8. How long a satellite stays in orbit depends partly upon how close it travels to the earth in its orbit and how heavy it is.
9. No matter how small the instruments of a satellite may be, they need to be operated by some source of power.

Using Your Ideas

(Do not write in this book.)

1. Compare the orbits of various satellites. Find out which satellite has remained or will remain in orbit longest. Why do some remain in orbit longer than others? What is the high point of an orbit called? What is the low point of an orbit called?
2. Find out what makes a water sprinkler like the one in the picture turn.

3. Find a way to launch a two-stage rocket using balloons to give thrust.
4. Find an article about a recently launched satellite or space probe in a newspaper or magazine. Keep a record of what happens to the satellite or space probe and report on it.
5. Read about the work of Robert H. Goddard and Wernher Von Braun.

10

Plants and Their Food

Without plants, there would be no animals. All animals depend upon plants for food. Some food you eat comes from plants. Fruits and vegetables are plant products. Some food you eat comes from animals. Milk and meat are animal products. Indirectly that food also comes from plants. Cows eat grass. Chickens eat seeds.

All living things must have food in order to live, grow, and change. Have you ever noticed how rapidly some plants grow and change? If you have ever mowed a lawn, you know how fast grass grows. Branches of many trees grow a foot or more each year. Some plants not only increase in size, but also produce fruits like the ones in this picture. How do plants get their food?

Green Plants: Chemical Laboratories

Plants need some source of food to grow and change. A green plant can produce its own food. However, a plant must obtain the materials with which it makes food. A green plant is a kind of chemical laboratory where chemicals from air and soil are changed into a kind of sugar called **glucose** (glü′ kōs′).

Glucose is a chemical compound. A glucose molecule contains six carbon atoms, twelve hydrogen atoms, and six oxygen atoms. Can you write the formula for glucose? Knowing that glucose is $C_6H_{12}O_6$ may not mean much until you know more about how this sugar is formed.

A plant must contain a special substance before it can make glucose. Do you know what this substance is?

DISCOVER

What substance does a plant that makes glucose contain?

What You Need

- fresh geranium leaf
- test tube
- alcohol
- pan
- water
- hot plate
- tongs

1. Put the fresh geranium leaf into the test tube and cover it with alcohol.
2. Put a pan of water on the hot plate. Use the tongs to hold the test tube in the water.
3. Heat the water until the alcohol in the test tube boils.

What color is the alcohol after it has boiled with the leaf in it? Where do you think the color came from? Many plants contain a green chemical compound called **chlorophyll** (klô′ rə fil). Only a plant which has chlorophyll can make glucose. A plant that contains chlorophyll is called a green plant. Chlorophyll in green plants can trap sunlight and use it in a way that causes the chemical changes necessary to form glucose. Without sunlight, chlorophyll cannot help to make glucose.

Leaves

Other things occur in a plant when glucose is formed. One important process occurs in the leaves of green plants.

DISCOVER

What is one process that occurs in the leaves of green plants?

What You Need

aquarium plant (elodea)	water
test tube	tape
small pan	magnifying glass

1. Put an aquarium plant such as elodea into the test tube.
2. Fill the pan three-fourths full of water. Put the test tube into the pan so that the test tube fills completely with water. Be sure the plant stays inside the test tube.
3. Be sure that there is no air in the test tube. Keep the open end of the test tube underwater. Raise the closed end of the test tube as shown in the picture. Do not let any of the water run out of the test tube.
4. Keeping the open end of the test tube underwater, tape the test tube to the side of the pan. At least half of the test tube should be out of the water.
5. Set the pan with the test tube and plant in bright sunlight for several hours. Watch the leaves of the plant with a magnifying glass.

What do you see? What happens to the water in the test tube? Can you see tiny bubbles collecting on the leaves? Where did these bubbles come from? What kind of gas do you think the bubbles are made of? Do leaves give off a gas?

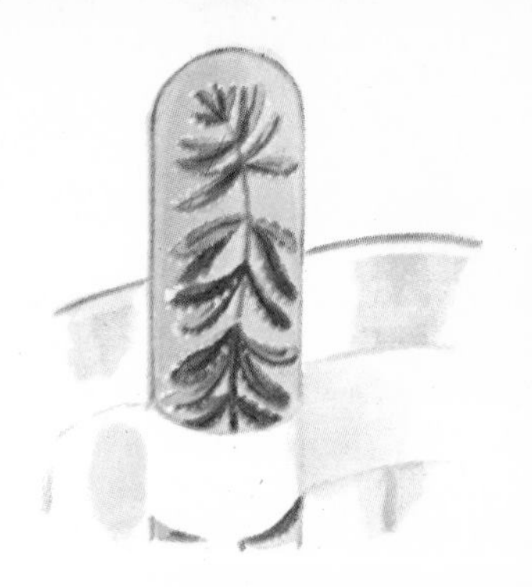

FIND OUT

Do the leaves of a green plant take in a gas?

EXPERIMENT

What You Need

limewater tablets	potted geranium plant
2 drinking glasses	pot of soil
2 coffee cans	label marked "one"
fresh grass clippings	label marked "two"
2 large cardboard boxes	teaspoon
scissors	water
tape	plastic wrap

1. Make limewater by dissolving a limewater tablet in water. Follow the instructions on the limewater tablet package. Remember that limewater becomes cloudy when exposed to carbon dioxide gas.
2. Fill the two coffee cans with fresh grass clippings. As they decay, the clippings will produce carbon dioxide by slow oxidation.
3. Cut the tops off the cardboard boxes. Seal all other openings in the boxes with tape.
4. Put the geranium plant, a can of grass clippings, and a glass of limewater into one cardboard box. Label this box "one."

5. Put the pot of soil, the other can of grass clippings, and a glass of limewater into the second box. Label this box "two."
6. Add three or four teaspoons of water to the pot of soil, to the geranium plant, and to the grass clippings in each box. Use tape to seal both boxes with plastic wrap.
7. Place both boxes where the plastic-covered tops will get direct sunlight. After two days, remove the glasses of limewater. What difference do you notice between the two glasses of limewater?

Did the limewater in box "one" become cloudy? Did the limewater in box "two" become cloudy? Did something decay in both boxes? What was different about the two boxes? What happened to the carbon dioxide in the box where the limewater stayed clear? What gas do the leaves of a green plant take in?

When plants produce glucose, they take in carbon dioxide and give off oxygen. What gas do animals take in from the air? What gas do animals breathe out? Plants also take in oxygen and give off carbon dioxide, but while they are making glucose it is hardly noticeable. This is because they take in much more carbon dioxide than oxygen and give off much more oxygen than carbon dioxide when they produce glucose.

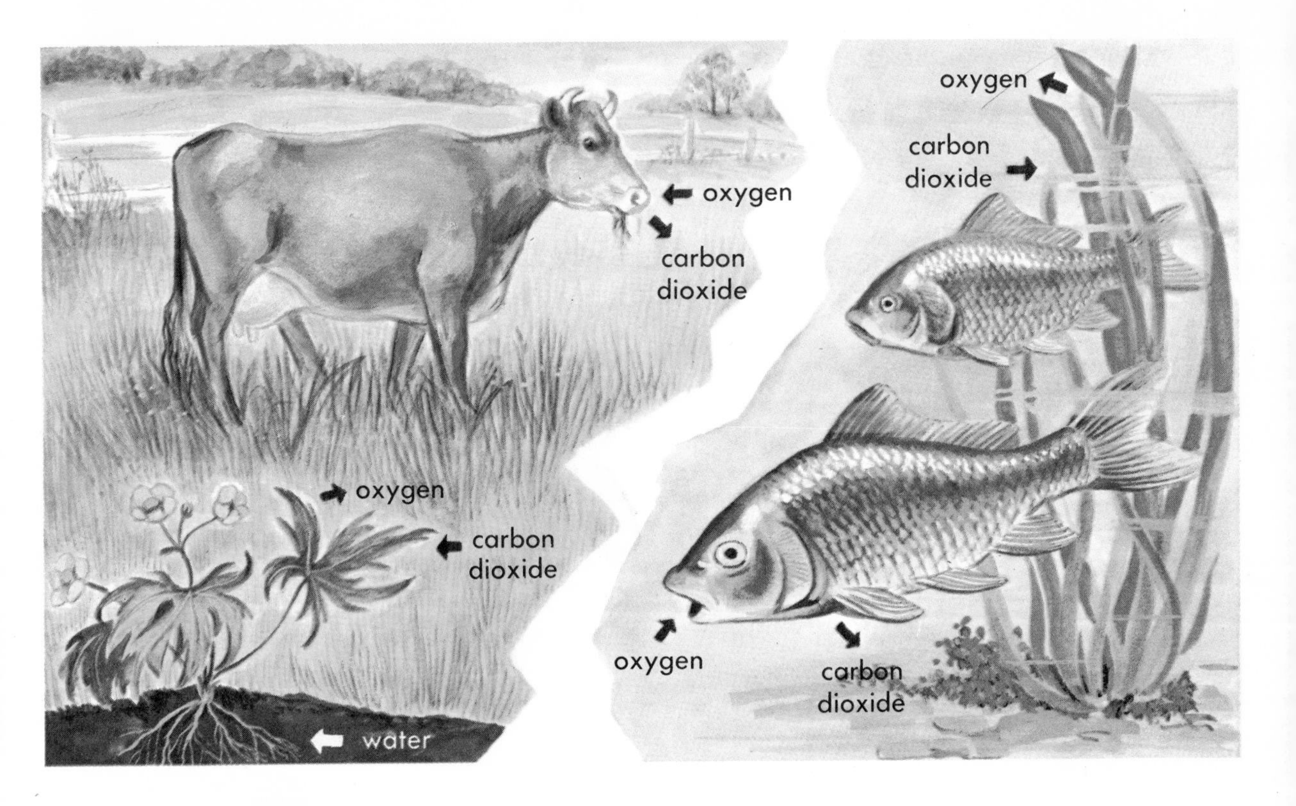

Plants and animals exchange gases in the air. Animals and plants that live in water exchange gases, too. However, the oxygen and carbon dioxide gases are dissolved in water.

Roots

Leaves can take from the air one compound that the plant needs. Both the carbon and the oxygen in carbon dioxide can be used to make glucose molecules. Look at the formula for glucose again. What other element is needed to produce glucose? What is the formula for water? From what compound might a plant get the other element of glucose? Where might the oxygen a plant gives off come from?

How do most plants take water from soil?

DISCOVER

How are the roots of a green plant important to the production of glucose?

What You Need

African violet or English ivy
scissors
flowerpot
clean sand
shallow dish
water
newspaper

1. Remove a leaf from the stem of an African violet plant or cut off a new branch of an English ivy plant.
2. Fill a small flowerpot with clean sand.
3. Push the leaf or branch about one inch into the sand.
4. Put the flowerpot on a shallow dish. You can keep the sand in the flowerpot moist by adding water to the dish. Keep the sand moist at all times.
5. Put the plant where it will receive sunlight for at least a few hours each day.
6. After two weeks, carefully remove the plant from the flowerpot. The best way to take a plant from a flowerpot without hurting the plant is to carefully shake the plant and sand over a piece of newspaper. Examine the plant. What do you observe?

Did the plant have sunlight? Could the plant get carbon dioxide from the air? Clean sand does not have any chemicals in a form which plants can use. What else did the plant use? Is water a compound containing an element a plant needs to produce glucose? To take water from the soil, most plants need roots. The parts of some plants, such as the African violet and English ivy, can produce roots which help keep the plants alive.

Why is water important for plants?

DISCOVER

Can plant roots take in materials dissolved in water as freely as they take in plain water?

What You Need

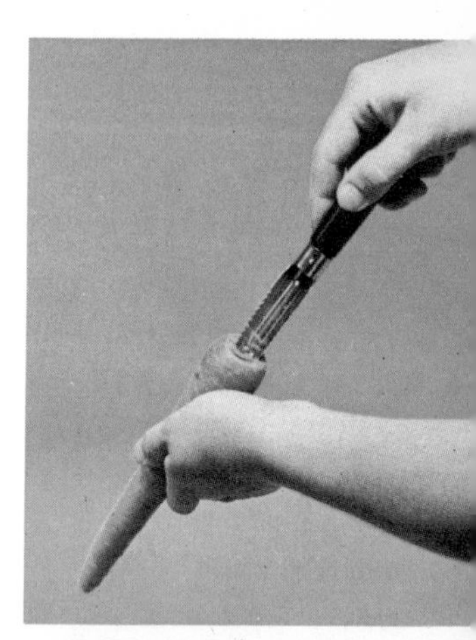

fresh carrot	tablespoon
apple corer	sugar
one-hole rubber stopper	water
plastic tubing	2 drinking glasses
wax or clay	grease pencil or marker

1. Get a carrot that has a wide top. Use an apple corer to hollow out the center of the carrot about one inch deep. Find a one-hole rubber stopper to fit the opening.
2. Put the end of the plastic tubing into the hole in the stopper. Seal the plastic tube to the stopper with clay or wax.
3. Dissolve two tablespoons of sugar in a half glass of water. Fill the hole in the carrot with the sugar water and put the stopper in place. Some of the liquid will probably move up into the plastic tube. Seal the space between the stopper and the carrot with wax or clay. Mark the height of the sugar water in the tube.

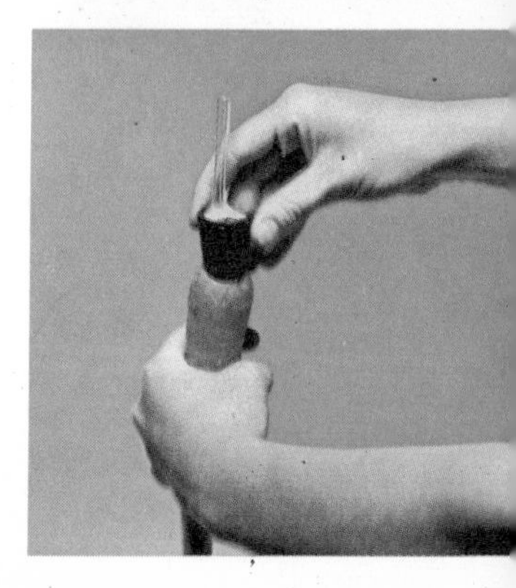

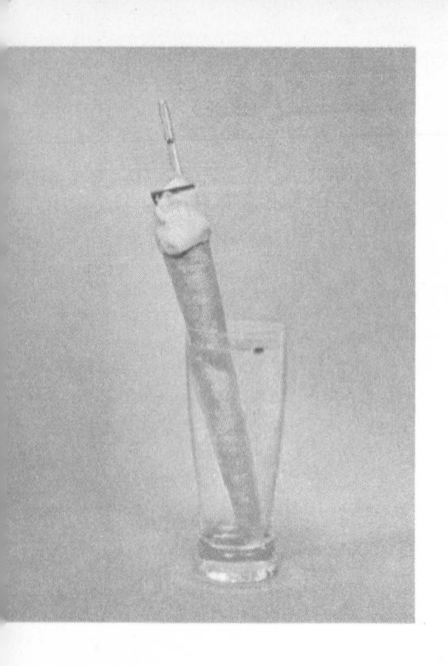

4. Set the carrot in a glass of plain water. Mark the height of the plain water in the glass. Observe the plastic tube after a few hours. What change do you notice?

What happened to the sugar water in the plastic tube? What happened to the plain water in the drinking glass? Does plain water pass through the carrot and mix with the sugar water? Does sugar water pass through the carrot into the plain water? You may wish to taste the glass of water and find out. Can sugar water pass through the carrot as freely as plain water can?

Some materials dissolved in water can enter and leave a plant rather freely. Other materials cannot.

Water is an important compound for plants because many chemicals can dissolve in it. Some elements and some chemical compounds dissolved in water can enter a plant through the roots. The plant uses these elements and compounds as it grows and changes.

Stems

Carbon dioxide enters a plant through the leaves. Water enters a plant through the roots. Carbon dioxide and water are used to make glucose in the leaves. How does the water get to the leaves?

DISCOVER

How are stems of a green plant important to the production of glucose?

What You Need

geranium or coleus plant	water
scissors	red food coloring
drinking glass	magnifying glass

1. Cut a young branch off a geranium or coleus plant. Put the cut end into a drinking glass half filled with water. This should be done right away so that the cut end is not in the air very long.
2. Add ten to twenty drops of food coloring to the water. Mix the food coloring and water completely.
3. After two hours, remove the stem from the water. Cut off about one inch of the stem from the bottom. Look at the cut edge through the magnifying glass. What do you observe?
4. Cut the one-inch piece of stem in half the long way. Examine the cut edges through the magnifying glass. What do you observe?
5. Cut across one of the leaves. Examine the cut edges through the magnifying glass. What do you observe? If you do not see any color in the leaves, put the stem back into the water for two more hours. Then, repeat this step.

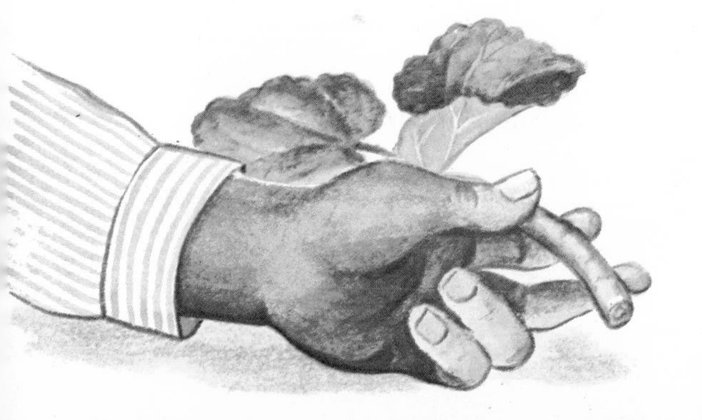

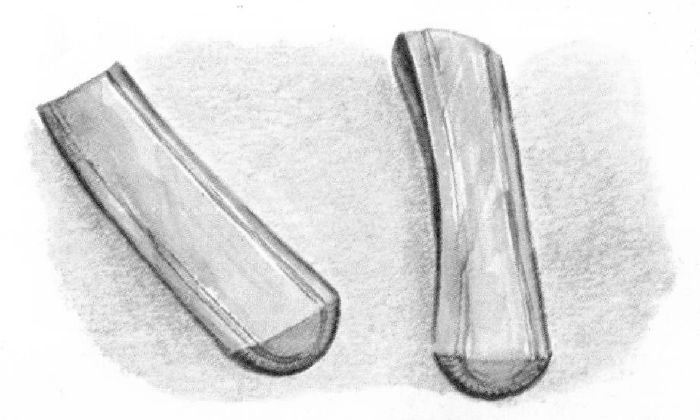

Where do you see color in the cut stem? Where do you see color in the cut leaves? The food coloring marks the path water takes as it moves up the stem. What do you notice about the path which water takes in both the stem and leaf? A stem has bundles of tiny tubes. Water travels from the roots to the leaves through these tubes. Why are stems important to the production of glucose?

Plant Products

When a green plant produces glucose, carbon dioxide from the air, and water from the soil are combined in a chemical reaction which is powered by the sunlight trapped by chlorophyll. This process of making glucose is called **photosynthesis** (fō tə′ sin′ thə səs). *Photo* means "light," and *synthesis* means "to make by putting together." Photosynthesis means putting together with light. What happens to glucose once it has been produced?

DISCOVER

How is glucose used in the leaves of a plant?

What You Need

aluminum foil
geranium plant

1. Make an envelope of aluminum foil as shown in the picture. Place it over one leaf of a geranium plant.
2. Put the plant in sunlight, and water it each day.
3. After three days, remove the aluminum foil from the leaf. What do you observe?

What has happened to the leaf which did not get any sunlight? How is this leaf different from the other leaves of the plant? Does this leaf contain chlorophyll? How can you find out if the leaf contains chlorophyll?

Some of the glucose produced in the leaves of a green plant is used as food in that part of the plant. The glucose may be used by the plant as it grows, or the glucose may be used to keep the parts of the leaf alive. Some glucose is used to produce other chemical compounds a plant must have to live. One of these compounds is chlorophyll. Why is chlorophyll necessary to keep a plant alive?

The green parts of a plant live and grow because they produce and use glucose. Are all parts of a plant green? Could any part of a plant which is underground produce glucose? Explain your answer. Many parts of a plant cannot produce chlorophyll.

Can a plant make sugar water?

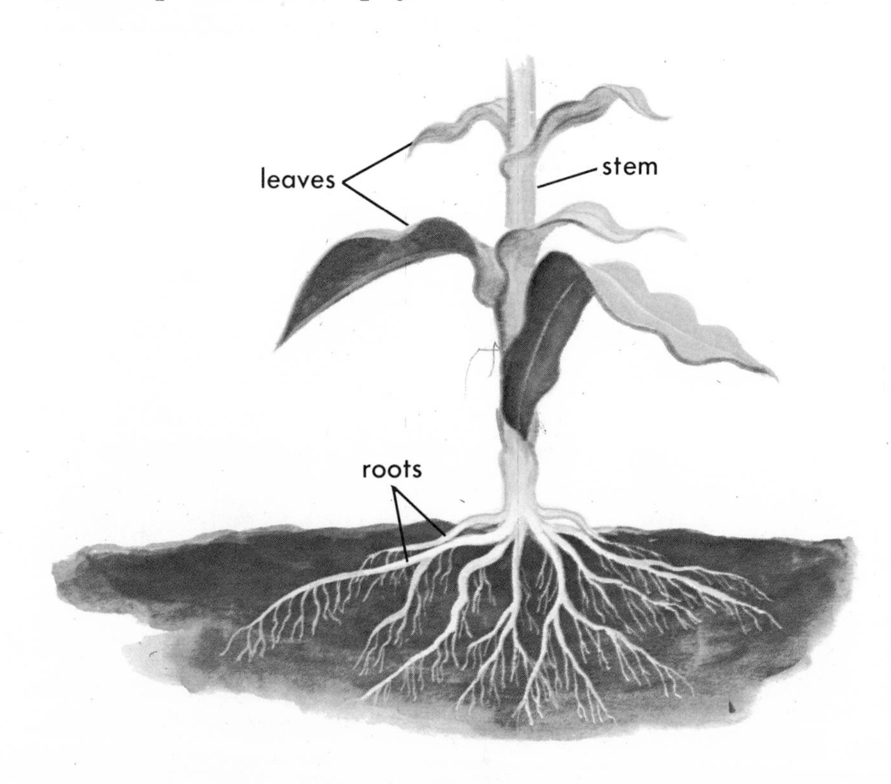

DISCOVER

How do the parts of a plant which are not green get the food they need to live and grow?

What You Need

geranium plant	water
scissors	red food coloring
drinking glass	

1. Cut a young branch off the geranium plant. Carefully cut all the leaves off the branch.
2. Add ten or twenty drops of food coloring to a drinking glass half full of water. Move the glass around until the food coloring is mixed with the water.
3. Put the branch into the glass of water so that the top part of the branch is underwater.
4. After two hours, take the branch out of the water and cut it in half. Examine the cut parts of the stem. What do you observe?

Was the branch upside down in the glass? Did the water still travel through the tubes in the stem? Do you think that water with chemicals dissolved in it can travel down a stem as well as up a stem?

Can sugar dissolve in water? Water containing sugar travels down the stem to parts of the plant which cannot produce their own food.

Water containing dissolved sugar which a plant has made is sometimes called **sap.** Maple syrup and maple sugar are made from the sap of a sugar-maple tree. The sugar you use at home is probably either cane sugar or beet sugar. These kinds of sugar are taken from sugar cane plants and sugar beet plants.

Taking sap from a sugar-maple tree.

Glucose produced in the leaves of a green plant may be used in the leaves, or it may travel to another part of the plant to be used. There is something else which may happen to glucose.

DISCOVER

What is another way in which a plant might use glucose?

What You Need

fresh potato	iodine
knife	water
drinking glass	medicine dropper
teaspoon	

1. Ask your teacher to cut a slice out of the center of a potato for you. Be sure your hands have just been washed. Rub one finger across the slice of potato and then taste the liquid on your finger.
2. In a glass, mix a teaspoon of iodine with a teaspoon of water. Use a medicine dropper to drop a bit of this mixture onto the slice of potato. What do you observe?

Are there chemicals in your mouth?

What is iodine used as a test for? Is starch present in the potato? In what two ways did you discover starch in the potato?

Put a piece of cracker into your mouth and chew on it for five minutes before you swallow it. What do you begin to taste?

Do you think that starch and sugar are chemicals which are alike in some way? There are chemicals in your mouth which can change starch into sugar. In a plant, starch can be changed into sugar, and sugar can be changed into starch. Why do you suppose this is important?

Many chemicals dissolve in water. Does starch dissolve in water? If you are not sure of the answer to this question, try mixing a teaspoon of flour, a common starch, with a glass of water. Starch is used in plants as a **storage** (stôr′ ij) **product.** A storage product is something which is produced that can be easily stored. Starch is a good storage product because it does not dissolve in water. Would oil be a good storage product? How can you test to find out?

A potato is a special part of a potato plant. Starch is stored in this special part. In the winter, the leaves and stem of the potato plant die. In the spring, starch stored in the potato is changed to sugar and the plant has food which it uses to begin growing again.

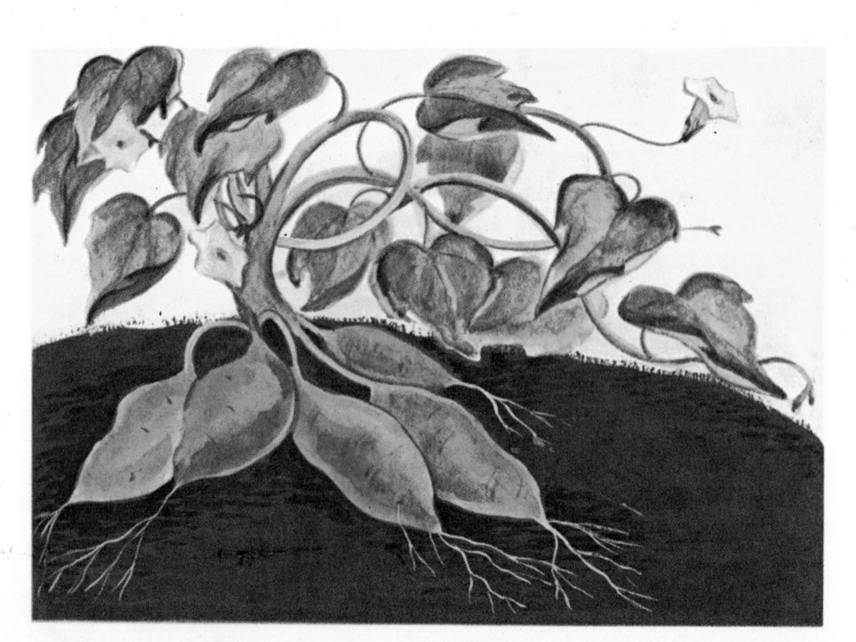

Sweet potato plant

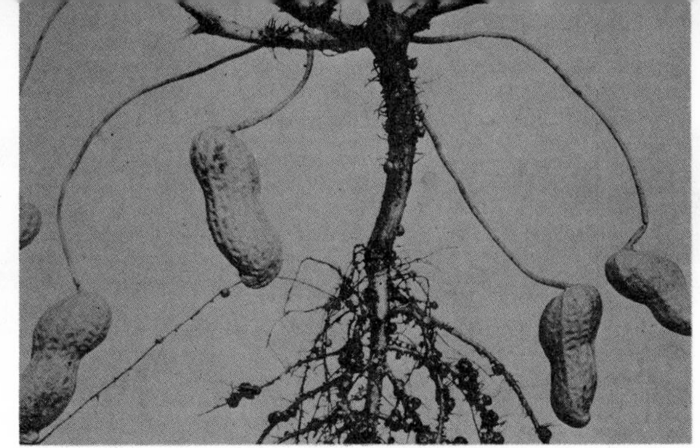

Carrots and peanuts are storage parts of plants.

Storage products are found in special storage parts of many plants. Starch or oil may be stored in roots, leaves, stems, and seeds. What parts of plants do you eat? Are any foods you eat the storage products of plants? Can you think of some?

Sugar, which is produced during photosynthesis, and starch, a storage product, are both **carbohydrates** (kär′ bō hi′ drāts). Carbohydrates are chemical compounds which contain carbon, hydrogen, and oxygen. All carbohydrate molecules contain two hydrogen atoms for every oxygen atom in the molecule.

Oils and fats are different from each other only in the amount of hydrogen in their molecules. Fat contains more hydrogen than oil does. Fats and oils are called **lipids** (lip′ īdz). Lipids are chemical compounds which contain carbon, hydrogen, and oxygen. Lipids contain much less oxygen in each molecule than carbohydrates do.

A third important food produced by plants is **protein** (prō′ tēn). Proteins are chemical compounds which contain carbon, hydrogen, oxygen, and nitrogen.

Testing for Plant Products

How can you tell if a food contains sugar? How can you tell if a food contains starch? How can you test for the other kinds of foods?

How can you discover some things a food contains?

DISCOVER

How can you test for lipids?

What You Need

olive oil	peanut butter
thin, white paper	spoon

1. Use your finger to rub some olive oil onto a piece of thin, white paper. Hold the paper up to the light. What change is there in the paper?
2. Use a spoon to rub some peanut butter on the paper. Turn the paper over and examine it.

Peanut butter is made from crushed peanuts. Do peanuts contain oil? How can you test for fats and oils? You may wish to use paper to test other materials for oils and fats.

DISCOVER

How can you test for protein?

What You Need

pan	hot plate
hair or feathers	dried lima beans

1. Place some bits of hair or feathers in a pan. Place the pan over high heat on a hot plate. Notice the odor.
2. Repeat this test using dried lima beans in place of the hair or feathers. Notice the odor.

Do burned lima beans have the same odor as burned hair or feathers? Hair and feathers are almost all protein. Do lima beans contain protein?

Which foods that you eat are proteins? Which foods contain carbohydrates or lipids? Are some foods both lipids and proteins? Are some foods both carbohydrates and lipids?

FIND OUT

Which foods produced by plants are lipids, which are proteins, and which are carbohydrates?

EXPERIMENT

What You Need

- teaspoon
- drinking glass
- iodine
- water
- medicine dropper
- thin, white paper
- pan
- hot plate
- foods such as peas, corn, lettuce, carrots, apples, potatoes, radishes, walnuts, oatmeal, corn oil margarine, maple syrup

What are some chemical elements found in your body?

Food	Sugar	Starch	Lipid	Protein
peas				
corn				
lettuce				

1. Taste each of the foods to see if they contain sugar. Record the results.
2. Do the activity on page 291 to see if the foods contain starch. Record the results.
3. Do the activity on page 294 to see if the foods contain lipids. Record the results.
4. Do the activity on page 294 to see if the foods contain protein. Record the results.

Plants get dissolved materials from the soil. Elements which plants take in from the soil are sometimes called **minerals** (min′ ər əlz). All foods contain some minerals. Your body has more than 18 different kinds of chemical elements in addition to carbon, oxygen, hydrogen, and nitrogen. How does your body obtain these elements?

Minerals such as sulfur, potassium, phosphorus, calcium, magnesium, and iron can be used by a plant to make **vitamins** (vī′ tə minz). Vitamins are chemical compounds which help control many processes that take place in plants and animals. Without vitamins, plants and animals cannot grow properly or remain healthy.

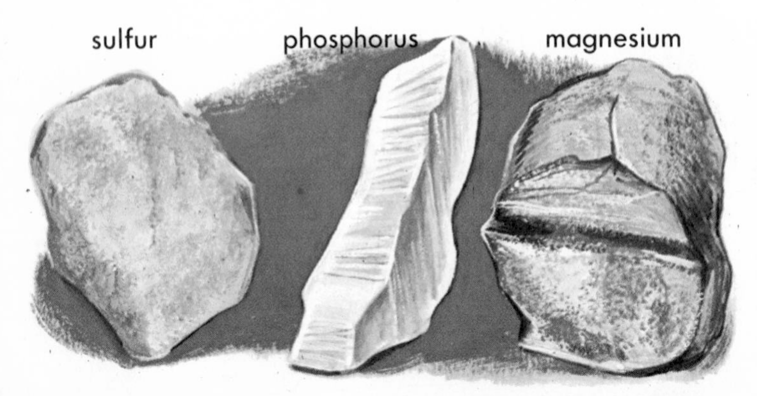

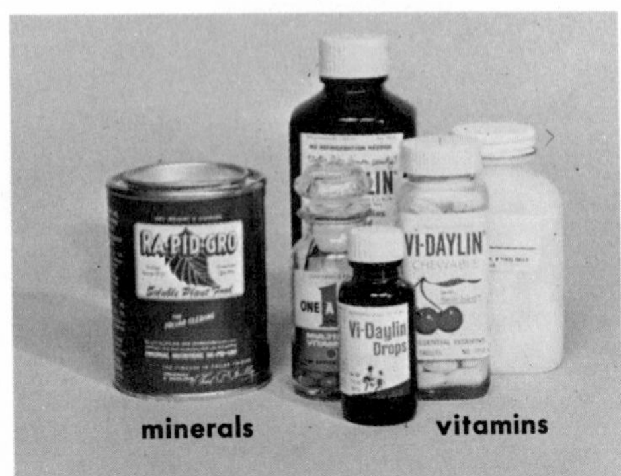

Mold growing on food

Courtesy Carolina Biological Supply Company

One kind of fungus as seen through a microscope

Fungus Plants

Do all plants contain chlorophyll? Can all plants make their own food?

Have you ever discovered a piece of bread on which some gray-green material was growing? You probably threw it away because it looked spoiled. That growth is called **mold.** You may have seen molds on fruits, cheese, or meat, too. Why do you think molds are usually found on foods?

Molds belong to a group of plants called **fungus** (fung′ gəs) **plants.** Fungus plants have no chlorophyll. Can they make their own food? Fungus plants grow on materials from which they can obtain food.

Mildew (mil′ dü) is a kind of fungus that grows on leaves and fruits of living plants. Some mildews grow on leather, paper, or cloth that has been stored in a damp place.

What are some fungus plants that could grow on your skin?

Mildew growing on an apple tree and books

Penicillin

Yeast

Some fungus plants grow on living animals and cause disease. Athlete's foot and ringworm are caused by fungus plants which grow on human skin. Other fungus plants may grow on animals which live in soil or in water.

Not all fungus plants are harmful. Some have been most valuable in saving human lives. A medicine made from a certain mold can help your body fight a serious infection. One of the most important of these mold drugs is called **penicillin** (pen′ ə sil′ ən). Other important drugs are made from fungus plants found in soil.

Yeast (yēst) is another kind of helpful fungus plant. It is used to make most kinds of bread.

DISCOVER

What happens to yeast as it grows?

What You Need

dry yeast	tablespoon
teaspoon	corn syrup
drinking glass	lukewarm water

1. Add half a teaspoon of dry yeast to a glass that contains one tablespoon of corn syrup and nine tablespoons of lukewarm water.
2. Watch the glass carefully. What do you notice happening?

Yeast plants can use sugar for food. As yeast plants grow, they form carbon dioxide gas. What gas forms the bubbles you see in the glass? Yeast is usually added to flour and water to make bread. Can you explain why a slice of baked bread has many small holes?

Some of the largest fungus plants are **mushrooms** (mush′ rümz). You may find some kinds of mushrooms growing in soil which has decaying wood or leaves. Other kinds grow on the bark of living trees. What do you think mushrooms use as food?

Mushrooms used for food are grown in beds of moist sawdust in dark buildings or caves. It is never safe to eat wild mushrooms because there are many poisonous kinds.

How many bacteria could be living on this page?

Poisonous wild mushrooms

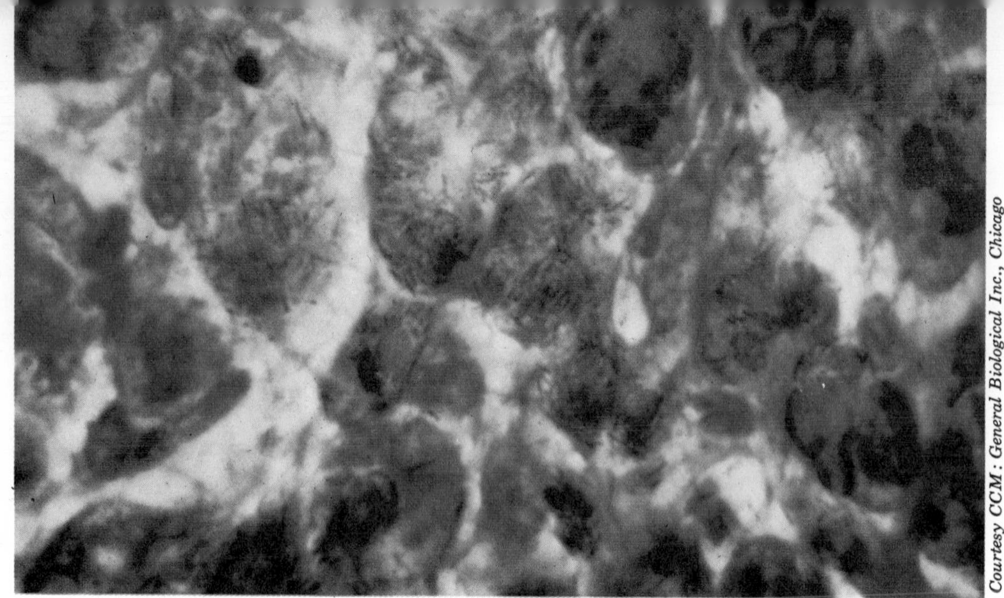
Courtesy CCM: General Biological Inc., Chicago

One kind of bacteria as seen through a microscope

Bacteria

Some very small living things called **bacteria** (bak tir′ ēə) cannot produce their own food. Bacteria are so small that several thousand could be placed on the period at the end of this sentence. Many bacteria cause illnesses in plants and animals. Other bacteria are helpful to man. Bacteria must have food on which they can grow.

FIND OUT

How can you grow some bacteria?

EXPERIMENT

What You Need

- 3 large jars with lids
- sharp knife
- 2 pans
- water
- hot plate
- potato
- tongs

1. Boil the jars, lids, and knife in a pan of water for 15 minutes.
2. Leave the jars in hot water, open end down, while you boil the potato in another pan. After the potato has boiled 15 minutes, pour off the water.
3. Have your teacher cut off three slices of the potato while it is in the pan. Take the jars out of the water with tongs. Place a potato slice into each jar, using only the knife.
4. Have a person cough into one jar. Then seal it immediately.
5. Place some scrapings from beneath fingernails on the potato slice in another jar. Seal this jar also.
6. Seal the third jar without adding anything to it. Place the jars in a warm, dark place for several days. What changes do you notice?

What can kill bacteria?

Some of the spots which can be seen on the potato are colonies of bacteria. Each spot has millions of bacteria. Some of the spots which can be seen on the potato may be mold. Because you boiled each jar, there were probably no live bacteria in the jars. Where did the bacteria that produced the colonies come from? Did bacteria grow in the jar which was sealed without adding anything? Can you see why it is important to use a handkerchief when you cough or sneeze? Tell why it is important to wash your hands thoroughly before eating.

Bacteria are found almost everywhere. They live in soil, in water, and in your body. They can enter your body through your nose and mouth as you breathe and through cuts or scratches in your skin.

Most bacteria around you are harmless and many are helpful. However, some can cause serious infections such as some kinds of pneumonia and tuberculosis.

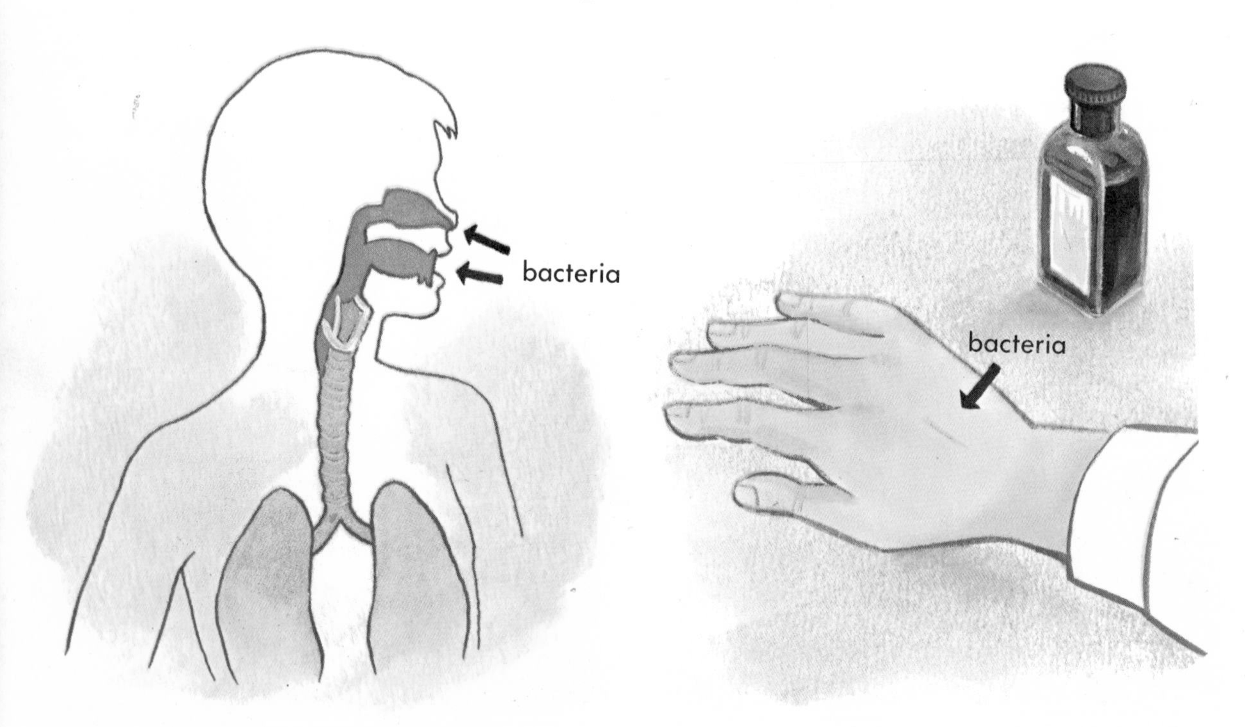

Food From Plants

Do animals need food to live and grow? Animals cannot produce their own food. Where do they get their food? Without green plants, could anything live? Could you live? When you eat eggs and milk, are you depending upon green plants? Where do chickens and cows get their food? In one way or another, green plants produce all the food that plants and animals use. Trace every kind of food you eat back to green plants.

Tell some things you know about plants.

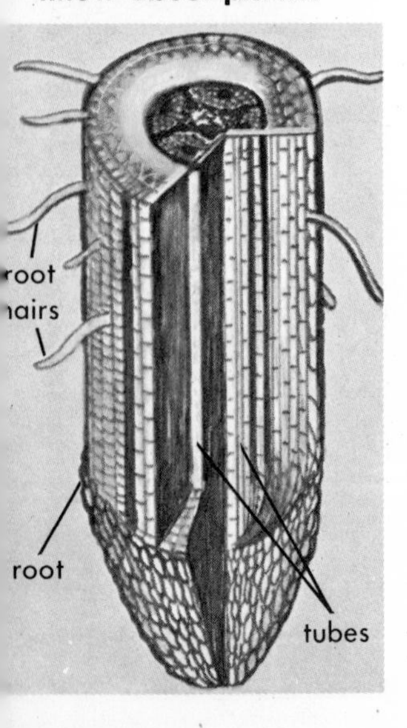

Exploring Your Learnings

Here are some ideas and vocabulary. What do these mean to you?

Words to Use

glucose (p. 278)
chlorophyll (p. 279)
photosynthesis (p. 288)
sap (p. 290)
storage product (p. 292)
carbohydrates (p. 293)
lipids (p. 293)
protein (p. 293)
minerals (p. 296)
vitamins (p. 296)
mold (p. 297)
fungus plants (p. 297)
mildew (p. 297)
penicillin (p. 298)
yeast (p. 298)
mushrooms (p. 299)
bacteria (p. 300)

Ideas to Use

1. A green plant is a kind of chemical laboratory where chemicals from air and soil are changed into glucose.
2. Sunlight used to cause some chemical changes in a plant is trapped by chlorophyll.
3. When plants produce glucose, they take in carbon dioxide and give off oxygen.
4. Carbon and oxygen in carbon dioxide, and hydrogen in water are used by green plants.
5. Water is an important compound for a plant because many chemicals dissolved in water enter the plant through roots.
6. A stem has tiny tubes through which water and dissolved materials travel between the roots and the leaves.

7. In photosynthesis, a green plant produces glucose from carbon dioxide and water in a chemical reaction which is powered by the sunlight trapped by chlorophyll.
8. Plants produce carbohydrates, lipids, proteins, and vitamins.
9. Fungus plants, such as mold, mildew, and yeast, do not have chlorophyll; they grow on materials from which they can obtain food.
10. Bacteria do not have chlorophyll; they grow on materials from which they can obtain food.
11. All living things depend upon plants which produce their own food.

Using Your Ideas

(Do not write in this book.)

1. Tell which of these plants can make its own food.
2. Find out which part of a bean seedling grows most rapidly. Use a pen to make black ink dots along the stem and the roots. How can you use these dots to see which part of the plant is growing fastest?
3. Find out what is meant by calling plants annuals, biennials, or perennials. Make a display showing each group of plants.
4. Find out about plant proteins which are called hormones. Plan and do an experiment to discover how plant hormones control plant growth.
5. Read about important mold drugs such as penicillin, terramycin, streptomycin, aureomycin, and chloromycetin.
6. Make two small batches of bread dough. Use yeast in one batch but not in the other. Bake the dough. Explain the difference.
7. Make a report on bacteria that are helpful.

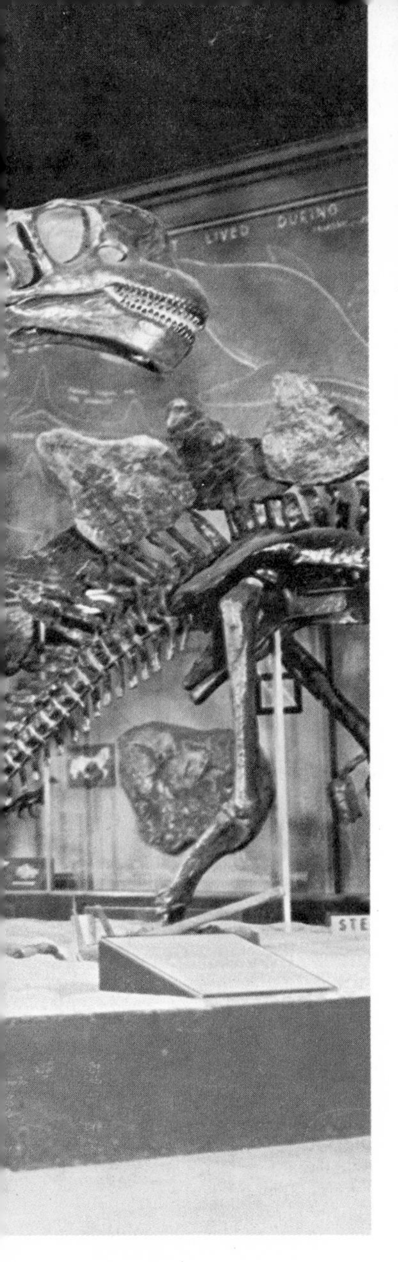

The Changing World of Animals

Are the animals that live on the earth today like those that lived on the earth long, long ago? Many dinosaurs used to live on the earth. Now some bones like those in the picture are all that is left of dinosaurs. What could have happened to the dinosaurs? Do you suppose that some animals alive today are relatives of the dinosaurs?

Each animal must fit in its surroundings in order to live. A polar bear is well suited for the icy north. A camel can live in hot, dry regions. Changes in the surroundings of animals are always occurring,but usually they are very slow changes. Over a period of time, much longer than your lifetime, there have been great changes in land and climate. Millions of years from now, the land and climates of the earth will probably be different from the way they are now. Do you think the kinds of animals that will live millions of years from now might also be different?

Different Environments

Would you be surprised to find a penguin on your school playground? What if you found a camel in your own backyard?

These animals may be entirely out of place in your neighborhood. They belong in other **environments** (en vī′ rən mənts). Environment is many things. An environment includes everything where a plant or animal lives. Air, water, light, rocks, soil, weather, plants, and animals are parts of a natural environment.

Describe your own environment. How is your environment different at school than at home? Is your environment changing?

There are as many environments as there are places on the earth. Each has its own particular kind of animals and plants. What makes one environment different from another?

If you look at the map in the picture, you can see one of the main differences in environment. A map of the earth shows large oceans and continents. Water is one kind of environment. What is another kind? On a map of your state, can you find lakes, rivers, and streams? Is an ocean environment the same as a small pond environment? What different kinds of land environments can you think of? Would you expect the same kinds of animals to live in these different kinds of environments?

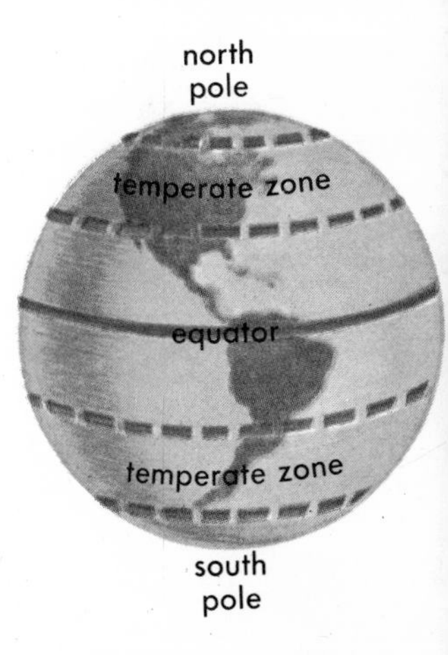

Different parts of the earth have different temperatures and weather. Land and water in some places receive more direct sunlight than other places. Very far north on earth and very far south, temperatures remain quite low most of the year. On part of the earth, it is very warm all year. Much of earth is in the **temperate** (tem′ pər it) **zones.** In the temperate zones, temperature and weather change a great deal from season to season.

The average weather of an environment is called **climate** (klī′ mit). Would you expect to see a camel or an elephant in a very cold, snowy climate? Would you expect to see a penguin or a polar bear in a climate that is hot and dry? How would you describe the climate where you live?

Animal Characteristics

No matter what environment an animal lives in, it must be able to get food, water, and oxygen. It needs room to raise its young. An animal must have some way to protect itself from becoming too warm or too cool. Most animals have special protections against enemies.

What kinds of characteristics do you think these animals have?

Every animal has characteristics (kar′ ik tər is′ tiks) which help it to live in its environment. What are some animal characteristics? How do they help the animal live in its environment?

How often do you look at a thermometer? You may not pay too much attention to changes in temperature unless they make you uncomfortable. Yet, these changes affect every living thing.

Groundhogs hibernate in winter.

Groundhogs are active in spring, summer, and fall.

Out of doors, the temperature changes continually throughout the day. Usually, there is quite a difference between night and day temperatures. Often, the greatest temperature changes take place from season to season. Animals that live in the temperate zones change their habits when there are great changes in weather. Would many animals stay alive if they did not change their habits? To some animals, a large temperature change means an entirely different way of life.

The amount of food which plant-eating animals can find depends a great deal upon the climate. In a warm, wet climate, there is usually a good supply of leaves, flowers, and grasses. Animals which use different parts of plants for food have plenty to eat. In the temperate zones, cold weather brings a complete change. Many plant-eating animals are without a food supply for several months each year.

Monkeys have a good supply of food all year long.

Animals like squirrels, beavers, chipmunks, and bees stay alive during the winter because they gather food in summer and fall and store it away. Other animals, such as the groundhog, that have no supply of food are able to spend the winter without eating. These animals have food stored in their bodies as fat. They find a sheltered place to **hibernate** (hī′ bər nāt) during cold weather. Hibernating is something like going to sleep for several months. But hibernation is more than sleeping. When an animal hibernates, its heart beats more slowly, its rate of breathing slows down, and its body temperature becomes lower. When an animal hibernates, its body uses food very slowly.

Squirrels must store food for use in winter.

Some birds **migrate** (mī′ grāt), or move to a different climate, during the winter. Some grazing, or grass-eating, animals such as caribou may move in search of mosses and grasses in the sheltered woods of warmer climates.

For fish and other water animals, temperature changes mean a change in the amount of oxygen in the water. Warm water has less oxygen than cold water. In warm weather, lake fishes move to deeper and colder water where they can obtain more oxygen.

Animals which live in places where temperatures get very cold have characteristics which protect them from freezing. During very hot, dry weather, other characteristics protect animals from the heat. Lizards which live in the desert find a sheltered spot where they can hibernate. Hibernation when there is much heat and little water is called **estivation** (es′ tə va′ shən).

Lizards like this one estivate.

An artist's drawing of what some scientists think these extinct animals looked like.

Animals of Long Ago

Suppose some changes occur in an animal's environment. What if the animal does not have characteristics which enable it to live in the changed environment? What do you think might happen to the animal?

Can you name the animals in the picture? Have you ever seen them in a zoo? None of these animals live on earth today. They are **extinct** (eks tingkt′) animals.

Many scientists think that about 200 million years ago, large animals such as triceratops roamed about in large numbers. Over millions of years, these animals became fewer and fewer. After a long time, none of these animals were alive. Many millions of years later, saber-toothed tigers lived on the earth. Since that time, the environment has changed and these animals are no longer living on the earth. These are just a few of the animals which became extinct as their environments changed. Many kinds of birds and fishes became extinct, too.

Has the earth always been as it is today?

Artist's picture of a saber-toothed tiger which is now extinct.

Today, there are many kinds of animals on earth. They are relatives of animals which lived long ago. Probably all of these animal groups did not appear on the earth at the same time. Why did some animals become extinct? Why were some able to continue living?

Environments on earth have not always been as they are today. Environments are always changing. Is the earth still changing slowly? A million years from today, many things may have changed on the earth.

Scientists think that at one time the earth was almost completely covered with water. At another time, much of the earth was warm and swampy. For a million years, most of the earth was covered with ice and snow. As environments changed, do you think the same kinds of plants and animals were able to stay alive?

The earth is constantly changing.

Some of the first organisms on the earth may have looked like this.

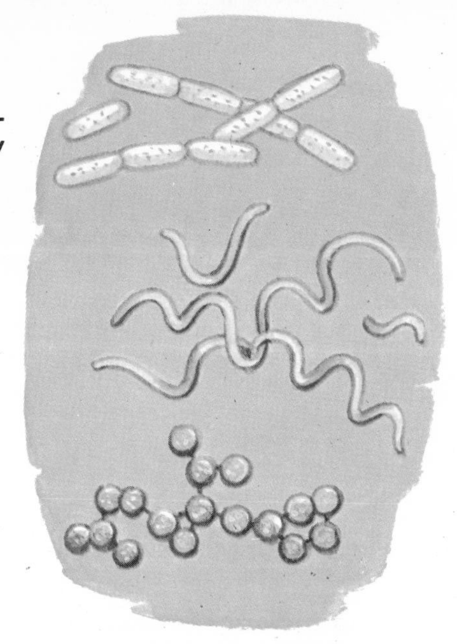

Soft-bodied Animals

A protozoan divides.

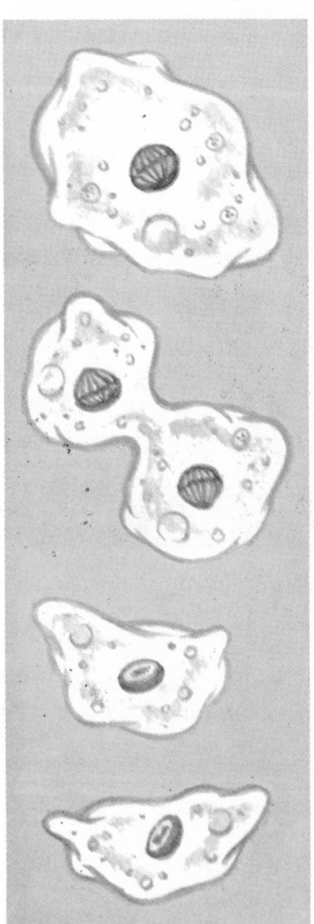

Every living thing is called an **organism** (ôr′ gən iz əm). For millions of years in the early history of the earth, there probably were no organisms. Some scientists believe the first organisms were very, very small. Each tiny organism could get and use food, water, and oxygen without any special body parts. Because plants can make their own food, scientists think the first organisms were plant-like. Animal-like organisms needed plants for food. Some of the first animal-like organisms are known as **protozoans** (prō′· tə zō′ ənz). Each protozoan can divide in half, forming two protozoans. In this way, protozoans increased in number. When animals produce more of their own kind, they **reproduce** (rē′ prə düs′).

Although every organism is much like the organism or organisms which produced it, no two living things are ever exactly alike. As protozoans increased in number, small differences were passed on from parent to young.

If these changes enabled an organism to live more easily in its environment, that type of organism continued to live and reproduce. What happened if the change was such that the organism could not live in its environment?

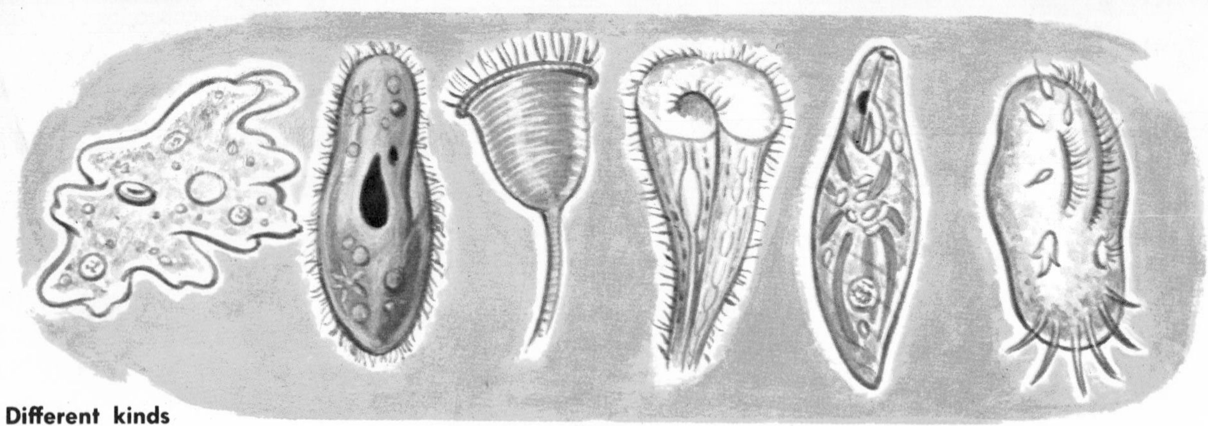
Different kinds of protozoans

After a long period of time, some protozoans had hair-like parts which enabled them to move about in their environment. Some of these tiny animals lived together in groups. Some parts of the group had special jobs. Parts on the outside helped the group to move about and capture food. Parts on the inside could digest food. These changes may have occurred as many small changes over millions of years. Each small change could have enabled these organisms to live as the environment changed.

Early jellyfish
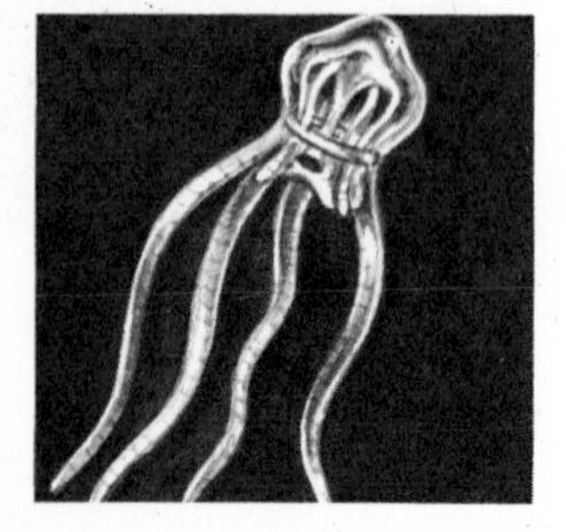

Some scientists believe that over millions of years, the parts of simple animals began more and more to do only one special job necessary to keep the animal alive. Through these changes, early sponge animals and their more complicated relatives may have appeared.

Because the oceans have changed much less than the land, scientists believe that simple ocean animals found today have changed very little since early times. If the oceans had changed a great deal, do you think the same kinds of living things would be living there? Do you think different kinds of organisms might have continued to live?

Scientists think that some groups of animals changed as the environment changed. Some groups of animals that did not change with the environment did not continue to live.

Animals With Hard Coverings

Shelled-animals probably appeared in the sea about 500 million years ago. Some had a one-part shell like snails do today. Others had a two-part shell which could open and close like today's clams and oysters. These animals formed shells from the minerals in seawater. The largest of these shelled animals were the ammonites. Some ammonites grew to a length of fifteen feet.

Trilobites were probably the first animals with outer skeletons that had jointed parts. Some trilobites were as small as tiny insects; some grew to more than one foot long. Although trilobites are now extinct, scientists believe that today's horseshoe crabs are living relatives of the trilobites. Why do you think trilobites became extinct?

Trilobites probably lived on the ocean bottom. A trilobite used its legs to crawl over mud and sand. Eyes along the side of its head and a flattened body were characteristics which enabled it to live in its environment.

Compare the picture of the trilobite with that of the horseshoe crab. How are they alike? How are they different?

One-part shelled animal

Two-part shelled animal

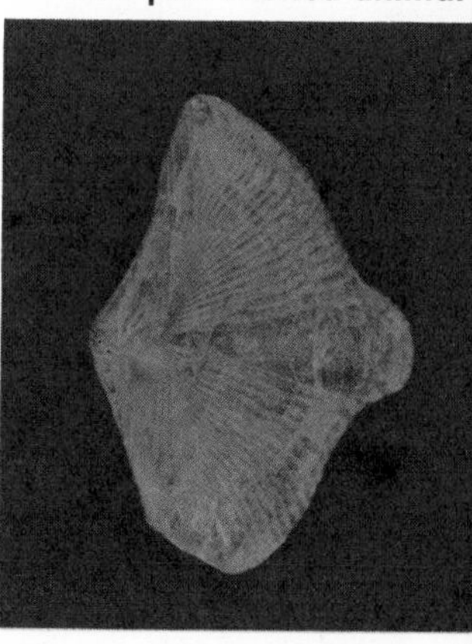

Trilobite fossil

What a trilobite might have looked like.

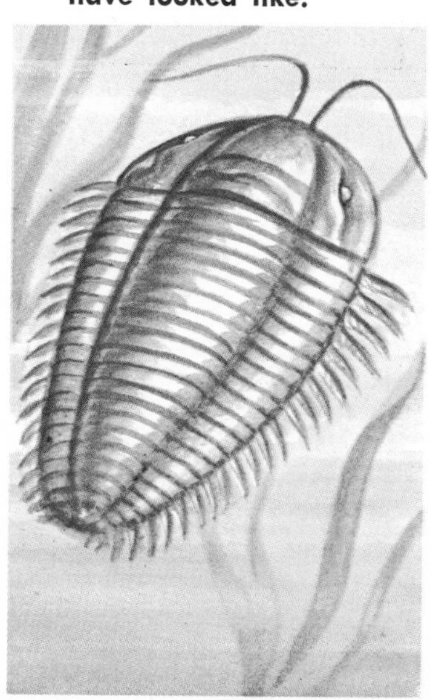

Horseshoe crab

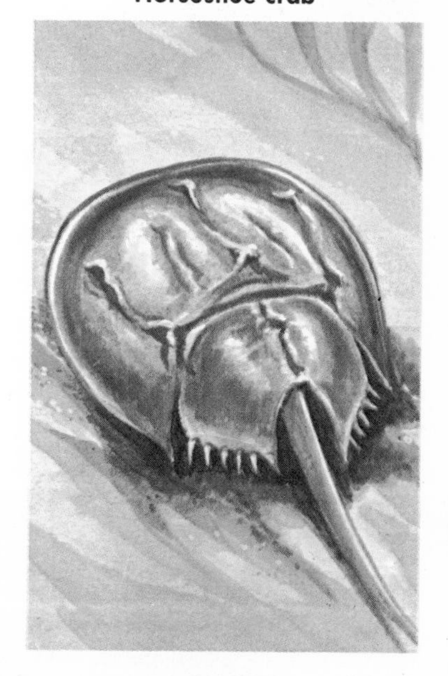

Artist's picture of what a giant sea scorpion might have looked like.

Trilobites probably were the most plentiful animals in the sea for a hundred million years. Later, giant sea scorpions became plentiful. Some sea scorpions were more than five feet long. Scientists believe that some of the later relatives of the scorpions may have had parts which enabled them to breathe air. These air-breathing animals probably were early relatives of the first insects. Would air-breathing insects have a different environment than the sea scorpion had?

Water Animals With Backbones

Probably the first animals with backbones were fish. The first fish probably lived in the oceans more than 500 million years ago. Some fish had soft inner skeletons and no fins. They wiggled through the water or over the bottom of the ocean. Some early fish had skeletons that were very strong. Some fish had fins that made them powerful swimmers. Some fish had hard bony plates which protected them. One of the largest of these armored fish was about twenty-five feet long.

Artist's picture of early fish

Artist's picture of an armored fish

The fins of some fish enabled them to "walk" along the bottom. Some later fish had a kind of lung and came to the surface of the water to breathe oxygen from the air. These lung fish began to spend time on the land. They were adapted to a new environment.

A. Artist's picture of an early fish which might have "walked" on ocean bottom.

B. Model of the fish caught near South Africa in 1938

A

B

In 1938, a strange looking fish was brought up in a net from the ocean near South Africa. Scientists discovered that the fish was a kind they believed had become extinct 70 million years ago. What do you observe about this fish? Do you notice that its fins have paddle-shaped soft parts? This type of fish was probably like the ones that first climbed up on the land. Scientists have made careful studies of living fish of this type which have been caught since.

Some early fish may have been the ancestors of today's frogs, toads, and salamanders. Frogs, toads, and salamanders are **amphibians** (am fib′ ē ənz). Amphibians spend part of their life in water and part of their life on land. Some of the early amphibians grew very large. How are lungs important to animals?

Look carefully at the picture of the amphibian. What characteristic besides lungs enabled it to live more easily on land than enabled its fish relatives?

What were some changes in amphibians that resulted in the development of large, fierce land animals?

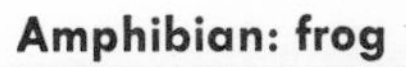

Amphibian: frog

Artist's picture of an early reptile

Early Land Animals

Amphibians spent more and more time out of the water. After a long time, some animals had scales which prevented their bodies from drying out. This group of animals had strong claws and sharp teeth. They were the first **reptiles** (rep′ tlz). Could reptiles live in an environment different from one in which amphibians live?

Reptiles did not need to stay near water as amphibians did. Reptiles laid their eggs on land. Teeth enabled reptiles to eat either plants or other animals. For many, many years, reptiles were plentiful on earth. Early reptiles were probably some of the largest and fiercest animals that ever lived. These early reptiles are known as **dinosaurs** (dī′ nə sôrz).

Some scientists think that some dinosaurs spent most of their time in the water. Other dinosaurs lived entirely on the land. A few kinds were able to fly.

Look at the pictures that show what dinosaurs might have looked like. Describe some of these animals' characteristics.

What some scientists think dinosaurs might have looked like

Today's reptiles, snakes, turtles, lizards, and crocodiles are probably much like the ancient dinosaurs. Some giant sea turtles and the crocodiles of today have changed very little from dinosaurs of long ago.

Today's reptiles

Many dinosaurs were very strong and powerful. There were many dinosaurs of many kinds, yet they became extinct. Why do you think this happened?

What feature of today's birds are reminders of their reptile relatives?

Scientists are not sure why dinosaurs became extinct, but they have several different theories. Some scientists believe that during the time of the dinosaurs, the climate changed, becoming too cold and dry for the dinosaurs to live. Others believe that new kinds of plants appeared which could not be eaten by the plant-eating animals. As the plant-eating dinosaurs died, the flesh-eating dinosaurs could no longer find food, and they died, too. There is also a possibility that dinosaur eggs laid on the ground were eaten in large numbers by other types of animals. Can you think of other possible theories to explain why the dinosaurs became extinct?

Fossil dinosaur eggs

A few of the smaller kinds of reptiles may have had feathers and hair. The feathers and hair would have kept their bodies warm. How would these characteristics have helped the animals to live?

Leg scales on a robin

Artist's picture of early flightless birds

Relatives of Reptiles

Many scientists think that after a long time, birds appeared. The ancient bird in the artist's picture was probably about the size of a pigeon. How was it different from birds today? Instead of a hard beak, it had teeth. It had a long tail with feathers growing from the sides. Claws on its wings enabled it to climb. Does this bird look somewhat like a dinosaur, too? What characteristics of dinosaurs might it have had? Today, birds have leg scales, much like reptiles.

At one time, there probably were many kinds of birds whose wings never grew large enough to be used for flight. They were flightless birds, much like an ostrich.

One animal in the bottom picture is a reptile; the other is a **mammal** (mam'l). Can you tell one from the other? What things about the animals look the same? How do they look different? The early mammals had only four toes instead of five like reptiles. Mammals are covered with hair, while reptiles have scales. Female mammals produce milk for their young.

A horse is one kind of mammal. Is a horse like the reptiles you know about? Scientists have been able to trace horses to their small relatives which lived on the earth fifty million years ago. The horse is a good example of a mammal which has not become extinct. Why has the horse been able to live so long?

The earliest known horse was probably about the size of a small dog. It had four toes on its front feet and fed on leaves of small plants. Later relatives of these small horses had a slender body and long legs. Perhaps these characteristics enabled the early horse to escape its enemies by moving swiftly.

Scientists think that slowly, through changes, members of the horse family became taller until they reached the size of today's horses. Other changes also took place. The toes and nails joined to form hooves. At a time when the climate became cooler and drier, most large forests disappeared and grasses began to grow. Horses had teeth which enabled them to chew the tough grasses.

What is the largest mammal that ever lived?

Today's horses

Artist's picture of early horses

Many other living animals are very different from their early relatives. Look at the pictures which show how the camel has changed since its first relatives lived. What changes can you name?

Probably, some of the first mammals were small insect-eaters, much like the shrews. Many early mammals were plant-eaters. Some fed on water plants. Others were able to reach the leaves of trees. Baluchithere was probably the largest land mammal that ever lived. It stood about twelve feet tall.

Flesh-eating mammals were probably relatives of dogs, bears, and cats. One of the fiercest, the saber-tooth tiger, had very long fangs. Saber-tooth tigers and other mammals that lived during the ice ages had a special protection against the cold. What was this protection?

Changes in the camel

Baluchithere is the largest animal in this picture.

Man Changes Environment

Some animals became extinct long before man lived on earth. These animals probably died out partly because of changes in the land and climate. Within the last few hundred years, some animals have become extinct.

An environment which is not changing or being changed is a **stable** (stā′ bl) **environment.** In a stable environment there are plants for animals that eat plants. These plant-eating animals are food for meat-eating animals. These, in turn, may have enemies which use them for food.

The number of animals in a particular stable environment stays about the same from year to year. This is called **natural balance** (nach′ ə rəl bal′ əns) because no single kind of plant or animal is too plentiful. Each animal's food supply is in balance with the animals which eat that food. However, man has often upset this balance. Can you think of ways he might have done this?

In some places, man killed many hawks and owls because they sometimes attacked his chickens. Killing hawks removed the natural enemies of rats and rabbits. In time, rats and rabbits became so plentiful that they were destroying farmers' crops.

In other places, mountain lions were killed to save deer. Then deer became so plentiful that they soon had eaten all the available food. Finally, there were so many deer and so little food that many deer starved. The deer that remained were smaller than normal. The deer were out of balance with their environment. It would take many years to restore that balance. In trying to save the deer, man had almost wiped out the mountain lion and had nearly ruined the deer herd and its food supply as well.

The early pioneers in America cut down many trees for lumber. They cleared the land for farming and plowed meadows and prairies. Year after year, they grew the same crops in the same fields until the soil no longer contained the chemicals that plants need to live and grow. Most animals cannot live where there are no plants.

Changing the environment in this way destroys animal homes as well as their food supply. As environments became crowded by cities and towns, animals could no longer move to find new homes. Soon some places had too many animals and not enough food. Many animals starved or were easily killed by enemies and disease.

To make land such as this more productive, man may drain the land, ruining the environment for some animals.

Other changes man has made in the environment affected the lives of animals that live in or near water. Some ponds and marshes were drained to provide farmland. Others were filled by soil carried by rainwater from cleared land. As cities grew, garbage, sewage, and waste chemicals were emptied into the water and air.

Man is constantly changing his environment. For too many years, these changes have harmed the environment. How have the air and water become polluted? How have air and water pollution harmed plants and animals?

What are some ways man can protect his environment?

Sometimes carelessness is responsible for changing the environment in ways which man is not aware of. Some plant and animal diseases are carried from one country to another. Plants or animals carried by man from one environment to another may ruin the balance of an environment.

Because man has changed the environment, many wild animals have become less plentiful. Many kinds that were once common are now extinct. When man changes the natural balance in his environment, he is often destroying the environment for himself, too.

Extinct passenger pigeons

At one time, millions of passenger pigeons made their homes in woods of North America. Yet today there are no passenger pigeons. Another animal, the California grizzly bear, has disappeared. Some other animals have become extinct, too. How did man help to make some animals extinct?

Conservation

Wise use of natural environments is called **conservation** (kon′ sər vā′ shən). Many people do not understand that conservation can help to make a healthy, stable environment for man to live in.

Some laws have been made to tell hunters how many animals can be killed and the times of the year when the animals can be hunted. Fish are also protected by law.

To provide places where animals can live, find food, and protect their young, some places called **wildlife refuges** (ref′ ūj əs) have been set aside. Many wildlife refuges are in state or national parks. No hunting or fishing is permitted in these places.

Many bears and buffalo are now protected from hunters by law.

Fish hatchery

In many areas, there are **fish hatcheries** (hach′ rēz) where fish eggs are hatched and the young are cared for. When these fish are large enough, they are flown or trucked to ponds, lakes, and rivers and released.

Because so many animals move from place to place, keeping a record of them is a difficult job. For this reason, many animals are trapped, marked in some way, and then released.

Bird being marked with metal band

Birds are usually marked by placing metal bands around their legs. Fish may have metal tags clipped to their gills or fins. Hunters and fishermen send these markers to the government and tell when and where the animal was killed. Information like this has enabled man to discover where animals travel, when they travel, and how long they live. Some animals are even marked with radios which send signals to tell where the animal is.

Records are kept of animal populations. Counts are made of ducks, deer, and other animals in a particular location. This is one way to find out if certain animals are becoming rare. Then the game laws may be changed to protect these animals. If animals become too crowded, game laws may be changed so that more of these animals will be harvested.

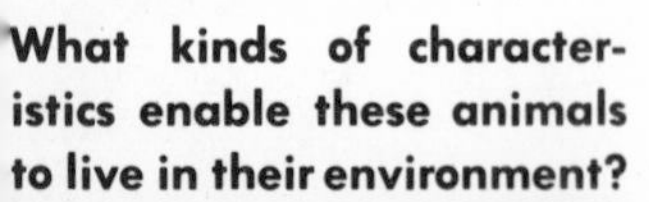

What kinds of characteristics enable these animals to live in their environment?

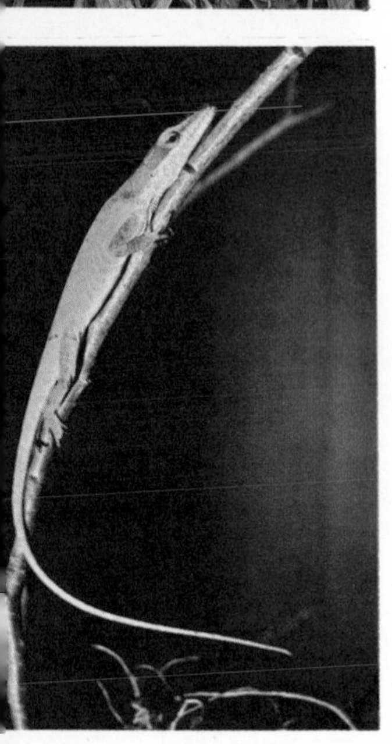

Exploring Your Learnings

Here are some ideas and vocabulary. What do these mean to you?

Words to Use

environments (p. 308)
temperate zones (p. 309)
climate (p. 310)
adaptations (p. 310)
hibernate (p. 311)
migrate (p. 312)
estivation (p. 312)
extinct (p. 313)
organism (p. 315)
protozoans (p. 315)
reproduce (p. 315)
amphibians (p. 319)
reptiles (p. 320)
dinosaurs (p. 320)
mammal (p. 322)
stable environment (p. 325)
natural balance (p. 325)
conservation (p. 328)
wildlife refuges (p. 328)
fish hatcheries (p. 329)

Ideas to Use

1. An environment includes everything where a plant or an animal lives.
2. Different parts of the earth have different climates.
3. Every animal has adaptations which enable it to stay alive in its environment.
4. Hibernation, migration, and estivation are adaptations which keep some animals from becoming extinct.
5. Animals on earth today are relatives of animals which lived long ago.
6. As environments on the earth change, the plants and animals in the environments change or become extinct.

Why do you think animals like this one are no longer living on the earth?

7. Although every organism is much like its parents, no two living things are ever exactly alike.
8. Man has often upset the natural balance of a stable environment.
9. When an organism is put into a new environment or removed from an environment, changes may occur in the natural balance.
10. The practice of conservation helps to make a healthy, stable environment in which man can live.

Even though these animals seem very much alike, no living things are exactly alike.

Using Your Ideas

(Do not write in this book.)

1. Make a shoebox display of a pond or desert environment. Show the kinds of animals that might be found in each environment.
2. Write to the conservation department in your state for information about game laws and wildlife preserves.
3. Plan an experiment to find out the effects of an environment for goldfish with and without plants, with and without light, and with and without salt.

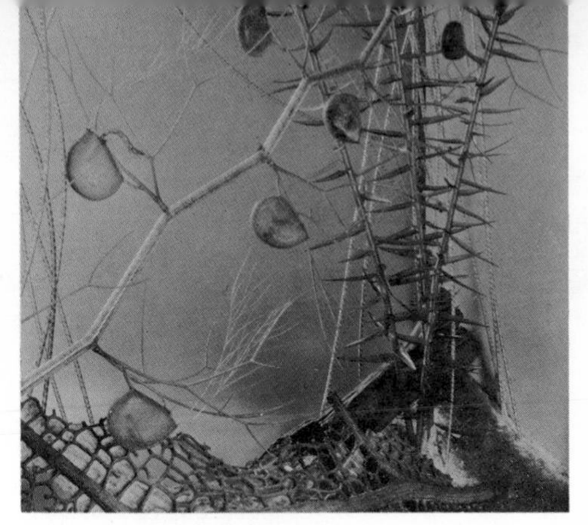

Pond water as seen through a microscope

4. Examine pond water with a microscope. Can you find any simple animals that look something like those on page 315?
5. Collect and care for eggs of frogs or toads. Make a record of the changes you observe with a magnifying glass or microscope.
6. Read about and report on such subjects as veterinary medicine, conservation, pollution, and wildlife management.
7. Report on the care of an animal you have or would like to have as a pet.
8. Plan a bulletin board which shows ways in which animals are adapted for moving, getting food, or protection.

Frog eggs

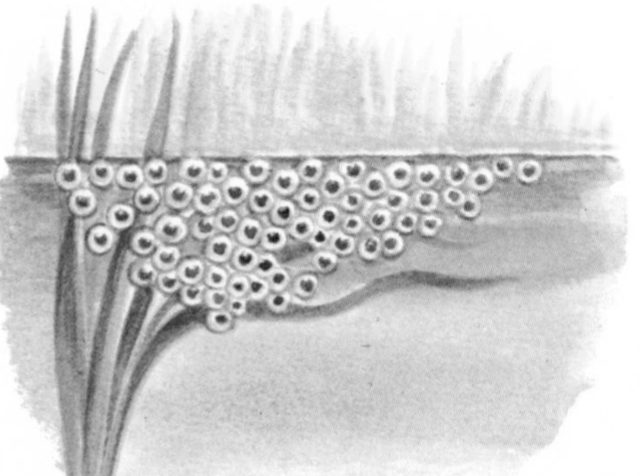

Pet turtle

GLOSSARY

In this glossary, you will find the science meaning of many important names and terms used in DISCOVERING SCIENCE. The pronunciation of many words is given in parentheses following each of these words.

The pronunciation key below will help you tell how the marked letters sound.

a	can	**ī**	hide, **by**	**ū**	**u**se, m**u**le
ā	came, **a**te	**o**	hop, doll	**u̇**	p**u**t, f**oo**t
ã	care, h**ai**r	**ō**	hope, gr**ow**	**ü**	r**u**le, f**oo**d
ä	car, st**a**rt	**ô**	corn, c**a**ll, s**aw**	**zh**	usual
ch	**ch**air, wat**ch**	**ou**	**ou**t, n**ow**	**ə**	*sounds like*
e	let, bell	**oi**	join, b**oy**		**a** about
ē	be, bab**y**	**sh**	**sh**e, fi**sh**		**e** under
ėr	learn, b**ir**d, f**ur**	**th**	**th**ank, ba**th**		**i** April
hw	**wh**eel	**t͟h**	**t͟h**an, ba**t͟h**e		**o** lesson
i	hid, win	**u**	**u**s, j**u**mp		**u** nature

absorb (ab sôrb′): to take in

accelerate (ak sel′ ər āt): speed up

acceleration (ak sel′ ər ā′ shən): increase in speed

acid (as′ id): chemical compound which dissolves in water, has sour taste, turns a vegetable dye called litmus red; separates into two or more electrically charged parts when it is dissolved in water

action-reaction (ak′ shən ri ak′ shən): forces of two objects acting on each other equally and oppositely

adaptation (ad′ ap tā′ shən): special characteristic which helps a living thing stay alive in an environment

air pressure (presh′ ər): weight of air

algae (al′ jē): single-celled plants that contain chlorophyll

alternating current (ôl′ tər nāt ing kėr′ ənt): electric current which flows back and forth

amoeba (ə mē′ bə): one-celled protozoan with a shapeless body

amphibian (am fib′ ē ən): animal which lives and breathes underwater part of its life but develops lungs and lives on land as an adult

anemometer (ãn ə mom′ ə tər): instrument used to measure speed of air movement

aneroid barometer (an′ ə roid′ bə rom′ ə tər): instrument used to measure air pressure; air pressure squeezes a metal box which moves a pointer

angle of incline (in′ klīn): angle at which an inclined plane slants

animal "clock": means by which an animal knows when to do certain things

annelid (an′ ə ləd)**:** invertebrate animal such as an earthworm with a body that appears divided by small rings

arm: long rod, pole, or plank of a lever

arthropod (är′ thrə pod)**:** invertebrate animal with an outer skeleton and jointed legs

artificial satellite (är′ tə fish′ əl sat′ l īt)**:** satellite made and sent into space by man

asteroid (as′ tə roid)**:** small body much like a planet that orbits the sun between Mars and Jupiter

astronaut (as′ trə nôt)**:** space explorer; word means "star sailor"

astronomer (əs tron′ ə mər)**:** scientist who studies heavenly bodies

astronomy (əs tron′ ə mē)**:** study of heavenly bodies

atmosphere (at′ məs fir)**:** gaseous mass around a heavenly body

atom (at′ əm)**:** bit of matter; smallest possible amount of an element

atomic decay (ə tom′ ik di kā′)**:** process in which an atom gives off radiation from its nucleus

attract (ə trakt′)**:** to pull together

attraction (ə trak′ shən)**:** pull, or force

axis (ak′ sis)**:** imaginary line about which a body rotates; imaginary line running through the earth between the geographic poles

axle (ak′ sl)**:** bar on which a wheel turns

bacteria (bak tir′ ē ə)**:** very small one-celled living things without chlorophyll that grow on materials from which they obtain food

ball bearings (bār′ ings)**:** small steel balls that roll around inside a wheel and help overcome friction

barometer (bə rom′ ə tər)**:** instrument used to measure air pressure

basalt (bə sôlt′)**:** dark rock formed from lava

battery (bat′ ər ē)**:** two or more electric cells connected together

beetle (bēt′ l)**:** insect with two pairs of wings, the outer pair form a hard covering for the inner pair

betatron (bā′ tə tron)**:** machine used to speed up subatomic particles

biological (bī ə loj′ ə kel) **clock:** change in an animal's body which acts as a signal for its life activities

boiling point: temperature at which a liquid boils

botanist (bot′ n əst)**:** scientist who studies plants

breathing (brēth′ ing)**:** movements which bring air into the body and force it out again

bristle (bris′ l)**:** short, stiff hair

bud: small, new growth on a plant that later may become a leaf, twig, or flower; cells that are not yet specialized

bulb (bulb)**:** underground bud with thick leaves around it

burrow (bėr′ ō)**:** hole in the ground made and used by an animal

calendar (kal′ ən der): record of time, giving the days, weeks, and months of the year

canine (kā′ nīn) **teeth:** long, pointed teeth on both sides of the incisors

carbohydrates (kär′ bō hi′ drāts): chemical compounds which contain carbon, hydrogen, and oxygen, with twice as much hydrogen as oxygen; one of the main classes of food

carbon (kär′ bən): element which makes up coal; also found in the form of diamonds and graphite; one of the most important elements in chemicals in living things

carbon dioxide (kär′ bən dī ok′ sīd): gas in the air; compound made up of carbon and oxygen atoms; CO_2

carnivore (kar′ nə vôr): animal that eats other animals

cell (sel): small living part of a plant or animal; basic unit of life

cell membrane (mem′ brān): thin covering around an animal cell

cell wall: covering which gives a plant cell its shape

Celsius (sel′ sē əs) **scale:** scale of a thermometer on which the freezing point of water is 0° and the boiling point of water is 100°

center of gravity (grav′ ə tē): point in an object around which its mass seems to be balanced

centrifuge (sen′ trə fūj): machine used to produce effects of gravity by whirling objects in a circle

Cepheid (sef′ ē əd): star which seems to grow larger and smaller over and over, at a certain rate

chain reaction (rē ak′ shən): series of reactions in which one reaction causes other reactions

chameleon (ka mē′ lē ən): small lizard whose skin color can change

characteristics (kar′ik tər is′ tiks): ways a living thing looks and acts which make it different from other living things

chemical (kem′ ə kl) **change:** change in which molecules are broken, changed, or combined to form different kinds of molecules

chemical equation (kem′ ə kl i kwā′ zhən): symbols and formulas used together to show how atoms and molecules react with each other, such as $2H_2 + O_2 \rightarrow 2H_2O$

chemical formula (fôr′myə lə): chemical symbols written together to show the atoms in a molecule, such as H_2O

chemical symbol (sim′ bl): one or two letters used to represent each known kind of atom, or element, such as H, O, and Na

chemist (kem′ ist): scientist who studies changes in matter and works with chemicals and chemical changes

chlorophyll (klô′ rə fil): material which gives plants their green color; chemical compound

chloroplast (klô′ rə plast′): green spot in a cell's cytoplasm which contains chlorophyll

chordate (kôrd′ ət): animal which has a spinal cord

chrysalis (kris′ ə lis): covering of the pupa stage of an insect

chuckwalla (chək′ wäl ə): lizard about two feet long that lives in the desert

circuit (sėr′ kit): path along which electricity travels

cirrocumulus (sir′ ō kūm′ ū ləs) **clouds:** cirrus clouds piled up

cirrus (sir′ əs) **clouds:** thin, curly clouds high in the sky

classification (klas′ ə fə kā′ shən): use of characteristics to divide things into groups

clay (klā): very fine-grained, light-colored substance often found in soil

climate (klī′ mit): overall kind of weather of an environment over a period of years

closed circuit: electric circuit with no gaps or openings

cockroach (kok′ rōch): flat, brownish insect that lives in dark, damp, and warm places and has a strong odor

cocoon: covering of the pupa stage of an insect

coelenterate (si len′ tər āt′): invertebrate animal such as coral which is hollow inside and usually has arms or tentacles

coil (koil): several turns of wire

cold air mass: large body of cold air

cold front: place where a moving, cold air mass meets a warm air mass

cold light: light given off with very little heat

colony (kol′ ə nē): group of cells living together

combustion (kəm bus′ chən): quick oxidation, or burning

comet (kom′ it): cluster of gases, dust, rock, and ice traveling through space

communication satellite (kə mū′ nə kā′ shən sat′ l īt): satellite used to help in sending messages from one place on earth to another

compass (kum′ pəs): instrument used to find directions

compass needle: small magnet shaped like a pointer and found inside a compass

compound (kom′ pound): substance that has more than one kind of atom; its atoms are bonded together into molecules

compound lever (lev′ ər or lē′ vər): two levers having the same fulcrum

compressed (kəm presd′) **air:** air molecules squeezed together

concave mirror (kon kāv′ mir′ ər): mirror which curves inwardly and collects light

condensation (kon′ den sā′ shən): changing of a gas or vapor into a liquid

condense (kən dens′): to change from a gas or vapor into a liquid

conduction (kən duk′ shən): movement of heat through a substance from molecule to molecule; movement of electricity through a substance

conductor (kən duk′ tər): material that electricity or heat travels along easily

cone (kōn): part that contains seeds on many evergreen plants; some cones produce pollen

conglomerate (kən glom′ ər it): rock formed from various-sized pebbles and stones pressed and cemented together

conservation (kon′ sər vā′ shən): wise use of natural environment

constellation (kon′stə lā′ shən): group of stars that appear to form a picture

contour plowing (kon′tur plou′ing): plowing by following the curves of a hill

contract (kən trakt′): to take up less space; decrease in volume as molecules move closer together

control (kən trōl′): part of an experiment which is not changed when testing other parts of the experiment; used as a comparison for the parts of the experiment that were changed

controlled pollination (pol′ ə nā′ shən): pollination done experimentally by botanists

control rods: metal bars in a nuclear reactor which help slow down or speed up nuclear reactions

convection (kən vek′ shən): movement of heat through a substance by the rising of warmer parts of the material and the settling of cooler parts of the material

convex mirror (kon veks′ mir′ ər): mirror curved outwardly which spreads light

coquina (kō kē′ nə): rough rock formed from skeletons and shells of animals such as crabs and clams, cemented together

coral (kôr′ əl): coelenterate with tentacles that uses minerals it obtains from water to build a hard wall around itself

core (kôr): soft iron center of an electromagnet; innermost part of the earth, believed to be made of heavy metals such as iron and nickel

corer (kôr′ ər): hollow pipe used to collect samples of materials

corona (kə rō′ nə): layer of glowing gases above the surface of the sun

crater (krā′ tər): hole in the ground formed by something hitting the earth or by volcanic action

crust: outer layer of the earth

crystal (kris′ tl): solid form of a substance in which the atoms are arranged in a pattern that gives the substance a particular shape

cultivation (kul′ tə vā′ shən): loosening of soil between crop plants; use of land by plowing, fertilizing, planting seeds, and growing and harvesting crops

cumulus (kūm′ ū ləs) **clouds:** rounded, puffy clouds

cumulonimbus (kūm′ ū lō nim′ bəs) **clouds:** large, tall cumulus clouds which produce thunderstorms or heavy rain

cutting (kut′ ing): part cut from a full-grown plant which may produce a new plant

cyclotron (sī′ klə tron): machine used to speed up subatomic particles

cylinder (sil′ ən dər): in an engine, a metal tube containing a piston

cytoplasm (sī′ tə plaz əm): liquid of a cell which contains minerals and other materials which a cell needs to live and grow

day: measure of the time it takes the earth to turn around, or rotate, once

degree (di grē′): unit of a scale on a thermometer; line or point on the earth determined by its distance from the equator; unit of measuring an angle

delta (del′ tə): land built up by soil deposited at the mouth of a river

density (den′ sə tē): amount of matter, or mass, in a certain volume of material

dew: droplets of water condensed on objects when the temperature falls

dew point: temperature at which a gas, or vapor, condenses to a liquid

diameter (dī am′ ə tər): distance from one side of a circle to the other through its center

diaphragm (dī′ ə fram): muscle in the body which moves up and down, contracting and expanding the lungs

dinosaur (dī nə sôr): large extinct reptile

dipping needle: magnetic needle used to chart magnetic lines of force

direct current (də rekt′ kėr′ ənt): electric current which flows in only one direction

direct light: light that comes from an original source rather than being reflected from something

discharge (dis′ chärj): to equalize the difference between two electric charges by one charged body giving up electrons to another

dissolve (di zolv′): to mix completely, molecule by molecule, throughout a material, usually a liquid

double concave lens (dub′ l kon kāv′ lenz): lens having both sides curved so that it is thinner in the middle than at the edges

double convex (kon veks′) **lens:** lens having both sides curved so that it is thicker in the middle than at the edges

double stars: two stars so close together that they look like one star

dune (dūn): hill of sand or other fine material

dust storm: strong winds that carry soil and fill air with clouds of dust

dwarf (dwôrf) **stars:** small stars; stars the size of the sun or smaller

eardrum (ir′ drum′): thin piece of stretched skin in the ear that vibrates when struck by sound waves

earthquake (erth′ kwāk′): movement of earth caused by the sudden movement of rocks below the earth's surface

echinoderm (i kī′ nə dėrm): invertebrate animal such as a starfish with spiny skin

echo: reflected sound

echo (ek′ ō) **sounder:** instrument used to study the ocean floor with reflected sound vibrations

eclipse (i klips′): passing of a body into the shadow of another body in space

electric appliance (i lek′ trik ə plī′ əns): household device run by electricity

electric cell: structure which is used to produce electricity by the action of chemicals; contains electrodes and an electrolyte

electric charge (i lek′ trik chärj): amount of electricity an object contains; basic unit of electricity

electric current (i lek′trik kėr′ənt): flow of electrons

electric motor (i lek′ trik mō′ tər): machine which can change electric energy into mechanical energy

electric resistance (i lek′trik ri zis′ təns): force which acts against the flow of electricity

electrolyte (i lek′ trə līt): material which, when dissolved in water, can conduct electricity

electromagnet (i lek′ trō mag′ nit): iron core within a coil of wire which is a magnet while electricity is flowing along the wire

electromagnetic (i lek′ trō mag net′ ik) **wave:** wave which travels at the speed of light

electron (i lek′ tron): subatomic particle with a negative charge; usually found orbiting an atom's nucleus

electron microscope (i lek′ tron mī′ krə skōp): microscope used to photograph very small things; uses focused electrons instead of light rays

electroscope (i lek′ trə′ skōp): instrument which is used to detect charges of electricity

element (el′ ə mənt): material that has only one kind of atom

ellipse (i lips′): special oval shape; has two foci instead of a center like a circle

energy (en′ ər jē): anything that is not matter; necessary for something to move or change; ability to do work

engine (en′ jən): machine that can change the stored energy of fuels to mechanical energy

environment (en vī′ rən mənt): all things that affect a living plant or animal; overall surroundings

equator (i kwā′ tər): imaginary circle around the earth halfway between the north pole and the south pole

equatorial (ē kwə tô′ rē əl) **air:** air from the equator, usually very warm

erosion (i rō′ zhən): process by which materials of the earth's surface are worn

escape tower (es kāp′ tou′ ər): frame with separate rocket engines and fastened to main space capsule; means of escape from rocket that has begun to lift off the launching pad

estivation (es′ tə vā′ shən): hibernation during the summertime

evaporate (i vap′ ə rāt): to change from a liquid into a gas or vapor

evergreen (ev′ ər grēn): plant that stays green all year long

expand (eks pand′): to take up more space; increase in volume as molecules move farther apart

experimental satellite (iks per′ ə men′ təl sat′ l īt): satellite with special equipment for detecting and recording information

extinct (eks tingkt′): no longer living and has no direct descendants

Fahrenheit (far′ ən hīt) **scale:** scale of a thermometer on which the freezing point of water is 32° and the boiling point of water is 212°

faulting (fôl′ ting): process of rock layers breaking and moving

fertilization (fėr′ tl ə zā′ shən): process in which a pollen cell nucleus joins with an ovule cell, or a sperm cell nucleus joins with an egg cell

fertilizer (fėr′ tl īz ər): material containing minerals that plants need for growth

fiberscope (fī bər skōp): instrument which is a long bendable tube filled with either thin glass or thin lucite threads, used for looking in different directions

filter (fil′ tər): object used to separate materials

fish hatchery (hach′ rē): place made by man where fish eggs are hatched and the young are cared for

flame test: test to identify elements by the color of a flame when they are heated in it

flood (flud): overflow of water

flood plain: land built up by soil left behind by a flooding river

fluorescent mineral (flü′ ə res′ ənt min′ ər əl): mineral that glows with colors under ultraviolet light but not under ordinary light

flyways: routes birds follow when they migrate

focus (fō′ kəs): point at which light reflected from a curved mirror comes together; point at which light bent by a lens comes together

fog: cloud of condensed water vapor near the ground

footcandle: unit used to measure the brightness of light; amount of light received from a candle flame at a distance of one foot

foot-pound: unit used to measure the amount of work done; amount of work involved in lifting one pound one foot high

force (fôrs): push or pull

fossil (fos′ l): any trace of an animal or plant that has been preserved from the past

fracture (frak′ chər): large crack in a rock or other material

freezing (frēz′ ing): changing a liquid into a solid as temperature decreases

friction (frik′ shən): force present when two objects rub against each other; resistance to rubbing

frictional electricity (frik′ shən l i lek tris′ ə tē): electric charges caused by rubbing one object against another; static electricity

frog: small, leaping animal that lives near water; spends the first part of its life as a tadpole

front: place where two air masses of different temperatures meet

frost: thin coating of ice crystals on objects; freezes directly from the air

fruit (früt): seeds and stored food of a plant ovary

fulcrum (ful′ krəm): point on which the arm of a lever rests

fungus (fung′ gəs) **plant:** plant with no chlorophyll that grows on material from which it can obtain food

furrow (fer′ ō): small ditch

galaxy (gal′ ək si): large star group with billions of stars, such as the Milky Way

galvanoscope (gal′ və nə skōp): instrument that is used to show when electricity is flowing along a circuit

gas: state of matter, neither liquid nor solid, that takes the shape of its container; has no definite shape or volume

gas bladder (blad′ ər): bag-like structure that can be filled with gas; found inside many fish

gear (gir): wheel with teeth in it

Geiger counter (gī gər koun′ tər): instrument which is used to detect radioactive materials

generator (jen′ ər ā′ tər): machine that changes water or steam power or other kind of mechanical energy into electricity

geographic (jē′ ə graf′ ik) **poles:** areas at both ends of the earth's axis

geologist (jē ol′ ə jəst): scientist who studies the earth and rocks from which the earth is made

giant (jī′ ənt) **stars:** large stars, many times the size of the sun

glacier (glā′ shər): huge mass of moving ice on land

globe (glōb): model of the earth or other such body

glucose (glü′ kōs′): type of sugar

gneiss (nīs): layered metamorphic rock similar to granite which has been changed by heat and pressure

graft: plant cutting attached to another plant

granite (gran′ it): hard igneous rock made of crystals of different minerals; composed mainly of feldspar and quartz

gravimeter (gra vim′ ə tər): instrument used to measure differences in the effect of gravity

gravitation (grav′ ə tā′ shən): force between all objects that pulls them together

gravity (grav′ ə tē): force which pulls things toward the center of the earth

groundwater: water which fills spaces below the surface of the ground

ground wire: wire connected to the ground through which an electric charge can easily be discharged

gully (gul′ i): ditch formed by running water

gypsum (jip′ səm): sedimentary rock made from sediments formed from calcium and magnesium chemicals, often used as chalk

habits (hab′ its): ways an animal lives and things it does

hailstone: stone-like object made of layers of ice that forms in some clouds and may fall to earth

heat: energy related to movement of molecules

heating coil: coil of wire which has a high resistance to electricity

heat shield (shēld): fire-proof material which keeps a space capsule from burning during reentry into the earth's atmosphere

herbivore (hər′ bə vōr): animal that eats only plants

hibernate (hī′ bər nāt): to spend a period of time in a state much like sleep

hive: nest of wax made by bees

hour (our): measure of time; one of 24 parts of one day

humid (hū′ mid): containing moisture

humidity (hū mid′ ə tē): amount of water vapor in the air

humus (hū′ məs): decaying plant and animal materials in soil

hurricane (hėr′ ə kān): huge storm hundreds of miles across with circular winds of great speed and much rain

hybrid (hī′ brid): new kind of plant produced by flowers which have been pollinated from a different kind of flower

hydrometer (hī drom′ ə tər): instrument used to measure the density of a liquid

hygrometer (hī grom′ ə tər): instrument used to measure humidity

ice: solid form of water

iceberg (īs′ bėrg): large piece of ice that breaks off and floats away from a glacier

igneous (ig′ nē əs) **rock:** rock formed from magma or from processes that involve heat

ignite (ig nīt′): to set on fire; to begin to burn

incandescent (in′ kən des′ ənt): giving off light when heated

incisors (in sī′ zərz): four upper and four lower front teeth; cutting teeth

inclined plane (in klīnd′ plān): tool or structure which has a flat surface which slants at an angle to the ground

infrared radiation (in′ frə red′ rā′ dē ā′ shən): part of the energy from the sun which reaches the earth; has longer wavelength than visible light

infrared rays (in′ frə red′ rāz): heat rays; rays that have a longer wavelength than visible light

insect (in′ sekt): small animal with three pairs of legs and a jointed body

insulator (in′ sə lā′ tər)**:** material that is a poor conductor of heat or electricity

internal combustion engine (in tėr′ nl kəm bus′ chən en′ jən)**:** engine which burns fuel directly in the cylinder

interplanetary probe (in′ tər plan′ ə ter′ē prōb)**:** rocket or satellite used to study other planets and the space around them

invertebrate (in vėr′ tə brit)**:** animal without a backbone

iris (i′ ris)**:** muscles in the eye that control the size of the pupil

iron filings (fīl′ ingz)**:** small pieces of iron that have been removed by a file

irrigation (ir′ ə gā′ shən)**:** bringing water to dry places

katydid (kā′ tē did)**:** insect that looks like a leaf and is much like a grasshopper

key: switch used to open and close an electric circuit when sending a telegraph message

kinetic energy (kə net′ik en′ər jē)**:** energy of motion

larva (lär′ və)**:** young insect form after hatching from an egg

laser (lā′ zər)**:** instrument which is used to produce very concentrated and almost perfectly parallel rays of light

latitude (lat′ ə tüd) **lines:** lines marked around a globe parallel to the equator and counted in degrees

launch (lônch)**:** to send into space

lava (lä′ və)**:** magma which reaches the earth's surface

law of conservation (kon′ sər vā′ shən) **of matter and energy:** law which states that, in all reactions, the total amount of matter and energy always remains the same

leaflet (lēf′ lit)**:** part of a compound leaf that has the shape of a simple leaf

leaf scar: place where a leaf was attached to a plant

lens (lenz)**:** piece of glass or other transparent material that refracts light and changes the direction of light which travels through it

lever (lev′ ər or lē′ vər)**:** simple machine consisting of an arm and a fulcrum

lichens (lī′ kənz)**:** small, gray-green plants which can grow on rocks and give off acids which soften rock minerals

lightning (līt′ ning)**:** flash of light caused by electrons moving between two objects of different charges

light-year: distance that light travels in one year at 186,000 miles per second, about 6 trillion miles; unit used to measure great distances

limestone (līm′ stōn′)**:** rock formed from skeletons and shells crumbled to a fine powder and cemented together

lines of force: lines showing the magnetic field around a magnet

lipids (lip′ īdz′)**:** fats and oils; chemical compounds which contain carbon, hydrogen, and oxygen; one of the main classes of food

liquid (lik′ wid)**:** state of matter, neither gas nor solid, that flows and takes the shape of its container

lodestone (lōd′ stōn′)**:** piece of magnetite; natural magnet

lodge (loj)**:** beaver's home made of twigs and mud

longitude (lon′ jə tüd) **lines:** lines marked on a globe from north pole to south pole and counted in degrees

loudness (loud′ nis)**:** characteristic of sound which makes sounds different from each other; related to volume or amount of energy in a sound

lunar eclipse (lü′ nər i klips′)**:** passing of the earth between the sun and the moon so that some or all the moon is in the earth's shadow

luster (lus′ tər)**:** way a mineral shines or reflects light

magma (mag′ mə)**:** melted rock under the earth's surface

magnetic (mag net′ ik) **field:** area of force around a magnet

magnetic poles: ends of a magnet; two places on the earth which attract the ends of a magnet

magnetite (mag′ nə tīt′)**:** magnetized mineral which contains iron

magnetometer (mag′ nə tom′ ə tər)**:** instrument used to study magnetism

mammal (mam′ l)**:** animal covered with hair; female produces milk for its young; has constant body temperature

mantle (man′ tl)**:** middle layer of the earth, beneath the crust

marble (mär′ bl)**:** metamorphic rock formed from limestone which has been changed by heat and pressure

mass (mas)**:** total amount of matter in an object

matter (mat′ ər)**:** anything you can touch, push, or hold; anything that takes up space and has weight or mass

megaphone (meg′ ə fōn)**:** cone-shaped object that reflects sound waves forward

melting (melt′ ing)**:** changing of a solid into a liquid

mercury (mėr′ kyə rē)**:** element which is a heavy liquid at room temperature

mercury cell: small, long-lasting electric cell

metallic luster (mə tal′ ik lus′ tər)**:** shine like that of metal

metamorphic (met′ ə môr′ fik) **rock:** rock changed by heat and pressure

metamorphosis (met′ ə môr′ fə səs)**:** change in form

meteor (mē′ tē ər)**:** piece of matter that moves from space into the earth's air

meteor crater: hole in the earth's surface made by meteorites

meteorite (mē′ tē ə rīt)**:** meteor that reaches the surface of the earth

meteoroid (mē′ tē ər oid): small piece of matter in space

microscope (mī′ krə skōp): instrument that makes very small objects look larger than they are

migrate (mī′ grāt): to move from one place to another

mildew (mil′ dü): fungus that grows on plants and other materials that are damp

mineral (min′ ər əl): natural substance in the earth; element or compound

mixture (miks′ chər): one or more things added to another

molars (mō′ lərz): teeth at back of the mouth; grinding teeth

molecule (mol′ ə kūl): very small bit of matter; smallest amount of a compound that has all the properties of that compound

mollusk (mol′əsk): invertebrate animal such as a clam with a soft body and a hard shell

molting (mōlt′ ing): process of shedding outer skeleton or skin

monaural record (mä nôr′ əl rek′ ərd): sound recorded with one microphone and played through one speaker

month (munth): measure of time; one of twelve parts of one year

moon: natural body in space that moves around the earth or other planets

moon probe (prōb): study of the moon with the use of rockets and satellites

moth (môth): winged insect that flies mostly at night; looks much like a butterfly but has a fatter body and its wings fold

mushroom (mush′ rüm): one of the largest fungus plants; some mushrooms are good to eat and some are poisonous

natural balance (nach′ ə rəl bal′ əns): number of animals and plants in a stable environment staying about the same from year to year

natural satellite (nach′ ər əl sat′ l īt): satellite in space which is not made by man

navigation (nav′ ə gā′ shən) **satellite:** satellite which sends radio signals back to earth to help navigators stay on course

nectar (nek′ tər): sweet liquid found in flowers

needles (nē′ dlz): thin, narrow leaves

negative charge (neg′ ə tiv chärj): minus charge; charge of an electron

nest: animal's home

neutral (nü′ trəl): having no electric charge

neutron (nü′ tron): subatomic particle with no charge

nimbostratus (nim′ bō strat′ əs) **clouds:** rain clouds in layers that are spread out

nimbus (nim′ bəs) **clouds:** storm clouds

nonmetallic luster (non′ mə tal′ ik lus′ tər): shine not like that of metal

nonporous (non pô′ rəs): not allowing water to pass through

north-pointing pole: pole of a magnet that points toward the north magnetic pole of the earth

nose cone: front end of a rocket

nova (nō′ və): fairly dim star which suddenly expands and becomes very bright before becoming dim again

nuclear energy (nü′klē ər en′ər jē): energy from nuclear reactions

nuclear fission (nü′ klē ər fish′ ən): reaction in which an atom splits and releases much energy

nuclear fusion (nü′ klē ər fū′ zhən): reaction in which atoms join and produce a different kind of atom and release much energy

nuclear reaction (nü′klē ər rē ak′ shən): changing of one kind of atom to another kind of atom

nuclear reactor (rē ak′ tər): machine which changes nuclear energy into some other form, such as kinetic or electrical energy; controls nuclear reactions

nucleus (nü′ klē əs): center of an atom made of protons and neutrons packed tightly together; central important part in the cytoplasm of a cell

nymph (nimf): young insect after hatching from an egg

observatory (əb zėr′ və tô′ rē): building made to hold a telescope to view the sky

observe (əb zėrv′): to pay careful attention to something

obsidian (ob sid′ i ən): rock in which no crystals can be seen; looks like dark colored glass

omnivore (äm′ ni vôr): animal that eats both plants and animals

opaque (ō pāk′): allowing no light to pass through

orbit (ôr′ bit): path of one object around a larger object; to move around a larger object

organ (ôr′ gən): tissues which work together

organism (ôr′ gən iz əm): living thing

ovary (ō′ və rē): part of the flower which produces ovules

ovule (ō′ vūl): large cell inside a plant ovary which, after fertilization, produces a seed

oxidation (ok′ sə dā′ shən): chemical change that takes place when oxygen joins with other atoms

oxygen (ok′ sə jən): element in the air which is a gas necessary for life; most abundant element on earth because it is contained in water and most rocks

penicillin (pen′ ə sil′ ən): drug made from a mold

periscope (per′ ə skōp): instrument made of prisms or mirrors and used to see around or over objects

petals (pet′ lz): bright parts of a flower seen when the sepals separate

phases (fāz′ əz) **of the moon:** changes in the way the moon appears

photon (fō′ ton): tiny particle or packet of energy that makes up light

photosynthesis (fō tə′ sin′ thə səs): process in plants in which water, carbon dioxide, and sunlight combine to form sugar and oxygen

physical (fiz′ ə kl) **change:** change in which molecules of a material stay the same kind of molecules

pigment (pig′ mənt): colored substance

pistil (pis′ tl): part of the flower which contains the ovary

piston (pis′ tən): movable part in a cylinder in an engine

pitch (pich): highness or lowness of a sound; up and down motion of part of a rocket or spacecraft

plain (plān): flat stretch of land

planet (plan′ it): large body in space that moves around the sun

planetarium (plan′ ə tār′ i əm): building where images of the stars are projected on a dome-shaped ceiling

planetary probe (plan′ ə ter′ ē prōb): study of a planet with the use of rockets and satellites

polar (pō′ lər) **air:** air from the area around the north pole or south pole

pole (pōl): each end of a magnet; each end of the earth's axis

pollen (pol′ ən): grains of powder-like cells produced by the stamens of a flower and needed in fertilization

pollination (pol′ ə nā′ shən): process in which a pollen cell from one flower reaches the pistil of the same flower or another flower of the same kind

polluted (pə lut′ əd): containing harmful wastes

poriferan (pə rif′ ə rən): invertebrate animal such as a sponge with its body full of holes

porous (pô′ rəs): allowing liquids to pass through

positive charge (poz′ ə tiv chärj): plus charge; charge of a proton

potential energy (pə ten′ shəl en′ ər jē): stored energy; energy of position

power plant: place where generators produce electricity

prism (priz′ əm): special piece of glass that separates white light into its colors; reflects and refracts light

protein (prō′ tēn): chemical compounds which contain carbon, hydrogen, oxygen, and nitrogen; one of the main classes of food

protist (prō′ tist′): one-celled living thing that has a nucleus

proton (prō′ ton): subatomic particle with positive charge

protozoan (prō′ tə zō′ ən): very small animal-like living thing; one-celled

pulley (pul′ lē): grooved wheel and axle machine used as a lifting tool

pumice (pum′ is): volcanic rock with small holes left from gas which escaped when the rock first formed

pupa (pū′ pə): resting stage in the development of an insect

pupil (pū′ pl): opening in the eye in which the lens is located

quality (kwol′ ə tē): characteristic of sound which makes sounds different from each other

quartzite (kwôrt′ sīt′): metamorphic rock formed from sandstone which has been changed by heat and pressure

radiant energy (rā′ dē ənt en′ ər jē): any form of energy which travels as waves

radiation (rā′ dē ā′ shən): given off as protons, neutrons, electrons, or energy by an atom; movement of heat rays away from something warm

radioactive element (rā′ dē ō ak′ tiv el′ ə mənt): element which gives off radiation in atomic decay

radioactive mineral (rā′ dē ō ak′ tiv min′ ər əl): mineral which gives off radiation

radioisotope (rā′ dē ō ī′ sə tōp): form of an element which is or has been made radioactive

radio telescope (rā′ dē ō tel′ ə skōp): instrument used to collect radio waves and focus them so that they can be recorded; used to detect distant stars

rain: water falling in drops that has been condensed from water vapor in the air

rain gauge (gāj): instrument used to measure the amount of rainfall

reentry (rē en′ trē): return of a spacecraft to the atmosphere of the earth

reflect (ri flekt′): to bounce off a surface

reflected (ri flek′ təd) **light:** light that bounces off an object

reflecting telescope (ri flek′ ting tel′ ə skōp): telescope which has a large concave mirror instead of a lens to collect light

reforestation (rē′ fôr is tā′ shən): planting new trees on land that once was forest

refracting telescope (ri frak′ ting tel′ ə skōp): telescope which has a lens to collect light

refraction (ri frak′ shən): change in direction of light as it passes from one material to another

regrassing (ri gras′ ing): planting new grass on bare soil that once was covered with grass

relative humidity (rel′ ə tiv hū mid′ ə tē): amount of water vapor in the air compared with the amount of water vapor the air can hold

repel (ri pel′): to push away from

reproduce (rē′ prə düs′): to produce offspring

reptile (rep′ tl): scaled animal that breathes with lungs and has a changeable body temperature

reservoir (rez′ ər vwär): lake, usually artificial, used for water storage

resistance (ri zis′ təns): force holding back something which passes through or over a material

retina (ret′ ə nə): back of the eyeball which receives light focused by the lens

retro-rocket (ret′ rō rok′ it): small rocket fired to steer or slow down a space capsule

revolution (rev′ ə lü′ shən): one complete trip of a planet around the sun, or of one body around another

revolve (ri volv′): to move around another body

roll: spinning or turning motion of a rocket

roller bearings (rōl′ ər bār′ ings): steel rollers that roll around inside a wheel and help overcome friction

root hairs (rüt hārs): tiny parts of plant roots that take in water from the soil

rotate (rō′ tāt): to turn around about an axis

salmon (sam′ ən): a kind of fish

sandstone (sand′ stōn′): rock formed from fine grains of sand cemented together

sap: food dissolved in water in a plant

satellite (sat′ l īt): object which travels around a larger object in space

satellite tracking (trak′ ing): using instruments to follow a satellite in orbit

scale (skāl): instrument used to measure weight

scales (skālz): flat, thin plates on the skin of an animal or covering a plant part

scoria (skôr′ ē ə): volcanic rock with small holes left from gas which escaped when the rock was first formed; more compact than pumice

screw (skrü): spiral inclined plane

sediment (sed′ ə mənt): material that settles out of water

sedimentary (sed′ ə mən′ te rē) **rock:** rock formed from materials which settle to the bottom of rivers, lakes, and oceans or from material deposited from the wind

seed plant: plant which produces seeds from which new plants can grow

seismograph (sīz′ mə graf): instrument used to record vibrations on and within the earth

sepals (sē′ plz): parts of a flower which protect the bud while it is growing

shale (shāl): smooth sedimentary rock formed from clay and silt

slate (slāt): metamorphic rock formed from shale which has been changed by heat and pressure

sleet (slēt): mixture of rain and ice

smog: air containing harmful wastes trapped by moisture

soil conservation (kon′ sər va′ shən): wise use and protection of soil

solar (sō′ lər) **battery:** two or more solar cells joined together

solar cell: object that contains materials which produce electricity when it receives light

solar eclipse (sō′ lər i klips): passing of the moon between the sun and the earth so that some or all of the earth is in the moon's shadow

solar furnace (sō′ lər fėr′ nis): large concave mirror, large lens, or series of flat mirrors that focus sunlight and produce a very high temperature

solar system (sō′ lər sis′ təm): the sun and many other smaller bodies, such as the planets and meteors, that move around the sun

solid (sol′ id): state of matter, neither gas nor liquid, that has its own shape

sonar (sō′ när′): instrument system that produces and detects ultrasonic vibrations

sonic (son′ ik) **boom:** sound much like an explosion caused by vibrations from something traveling faster than sound

sounder: part of a telegraph that changes electricity into sound vibrations

south-pointing pole: pole of a magnet that points toward the south magnetic pole of the earth

space (spās): area surrounding the earth in all directions

space capsule (kap′ səl): special compartment equipped to carry living things into space

specialized (spesh′ əl īzed) **cell:** cell which has a particular function, but can do only part of what is needed to keep a living thing alive

spectroscope (spek′ trə skōp): instrument used to separate light into its colors, or spectrum; used to discover elements in a star

spectrum (spek′ trəm): bands of colors produced when white light is separated

sperm (spėrm): special cell from one living thing that can join with an egg in another living thing and produce a new living thing

sphere (sfir): object shaped like a ball

spider (spī dər): animal with eight legs that spins a web

sport (spôrt): natural hybrid

squirrel (skwėr′ əl): small animal usually living in trees; mammal with gray or brownish fur and usually eats seeds

stable environment (stā′ bl en vī′ rən mənt): environment which is not changing or being changed

stage (stāj): one part of a rocket

stamens (stā′ mənz): parts of the flower that produce pollen

star: object in space that makes its own light; ball of incandescent gas that glows by nuclear reactions

star cluster (klus′ ter): faint spot of light in distant space made up of many hundreds or many thousands of stars

static electricity (stat′ ik i lek tris′ ə tē): electric charges that do not move

steam (stēm): a gas; water vapor

stereophonic (ster′ ē ə fän′ ik) **record:** sound recorded with two or more microphones and played through two or more speakers

storage (stôr′ ij) **battery:** large battery of several cells

storage product (stôr′ ij prod′ əkt): something that can be easily stored in the plant where it was produced

stratocumulus (strat′ ō kūm′ ū ləs) **clouds:** cumulus clouds in a layer

stratus (strat′ əs) **clouds:** flat, spread out clouds

streak (strēk): mark of a mineral made by scratching it against a hard white surface

subatomic particles (sub′ ə tom′ ik pär′ tə klz): parts which make up an atom

subsoil (sub′ soil′): layer of soil below topsoil

subsonic (sub son′ ik): vibrations that are too slow to be heard

sunspot: spot on the sun which is cooler than the rest of the sun's surface

supersonic (sü pər son′ ik): speed that is faster than the speed of sound

surface (sėr′ fis) **water:** water which stays above the ground

switch (swich): device used to open and close a circuit

system (sis′ təm): group of parts working together as a unit

tadpole: young amphibian after hatching from an egg

talons (tal′ ənz): sharp, curved nails on the feet of some birds

telescope (tel′ ə skōp): instrument that makes objects in the distance seem closer

temperate (tem′ pər it) **zone:** zone of the earth where temperature and weather change a great deal from season to season

temperature (tem′ pər ə chər): measurement of the warmth or coldness of an object

tendril (ten′ drəl): curly part of a plant that winds tightly around other objects and helps to support the plant

tentacles (ten′ tə klz): structures much like arms around the mouth or head of some animals

terminal (tėr′ mə nl): place at the top of an electric cell to which an electric circuit can be connected

terminator (tėr′ mə nā′ tər) **line:** area on the moon where light meets dark

theory (thē′ ə rē): best explanation you can give with the information you have

thermocouple (thėr′ mō kəp′ əl): instrument used to measure temperature differences in stars

thrust (thrust): push opposite to the force of gravity; usually related to the push of rocket motors

tide (tīd): one of the movements of water in the ocean; the rise and fall of the ocean

tissue (tish′ ü): similar cells grouped together

tongue (tung): movable muscle attached to the floor of the mouth

tool (tül): kind of machine which is used to do work in an easier way

topsoil (top′ soil′): top, rich layer of soil

tornado (tôr nā′ dō): large storm with funnel-shaped clouds and whirling winds

tortoise (tôr′ təs): turtle that lives on land

tracer (trā′ sər): small amount of a radioisotope used in scientific studies to trace certain materials and to show what happens to them

translucent (trans lü′ sənt): allowing some light to pass through

transparent (trans pãr′ ənt): allowing most light to pass through

troposphere (trop′ ə sfir): layer of atmosphere closest to the earth

turbine (tėr′ bən): series of blades arranged around an axle

ultrasonic (ul′ trə son′ ik): vibrations that are too fast to be heard

vacuum tube (vak′ yəm tüb): tube which has very little air in it, often used to control the flow of electrons in a circuit

variable (vãr′ ē ə bl) **star:** star that changes in size and brightness from time to time

vertebrate (vėr′ tə brit): animal which has a backbone

vibrate (vī′ brāt): to move back and forth several times

vibration (vī brā′ shən): motion back and forth several times

visible (viz′ ə bl) **light:** radiant energy which can be seen

vitamins (vī′ tə minz): chemical compounds which help control many processes that take place in plants and animals

vocal cords (vo′ kl kôrdz): two bands of skin in the throat that vibrate and make sounds

volcano (vol kā′ nō): mountain formed from lava

volume (vol′ yəm): measure of an amount of space

wading (wād′ ing) **bird:** bird that walks in shallow water

walking stick: insect that looks like a twig

warm air mass: large body of warm air

warm front: place where a moving warm air mass meets a cold air mass

waterspout: tornado over water

water table: height of the top surface of the groundwater

water vapor (wô′ tər vā′ pər): water in the air as a gas that you cannot see

waterwheel (wô′ tər hwēl): engine run by moving water

watt (wot): measure of the amount of work done each second by flowing electricity; unit used to measure the brightness of a light bulb

wavelength: distance from the high point of a wave to the high point of the next wave

weathering (weth′ ər ing): changes in rocks caused by air, sun, rain, or wind

weather satellite (weth′ər sat′l īt): satellite with instruments which sends weather information back to earth

weather vane (vān): instrument that shows the direction of the wind

webbed (webd) **foot:** foot with skin between much of the length of the toes

wedge (wej): triangular-shaped tool formed by two inclined planes put together

weed (wēd): wild plant that interferes with growth of desired plants

week (wēk): measure of time; period of seven days

weight (wāt): heaviness of matter, measured on a scale and caused by gravity

wheel (hwēl): round object that turns on an axle

wildlife refuge (ref′ ūj): place man has set aside where animals can live, find food, and protect their young

wind (wind): moving air

windlass (wind′ ləs): wheel and axle machine used as a lifting tool

windmill (wind′ mil): engine run by wind

work: force through a distance

yaw (yô): right to left motion of a rocket

year (yir): measure of time that it takes the earth to go around the sun once

yeast (yēst): fungus that is used to make most kinds of bread

INDEX

4 5 6 7 8 9 10 11 12 13 14 15-80 79 78 77 76